Understanding Entrepreneurship

Understanding Entrepreneurship

Björn Bjerke

Professor of Entrepreneurship, Malmö University and Guest Professor, Stockholm University, Sweden

Edward Elgar

Cheltenham, UK • Northampton, MA, USA

Published by
Edward Elgar Publishing Limited
Glensanda House
Montpellier Parade
Cheltenham
Glos GL50 1UA
UK

Edward Elgar Publishing, Inc.
William Pratt House
9 Dewey Court
Northampton
Massachusetts 01060
USA

A catalogue record for this book
is available from the British Library

Library of Congress Cataloguing in Publication Data

Bjerke, Björn, 1941–   .
    Understanding entrepreneurship/Björn Bjerke.
        p.   cm.
    Includes bibliographical references and index.
    1. Entrepreneurship. I. Title.
    HB615.B595   2007
    338'.04—dc22

                                    2007000146

ISBN 978 1 84720 066 2 (cased)
ISBN 978 1 84720 067 9 (paperback)

Printed and bound in Great Britain by MPG Books Ltd, Bodmin, Cornwall

Contents

Preface

My interest in entrepreneurship started in the early 1980s. As a member and one of the owners of a consulting company (and as a Professor of Business Administration at University of Lund, Sweden) I was in 1981 given an assignment to assist in finding suitable people, that is, entrepreneurs, who were interested in starting new business ventures with financial assistance that I could arrange on the site of a nearby shipyard which had closed down with effect on about 4000 employees. During a period of two years I came in contact with about 1000 potential entrepreneurs and listened to several hundred business ideas and business plans. I played a part in establishing about one hundred new business firms on the old shipyard. This was an unforgettable experience and it had a major influence on my career thereafter.

I wanted to do a good job in recruiting potential entrepreneurs so I read the existing academic literature, which turned out to be very meagre and entirely concerned with the United States. It was wholly useless for any practical application in Sweden at the time. In an angry response or perhaps in protest, I wrote a book of my own which was published in 1989. Its title was *Creating New Business Ventures* (published only in Swedish). It was very well received, and was even given the Book of the Year Award by the Swedish Marketing Association in 1991.

This was very early in the development of entrepreneurship as a modern academic subject. At that time, the number of professors in the world who had the word 'entrepreneurship' in their title could be counted in single figures.

This book is, in a way, a continuation of *Creating New Business Ventures*, but there are differences as well as similarities between the two books. The similarities are:

- I still stress the importance of the entrepreneur as a human being strongly.
- I still claim that the subject of entrepreneurship belongs to the whole of society, not only to its economy.
- I still think that entrepreneurship is closer to art and aesthetics than science and mathematics.
- I still assert that philosophy is a good ground to stand on when trying to understand entrepreneurship.

- I still believe that language plays a decisive role when we try to come to grips with what entrepreneurship is all about.

But there are differences between the two books as well:

- I talked in my earlier book about two different approaches to researching entrepreneurship, that is, explaining and understanding, which I then believed could be combined to some extent. I now believe that such combinations are self-delusions and potentially dangerous and I place myself firmly in the understanding camp (hence, the title of this book).
- I believed earlier that it was possible, at least to some extent, to speak of a 'typical' entrepreneur and to provide a general presentation of a good way to run and to support an entrepreneurial effort. I do not believe this any more.
- I am more convinced than ever that entrepreneurship cannot be planned to any major extent in advance, and that planning even goes against the very entrepreneurial idea. Entrepreneurship is rather about courage and willpower, being venturesome when experimenting and networking, and about exploiting necessary mistakes as moments of learning.
- I stress much more strongly the differences between entrepreneurship and small business management in this book. The first comes before the second in the development of a new venture and the two are definitely based on different thinking. Among other things, business plans are more relevant in the latter case.

In the 1990s, the interest in entrepreneurship took off. The fundamental reason for this was simply an understanding, in all camps, that the growth and development of any economy, any region, any industry and any business and social activity stands or falls with its ability to be entrepreneurial. The number of courses and programmes at university level in the world exceeds 1000 today. And numerous entrepreneurship research projects are going on everywhere.

It is not surprising that most research on entrepreneurship is of a positivistic, logical-empirical type, that is, based on some kind of explaining approach. After all, the subject of entrepreneurship has existed academically since the eighteenth century but was studied only by economists until some 30–40 years ago, when subjects like psychology, sociology, geography and history entered the scene. Also, studies of modern entrepreneurship started in the United States and most entrepreneurship research still goes on there; transatlantic research traditions are dominated by a objectively rational logical-empirical thinking (Neergaard and Ulhøi, forthcoming).

However, I have become increasingly convinced that a logical-empirical, explaining type of research is not enough to move our knowledge of entrepreneurs forward to any major extent in many situations. This approach will often not do justice to what entrepreneurship and entrepreneurs are all about. Entrepreneurship belongs to the whole of society, not only to its economy, and entrepreneurs do not, most of the time, behave logically and rationally in any objective sense. On many occasions (maybe most) of our research efforts here, it seems, in my opinion, wiser to use a more interpretive, qualitative, understanding research approach.

I see islands of entrepreneurship research, built on understanding, appearing everywhere, increasing in numbers. This book is a map of those islands, including one which I have built myself during my years of researching entrepreneurship.

1. Our new entrepreneurial society

WE LIVE IN A TIME OF CHANGE

The society of today is a society of change. There is not much firm ground left. This can be seen in all areas of society: in public life, in private life, in the business sector. Politicians have to live with the fact that their popularity ratings are roller-coasting. We are constantly reminded of the unsettled world around us through our television screens, and we are disappointed in the business giants who are unable to maintain their levels of employment or to restrain the unethical behaviour of their senior managers.

There are, however, still many people who try to deny the process of drastic change that characterizes our present society. They assume – and live their lives accordingly – that the world they know today will be the same tomorrow. They have problems imagining a genuinely different life for themselves. Of course they notice that things change around them. But they assume that the changes of today are minor variations to a basic solid economic system, social framework and political structure, and they are convinced that tomorrow will be a continuation of today. And if change and innovation become too insistent, the response may be to struggle to restore what is perceived as the status quo.

This kind of linear thinking takes many forms. Individuals may choose not to question the premises on which establishment decisions rest and, even if they seem doubtful, may feel that nothing can be done about them. Public statistics might represent lists of trivialities with little sign of intelligent interpretation. Both imply that the future is a continuation of the path we are already on, that the future is situated around the next bend of the path, waiting for us.

Change can be seen and experienced in different ways. If it is not understood, change can be felt as hostile, as beyond our control and as a threat. Change can be seen in a more positive light however, if an individual has a feeling of being in control of the process. Changes can even be seen as opportunities if a person believes that he or she has a way to use them to his or her advantage.

To live with change in the latter case is to replace the belief that securing lies in an unaltered reality, with a constructive sense of being able to participate, even if only to a small extent, in creating the future.

1

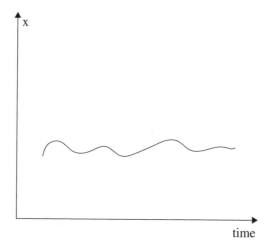

Figure 1.1   Variation

But one change is not like another. As Kelly (1998) puts it, changes come at different wavelengths. There are changes in the way the game is played, changes in the rules of the game and changes in how those rules are changed. Changes in the way the game is played produce winners or losers, firms that are doing well and those doing less well in a specific business area. Examples could be Ericsson, Nokia and Motorola. Changes in the rules of the game produce new industries or force old industries to restructure, they generate new sectors in the economy and new kinds of games. The IT boom could be an example, or laws regulating what is meant by a bank. The third level of change generates changes in how the rules of the game are changed. Changes change themselves, they become autonomous as it were. Changes become so complicated that it is impossible to identify separate and individual causes. Old change paths are turned upside down.

Change can also be classified by distinguishing between variations, structural changes (also called displacements) and paradigmatic changes (also called paradigmatic shifts) (Bjerke, 1989). The first one, that is, variations, could also be called changes with retrogression. This means a variation in the environment around a normal position, for instance when a hard winter forces traffic to use land transport around a frozen lake, where shipping on the lake is the normal case. This principle is shown in Figure 1.1.

Structural and paradigmatic changes constitute changes without retrogression. A structural change (structural displacement) means that an environmental factor takes a permanent new position. One example could be a new law governing when shops are allowed to open and to close. This principle is shown in Figure 1.2.

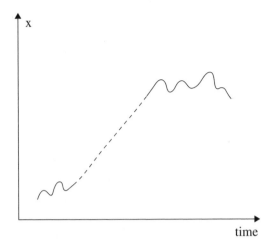

Figure 1.2   Structural displacement

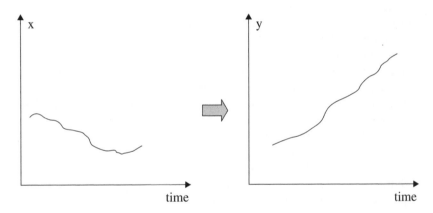

Figure 1.3   Paradigmatic shift

Neither of these two first models of change is adequate to conceptualizing a paradigmatic change (paradigmatic shift). In this case, changes in the environment have become so large (or so numerous) that previous explanatory patterns no longer suffice and new ways of explaining events must be found (Figure 1.3).

A paradigmatic shift in the environment can only be understood in the context of a complete change in our basic frame of experience. Anomalies will be placed in a new frame, and in consequence they will no longer be perceived as anomalies, but will become understandable and natural. There are similarities between Kelly's third level of change (changes in how the rules are changed) and what is here referred to as a paradigmatic shift. It is important for a company to understand which type of changes are taking place in its environment so that problems are neither underestimated nor overmanaged.

THE PARADIGM CONCEPT

The concept of the *paradigm* (paradigm = model, pattern) was established, above all by the historian of science Thomas Kuhn (1922–96). Kuhn (1962) pointed out that major changes (whether in day-to-day context or by researchers) in understanding take place only on rare, but intensive, occasions, with what he referred to as shifts of paradigm. At this point, existing assumptions become so inadequate that they collapse and are replaced by a new set of assumptions. Our social and economic (and for Kuhn, our scientific) history is characterized by long periods of stable paradigms punctuated by relatively short periods with a high degree of instability – history as a staircase rather than as a ramp.

The researcher's task is to describe, explain and/or understand, but these processes cannot replace a paradigm; they can only articulate the paradigm in use. Generally speaking, a shift of paradigm cannot occur through what Kuhn refers to as 'normal research'. Such shifts tend rather to start with awareness of an anomaly, that is, the discovery that the situation being studied does not correspond to the expectations ruling normal research within a given paradigm. Such anomalies may be critical. They cannot be dealt with through reinterpretation or afterthought, but only through a relatively sudden and restructuring event, with (to use a psychological term) a change of Gestalt. New solutions seem possible for the first time. A new paradigm has been established. A new period of normal research can take place. One may refer to a shift of paradigm as a cognitive revolution.

Kuhn describes a paradigm as consisting of four parts:

1. *Symbolic generalizations*, that is, typical expressions which are used by researchers working in the paradigm. We may call this a jargon.
2. *Metaphysical aspects*, that is, typical models, everything from philosophical assumptions about the fundamental construction of reality to rules of thumb for what is the 'correct' way to do research. These aspects also provide researchers with suitable and acceptable analogies and metaphors. Furthermore, they assist in deciding what can be accepted as a solution, which also means that they determine what constitutes unsolved problems.

3. *Values*, which are used to judge research results (for instance, that they allow problems to be formulated and solved and, when possible, that they shall be simple, consistent and probable) and other values (such as utility to society).
4. *Ideal examples*, that is, concrete problem solutions which students face in their education or which can be read in recognized scientific journals.

IS THERE A NEW SOCIETAL PARADIGM DEVELOPING TODAY?

Around three hundred years ago life changed for millions of people in that part of the world which we in the west refer to as 'civilized'. Until then, land had been the basis for all economies, for culture, for family and for politics. People lived in villages. Power was held in a few hands. Civilization was based on agriculture. This seemed likely to continue for ever. We may call this *the first wave* (Toffler, 1984).

Out of this world came the industrial revolution. This *second wave* created a strange, powerful and very energetic counter-revolution. The industrial revolution was more than smokestacks and assembly lines. It was a system that touched every aspect of human life. The first wave passed into history.

Traits which characterized industrial society are now in a process of being erased by *a third wave*. This too is affecting everybody. Our established systems are questioned, our power systems are weakened, our values are scattered and our economies are shaken. This new society contains contradictions, at least in its early stage: it is both highly technological and anti-industrial. But, above all, it questions our old assumptions. It points, for instance, to 'anomalies' in our 'normal handling' of our companies. Old ways of thinking, old formulae, dogmas and ideologies, no matter how valuable they might have been in the past, no longer fit the facts. We cannot force the dawning world of tomorrow into the pigeonholes of yesterday.

This concept is central to an understanding of the present situation and the immediate future. The times are as revolutionary as those that saw the invention of agriculture or the industrial revolution at its height. Mankind is taking a leap forward. Unseen by many, we are building a new civilization from below. This is the meaning of the third wave (Toffler, 1984). Industrial society, as we know it, is dying out to be replaced by something irreversibly new.

Many names have been given to this new society, among them the *new economy*, but I believe this concept can be misleading. Certain basic economic rules turned out to be valid even during the so-called IT revolution, for instance:

- In order for a business to survive in the long run, it has to generate more resources than it consumes.
- If cash is out, business is out.

Apart from the third wave and the new economy, it has been suggested that are new society should be called the information society, the risk society, the post-industrial society, the service society, the game society, the knowledge society, the network economy, the negotiation economy or the experience economy.

In our new society, in order to survive mentally, we have to learn to live with change, understand change and act in change, we have to take care of our own future, we have to engage with society, we have to be entrepreneurial (in the wide sense of the term, which will become clear as we move on in this book). Therefore, I propose that we decribe our present situation as *our new entrepreneurial society*. And what we call things will lead our ideas into specific directions:

> Expressed simply, words do things. It is not possible or meaningful to separate rhetoric and practice. Journalists, academics, business professionals and consultants are all practising the rhetoric, and it is the change of rhetoric and practice that opens up an understanding of contemporary society. New words produce new actions, and it is this interplay that provides an interesting focus. Looking back on the actions carried out in the name of the new economy while looking at the words constructing these actions, we realize that the new economy is not concerned with the past or the present, but the focus is completely on and in the future. (Holmberg et al., 2002b, p. 268)

CHARACTERISTICS OF OUR NEW ENTREPRENEURIAL SOCIETY

I find the type of 'wave front analysis' being used here very rewarding. It looks at history as a sequence of different waves of change and asks questions about where they lead us. It directs our attention not so much to continuous change (which is important as well) as to discontinuities, innovations and breaking points. It gives us patterns of change so that we can participate in them.

There are also risks associated with such an approach. It is worth mentioning two of them here:

1. The stress is strongly on difference, although society is subject to both discontinuous and continuous change. There are, furthermore, aspects of society that hardly change at all, for instance, religion, basic laws and educational systems.
2. In most countries, agriculture and industrialism persist to some degree alongside post-industrialism. These elements coexist, but in different proportions depending on the development stage of the society. It is usually the case that a developed society has less of the first and more of the last. This does not, for instance, prevent the United States from being the biggest agricultural producer in the world.

Let us look at some of the characteristics that we can associate with our new entrepreneurial society, that is, the society where we have to be entrepreneurial. Taken individually these characteristics may not look particularly significant, but taken together they definitely point to the fact that a new society is developing – a new society where none of us should sit still and rely on the past (Table 1.1).

A New Kind of Change

I have mentioned already that change plays a dominant role in the working environment of today, but this needs to be emphasized. Many changes are of a new kind in that they contain genuine uncertainty. Such uncertainty cannot be eliminated or erased by more extensive or more careful planning. Our *changes have changed* (Ferguson, 1980). Furthermore, more and more aspects of our new society are affected by change.

Table 1.1   Our new entrepreneurial society

Some characteristics of our new entrepreneurial society
• A new kind of change
• IT and other technologies play a decisive role
• Knowledge is central
• Business has a new content
• New kinds of organization and work
• Relationships and networks are more important to us
• Globalization
• A new view of distance and time
• New types of capital
• Industrial boundaries are more blurred
• Members of the economy are, on average, older
• Words are more important

IT and Other Technologies Play a Decisive Role

Castells has provided a date for and localized the start of what he calls the 'new economy':

> The new economy arose at a certain point in time, the 1990s, at a certain place, the United States, and around/from specific industries, mainly information technology and finance with biotechnology standing out in the horizon. It was at the end of the 1990s that the seeds of the information technology revolution, planted in the 1970s, were seen to start to grow in a wave of new processes and products which spurred productivity and stimulated economic competition. Every technical revolution has its own speed of diffusion to social and economic structures. For reasons, which are the object of the historians to determine, this specific technical revolution seems to need about a quarter of a century to equip the world with new tools – a much shorter time than the predecessors. (Castells, 1998, p. 169; my translation)

Technology is more than information technology (IT), but it is this technology which is most widely associated with our new entrepreneurial society. IT can be defined as the infrastructure and knowledge necessary to make information quickly and easily accessible (increasingly it applies to the software and the communication services that link the hardware).

However, IT is not essentially about new firms in a new sector but about new conditions for the whole economy ('Det nya näringslivet', 2001, p. 20):

> The popular distinction between the old and the new economy completely misses the point. The most important aspect of the new economy is not the shift to high-tech industries, but the way that IT will improve the efficiency of all parts of the economy, especially old-economy firms. (*The Economist*, 2000, p. 13)

IT is central to modern society. It moves faster and faster, it invades all sectors, all that can be digitalized will be. It has created completely new industries (for instance, e-commerce, information services online and mobile communication) and it eases boundaries between nations, industries, companies, goods and services, working time and leisure time ('Det nya näringslivet', 2001, pp. 11–12).

In addition to lowering prices, IT has four other noteworthy features (*The Economist*, 2000, p. 10):

- It is pervasive and can boost efficiency in almost everything a firm does, from design to marketing and accounting, and in every sector of the economy.
- By increasing access to information, IT helps to make markets work more efficiently.
- IT is truly global.

- IT speeds up innovation itself, by making it easier and cheaper to process large amounts of data and reducing the time it takes to design new products.

IT can give the same advantages to small firms as to big ones (ibid., p. 34), but, as we have already observed, not only IT but technology in general is characterizing our new entrepreneurial society. Technology occupies a strategic position like never before. 'Technology has become our culture, our culture technology' (Kelly, 1998, p. 49; my translation). Technology increases the rate at which our economy is changing and it is spread at an accelerating rate (Coulter, 2001, pp. 34–8).

Today's technology is not only know-how, but also know-when, know-where and know-why, sometimes also know-whom.

Knowledge is Central

Society has become knowledge society. Knowledge and competency are its key resources, 'the' only meaningful resources, according to Drucker as long ago as 1969 (Drucker, 1969, p. ix), and knowledge workers are the dominant group in the workforce. It is a society where opportunities are greater than ever before, but so are the chances of failure (*The Economist*, 2001, p. 4). But according to Castells, the relevant border line is not between the industrial and post-industrial economies but between two types of production. The analytical emphasis should, according to him, be moved from post-industrialism to informationalism (Castells, 1998).

> Economies are increasingly based on knowledge. Finding better ways of doing things has always been the main source of long-term growth. What is new is that a growing chunk of production in the modern economy is in the form of intangibles, based on the exploitation of ideas rather than material things: the so-called 'weightless economy'. In 1900 only one-third of American workers were employed in the service sector; now more than three-quarters are. (*The Economist*, 2000, p. 29)

An interesting aspect of knowledge is that it does not obey the traditional economic laws of scarcity. It does not matter how much knowledge is used, it is still not used up. Also important is that it is not really knowledge and competency in itself that signify but those people who have these qualities and/or that know how to use them. Among them are many of those agents for change who are of interest in this book, that is, entrepreneurs.

Furthermore, when talking about new knowledge we should remember that it might be equally important to unlearn the old as to learn the new.

Business has a New Content

Our new society concerns difficult immaterial entities such as information, relationships, copyright, entertainment, security, and what is derived from them (Kelly, 1998, p. 11). The economy is about services as never before.

Most revolutionary – and this is touched upon above – is that our new entrepreneurial society defies the traditional economic laws of diminishing returns. Instead there are opportunities for increasing returns. The fixed cost of setting up a new business may still be high, but the product of such a business may cost almost nothing to manufacture per unit!

New Kinds of Organization and Work

New kinds of organization appear as hierarchical and centralized structures decline. But society does not collapse. Far from it. Some ambitious people transform society from below in order to make it stronger, more well-balanced and more multi-faceted (Bjerke, 1989, p. 64).

However, work becomes less permanent (Holmberg et al., 2002a, p. 14) and more informational (Castells, 1998, p. 278).

Relationships and Networks are More Important to Us

Contemporary society is underpinned by all-encompassing electronic networks; the network is the primary symbol of our new entrepreneurial society (Holmberg et al., 2002a, p. 13). One characteristic of the new info-technological paradigm 'is *the logic of networks* in every system and arrangement of relationships using the new information technology. The network morphology seems to be well suited to the increasingly more complex interaction and the unpredictable patterns of development emerging through the creative power of this interaction' (Castells, 1998, pp. 92–3; my translation). Our new entrepreneurial society is based on networking 'because under the new historical conditions, productivity is generated through and competition takes place in a global network of interacting business networks' (ibid., p. 99; my translation).

> By transforming the processes for managing information, the new information technology is influencing the activity field of all human beings and makes it possible to create an infinite number of connections between separate areas as well as between different elements and agents of various operations. A network-based economy emerges with far-reaching internal interdependencies which is increasingly more able to apply its advances within technology, know-how and business organizations on technology, know-how and organizing businesses themselves. Such a virtuous circle should lead to improved productivity and

efficiency, given the right conditions in terms of equally dramatic organizational and institutional changes. (Castells, 1998, pp. 99–100; my translation)

I mentioned earlier in this chapter that there is a kind of change in our new entrepreneurial society which may have a paradigmatic content. It is possible to see the logics of networks as an answer to such a situation, because the network economy has moved 'from change to a situation where everything is in a state of flux' (Kelly, 1998, p. 144; my translation). Understanding how these networks are working is the key to understanding how our new entrepreneurial society is working, and the greatest profits in this society are to a large extent to be found in researching and exploiting the power of decentralized and autonomous networks (Kelly, 1998).

It is even possible to say that the network economy is changing our identities. What matters today is whether a person belongs to 'the network' or not (Kelly, 1998). At the same time, the more high-tech we become the more 'high-touch' we need (Naisbitt et al., 2001).

Globalization

But we do not only need each other more as humans. We also need each other more as nations. Our new entrepreneurial society is global because its central activities and its components are organized globally (Castells, 1998). Jonung (2000) associates this new globalized economy with a free and extremely fast flow of ideas, information and capital, a flow which to a large extent is a result of the IT revolution. Others, such as Eriksson and Ådahl (2000), discuss the new economy in somewhat more political terms, with the market economy (with the United States as a forerunner) as a model. The supporters of this thesis claim that the globalization process facilitates high economic growth for all participants. Its opponents claim, on the other hand, that it is increasing the rifts between rich and poor countries.

At any rate, global markets add to our inability to make meaningful forecasts.

A New View of Distance and Time

The limitations of physical distance on decisions and actions in our companies and organizations as well as limitations of time have, by and large, disappeared (Coulter, 2001). 'The linear time-regime of industrial society has been substituted by a time which has no beginning or end, which operates worldwide in real time and without respect to geographical demarcations' (Benner, 2002, p. 136).

The winners in the competition between participants in our new entrepreneurial society often seem to concentrate on being the fastest rather
than being the fittest (Bjerke and Hultman, 2002).

New Types of Capital

The view of business capital has changed in our new entrepreneurial
society. Today we speak not only of financial capital but also of capital
invested in, say, business knowledge, local data bases, willingness to learn,
networks, contacts and so on.

Arbnor (2004) makes a distinction between financial and real capital,
human capital, structural capital, relationship capital and visual capital
(see Figure 1.4).

Industrial Boundaries are More Blurred

Our industrial boundaries are becoming less distinct and are often impossible to maintain. Traditional industries invade each other's territory or
merge. An example is telecommunications, computers and entertainment.

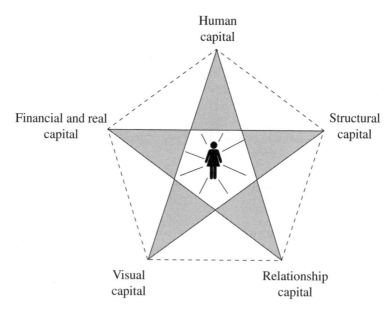

Source: Arbnor (2004, p. 383).

Figure 1.4   New types of capital

Members of the Economy are, on Average, Older

One irreversible and widespread change in our new society that could be called a paradigmatic shift is the growth in the number of older people and, at least in industrialized societies, a correspondingly rapid reduction in the number of children being born. Consequently, older people will participate in working life in many new and different ways. Within 20–25 years perhaps as many as half of those who work for an organization will not be employed in a particular place, at least not full-time (*The Economist*, 2001, p. 3).

Words are More Important

It is obvious that actions, if new, must be based on new ideas, new concepts or at least new understandings of old concepts. It becomes increasingly difficult to separate rhetoric and practice.

This can also be formulated such that we *live in the fourth dimension* (Bjerke, 1989). The concept of *process* becomes more and more part of our vocabulary:

> Goals and endpoints matter less. Learning is more urgent than storing information. Caring is better than keeping. Means *are* ends. The journey is the destination. When life becomes a process, the old distinctions between winning and losing, success and failure, fade away. Everything, even a negative outcome, has the potential to teach us and to further our quest. We are experimenting, exploring. In the wider paradigm there are no 'enemies', only those useful, if irritating, people whose opposition calls attention to trouble spots, like a magnifying mirror. (Ferguson, 1980, p. 101)

WE NEED MORE ENTREPRENEURSHIP

> Innovation is on its way to become a major theme on the economic-political agenda in all industrial countries. As a consequence we also start to dig deeper into the complexity which concerns the very core of all economic development. The fact is that stressing innovation is the only known way to manage intensified competition without reducing the living standard of the citizens. No company, region or nation can reach sustainable growth without innovation. (Lans, et al., 1997, p. 3; my translation)

In our new entrepreneurial society, success comes from innovation, not optimization; growth is achieved less by doing what you know best than by attacking and, hopefully, managing what you know less well. Results are appreciated less by how much work and capital go into them and more by how innovative they are and how they differ from other results that aim at fulfilling the same need. In our new entrepreneurial society learning is necessary in order to make individuals proactive, adaptive and more effective. Learning is no longer a choice but a necessity and the important thing is to learn how to learn. The learning curve should never flatten out, neither in relation to individuals nor to organizations. Our new entrepreneurial society could therefore also be called the *innovation society*.

What is needed today is innovation at all levels and in all camps, not only in the traditional sense of new goods and services, but in the very way in which our societies operate, in the way in which we look at ourselves, and in those mechanisms, groupings and organizations which can develop and commit our resources in the most meaningful way to changing our setup in order to start a normal, steady and continuous innovation process (Kanter, 1983). And it is precisely those everyday innovations – which are not necessarily planned but aimed at possibilities and needs – which will keep any society, economy, industry or company flexible and in a continuous flux.

Creativity has always been important, but in our new entrepreneurial society it will be more obvious that the success of a business stands and falls with this quality – and with the company being able to involve all employees at all levels in this process. It is obvious today that a modern progressive society must get involved in genuinely creative activities and that these activities must be reflected in all sectors. This is the only guarantee that the outcome will be a sustainable success; results in all sectors are completely dependent on individuals who take the initiative to develop new methods, processes, organizations, goods and services, alone and/or in cooperation with others. Some routine work remains and will remain, of course, just as there existed some mentally stimulating work before, but the emphasis is clearly shifting.

Still, initiatives do not happen by themselves nor do innovations develop on their own. Public debate calls for 'better models', 'more effective innovation systems' or 'institutions and incentives for innovative activity'. But, in my opinion, most important in our new entrepreneurial society are not models, systems, institutions and/or incentives but entrepreneurs themselves. We will look below at definitions and a conceptualization of what we could mean by 'entrepreneurs', but let me indicate here that, when talking about entrepreneurs I think of agents for change who understand that the future cannot be modelled, systematized or institutionalized, but are enterprising enough to come up with innovations of all kinds, innovations which ordinary people adopt and find useful, innovations that build our future – now! These people are crucial to the success of our new entrepreneurial society.

Arbnor claims that most so-called modern industrialized societies have already come to a halt:

As members of our society, we have only been provided with more of that mechanical oil, by which we were already grafted, in order to think instrumentally. Old premises of thinking were structured by prefabricated knowledge. New knowledge, however, comes from *within* people. Important driving forces like courage, imagination, ingenuity, drive, joy, near and genuine relationships, empathy, dialogue and social intelligence; they come, by and large, only from within individuals. These driving forces are absolutely essential to develop in the knowledge-based society. *No longer* is the intensity of the knowledge-repetitive work determining development of productivity and new businesses in postmodern enterprising. [Modern societies] need a rich *imagination lift*, if research and development are to lead to economic growth. (Arbnor, 2004, pp. 9–10; my translation)

Entrepreneurship at its best creates new ideas, new products and more jobs and is vital for the economic development of a country. This is proven over and over in various studies and reports, for instance:

This analysis does not suggest that entrepreneurial activity is by itself a source of economic growth. It does, however, indicate that changes in the economic structure and market processes within a country leading to economic growth may occur more quickly when an active entrepreneurial sector is available to implement such changes. (*Global Entrepreneurship Monitor*, 2002, p. 22).

Henrekson (2001b, pp. 41–2) has gathered together important milestones in the literature, which explain the trend-break of the dominance of the big companies and their previous taken-for-granted role as the backbone of economic development through their mass production of relatively standardized products, using specialized machinery and technology. This trend-break is believed to have taken place during the 1970s in leading industrial countries (Henrekson, 2001b, pp. 41–2):

- Based on theories from Coase (the father of transaction cost analysis, see for instance Coase, 1937), it is possible to show that technological development has led to a situation where the transaction costs on a market in many cases have become so drastically low that it is profitable for many companies to concentrate on their core business and to outsource other activities (Carlsson, 1999; Piore and Sabel, 1984).
- Development has gone the way of more service-dominated businesses and away from big manufacturing companies and their establishments (see for instance, Davis et al., 1996).
- Consumers increasingly demand more differentiated rather than mass-produced products (Piore and Sabel, 1984; Carree and Thurik, 1999).

- Big companies have proven to be in a class of their own as far as improved productivity of existing products is concerned. However, new products are often best produced in new firms, sometimes established just for this purpose (Baldwin and Johnson, 1999; Audretsch, 1995).
- Entrepreneurial small firms can function as agents of change and act as important engines in the growth process of an economy (Carlsson, 1999).
- The small business sector can prove very fruitful for the identification and development of future business leaders and entrepreneurial talents (Davis and Henrekson, 1997; Lucas, 1978).

The role of entrepreneurship in an economy can be summarized as follows (Ushido, 1995; Coulter, 2001; 'SMEs in Europe . . .', 2002):

- Entrepreneurs are agents of change, creating innovations of all sizes.
- Entrepreneurship liberates the creativity in individuals.
- Entrepreneurship contributes to job creation and growth.
- Entrepreneurship is crucial for competitiveness.
- Entrepreneurship increases consumers' choices.
- Entrepreneurship can contribute to promoting social and economic solidarity in a region.

DEFINING ENTREPRENEURSHIP

Entrepreneurship can– and has – been studied within many different disciplines. This has led to a variety of opinions about its meaning. There are, in principle, three different ways to define entrepreneurs and entrepreneurship (Davidsson, 2003):

1. Using those skills characterizing entrepreneurs.
2. Using those processes and events which are part of entrepreneurship.
3. Using those results that entrepreneurship leads to.

Most definitions are a mix of these three. A few examples:

> Entrepreneurship is a way of thinking, reasoning, and acting that is opportunity obsessed, holistic in approach, and leadership balanced. (Timmons, 1999, p. 27)

> Entrepreneurship: the process whereby an individual or a group of individuals use organized efforts and means to pursue opportunities to create value and grow by fulfilling wants and needs through innovation and uniqueness, no matter what resources are currently controlled. (Coulter, 2001, p. 6)

An entrepreneur is one who creates a new business in the face of risk and uncertainty for the purpose of achieving profit and growth by identifying opportunities and assembling the necessary resources to capitalize on them. Although many people come up with great business ideas, most of them never act on their ideas. Entrepreneurs do. (Zimmerer and Scarborough, 2002, p. 4)

Entrepreneurship is a dynamic process of vision, change, and creation. It requires an application of energy and passion towards the creation and implementation of new ideas and creative solutions. Essential ingredients include the willingness to take calculated risks – in terms of time, equity, or career; the ability to formulate an effective venture team; the creative skill to marshal needed resources; the fundamental skill of building a solid business plan; and, finally, the vision to recognize opportunity where others see chaos, contradiction, and confusion. (Kuratko and Hodgetts, 2004, p. 30)

My opinion is that entrepreneurship (in its modern sense) appears in so many contexts that it is impossible to limit the understanding of an entrepreneur to a specific character. Furthermore I do not see any generally applicable or useful road on which an entrepreneur will succeed; it would therefore do entrepreneurs a disservice to try to provide a too precise picture a priori of what an entrepreneur is and/or of how entrepreneurship is done. For this reason I believe that in order to better understand our new entrepreneurial society entrepreneurship should only be specified by its results. In other words:

Entrepreneurship = to create *new* user value

I do not want to call this a *definition* (from Latin = *definire* = to mark off) but would prefer to call it a *conceptualization* (from Latin = *concipere* = to summarize). I look at the relationships between creativity, innovation and entrepreneurship in the following way:

1. Creativity = to come up with new ideas
2. Innovation = to apply these new ideas
3. Entrepreneurship = to come up with new applications which others can use (as well) to fill a need and /or satisfy some demand, existing or created.

This conceptualization of entrepreneurship is close to some conceptualizations of marketing to which entrepreneurship is intimately related: successful entrepreneurs are good marketers (Bjerke and Hultman, 2002). Conceptualizations of entrepreneurship and marketing often overlap; both are concerned with creating user value. However, the way I see it is that entrepreneurship always has to do with creating 'new' value, which is not always true of marketing, especially mass marketing, where the aim is to satisfy existing values rather than creating new ones.

Still, the concept of 'new' should not be interpreted too radically in an entrepreneurial context. 'New' may only be a new aspect of an existing application; for instance, making a solution more accessible or more practical. Most entrepreneurial efforts are, in practice, not much more than decent modifications of what exists already. Few of them change our lives as consumers to any major extent. For this reason an entrepreneur should possibly rather be called a 'user value maker' than a 'user value creator' (compare Chapter 4).

In principle, all business startups which succeed in establishing themselves contain some, even if small, entrepreneurial aspects. The fact that they may subsequently no longer be worthy of the label entrepreneurial is another matter (and they still continue with marketing). We will have reason to return to this several times in this book.

ARE THERE MORE ENTREPRENEURS TODAY?

Having considered a new entrepreneurial society, are there more entrepreneurs today? There are those who claim that entrepreneurship today occurs at significantly higher rates than ever before (at least over the past 100 years) (Gartner and Shane, 1995).

However, numbers refer to the market sector (where products and services are offered for a price with the hope of a profit), While, as I see it, today's entrepreneurship is found (and should be found) in all sectors of society and is more of a lifestyle choice than anything else (more of this later). So, while figure for entrepreneurial activities in the market sector are higher than before, the understanding of and feeling for entrepreneurship is higher everywhere. This, in my opinion, is the true sense of our new entrepreneurial society.

However, concentrating on the market sector, tends to lead to too great an emphasis on a few near legendary successful business leaders in senior positions in big companies who already have high public profiles. They are considered to be more interesting to the media and to the general public (who may perceive them as 'odd') than those many small-business owners that operate in all western countries. But, while the former may constitute outstanding examples of what you can achieve as an entrepreneur, they do not constitute the bricks and mortar of the continuously innovative society. Consider instead the following question: 'How can we turn a larger number of all kinds of members of our society into entrepreneurial champions?'

During the industrial revolution (we will be back to the history of entre-preneurship in Chapter 3), most companies grew out of their founders' activities as craftsmen, day workers or middlemen. There were no estab-lished organizations to start from or copy. The whole process of recruiting and organizing people, material and capital had to be learnt from scratch, often, of course, with painful social results.

Some of the small baronies that were built up during the industrial revo-lution grew up to become great corporate kingdoms. Some achieved this through their own strength, others grew by conquering companies which lacked the power and/or initiative to expand on their own (Jay, 1970).

A period of approximately half a century, from roughly the 1920s, could be considered as the great era for the growth of the big corporate organi-zations. From small, insecure and perhaps temporary beginnings, these companies became vast and permanent. The aim was to achieve mass pro-duction and standardization of the operations. More and more employees were incorporated into bigger and bigger units. Gigantic concerns and multinational corporations became economic facts. Public discussion was increasingly concerned with the role of these giants in the economy, but few people questioned their value.

What happened to entrepreneurship during this period? During the 1970s, questions such as these began to be asked:

- Has the entrepreneurial breed died out? Is the mould broken?
- Are entrepreneurial interests stifled by the internal cultures of the giants?
- Are potential entrepreneurs discouraged by the societal climate and the tax system?

The debate at this time was simplistic and biased. For one thing, most people were not really interested in the debate at all. Most people still had jobs. And why should workers have any interest in doing something different, and where were the opportunities to do it, as little more than components in an ever bigger and more complex system? Further, there was a still a tendency to define an entrepreneur as the single, capital-raising, risk-taking generalist of the old type, and to see companies as hier-archies with room for only one entrepreneur at the top. It was easy to draw the conclusion (which was probably right) that this archetype had disap-peared and the entrepreneurial spirit with him at a time when occupations and employment became more and more specialized; when capital seemed to exist only in the banks, in various public funds and with high finance; when society took care of its citizens from the cradle to the grave; and when most new jobs seemed to be created by established institutions.

Table 1.2　Entrepreneurs then (15–20 years ago) and now

Entrepreneurs then	Entrepreneurs now
Small-business founder	True entrepreneur
Boss	Leader
'Lone Ranger'	Networker
Secretive	Open
Self-reliant	Inquisitive
Seat of the pants	Business plan
Snap decisions	Consensus
Male ownership	Mixed ownership

Source:　Dollinger (2003, p. 9).

Those who became consultants, who established advertising agencies, who started pop groups or who led environmental movements, were not considered 'real' entrepreneurs.

Given that there are so many and shifting opinions of what is meant by an 'entrepreneur', that we have a much broader conceptualization of the concept today (which is reflected in this book as well) and that we have the spread of entrepreneurial ideas to all sectors of our new society, I find it difficult to claim, in any meaningful comparable sense, that entrepreneurial scale and intensity is higher today than ever before. Maybe it is just that, because the interest in entrepreneurship has risen and we have learnt the importance of entrepreneurial efforts to our economic welfare and growth and job creation, we simply 'see' more entrepreneurs than before!

There are also those who claim that we have a new type of entrepreneur today, compared to just 15–20 years ago (Table 1.2).

ENTREPRENEURSHIP, SMALL BUSINESS AND NEW BUSINESS

There are similarities between entrepreneurship and small business. They should, however, be seen as different phenomena, even if they may coincide. A small company is not necessarily entrepreneurial once it is established. To be entrepreneurial means to create new user value. A common picture is that the successful small firm start's as entrepreneurial and then transforms itself, exploiting the formula that underlies its success and the market niche it has found and/or established. This uses skills of management and marketing rather than entrepreneurship (more of this in Chapter 6).

Neither is entrepreneurship necessarily the same as starting a new business, even if the two may coincide. Many companies start without being very entrepreneurial, although these startups probably have little chance of surviving in the long run.

There is nothing, in principle, preventing big companies or established small companies from having recurrent entrepreneurial periods and activities, that is, developing new user value starting from what they have already. This is sometimes called *intrapreneurship*.

Small Business and New Business are Dominating Our New Entrepreneurial Society

It seems to be generally accepted among researchers as well as among politicians and other commentators that small business dominates our new entrepreneurial society. There are several explanations for this (Bjerke and Hultman, 2002, pp. 3–5). Some of which we have been already:

- In broad terms, an increasing number of work tasks have to do with managing information, a decreasing number with managing physical objects. Small firms have a better chance of establishing themselves and succeeding in a knowledge-based economy.
- Many industry entry barriers have been erased, and there are fewer natural economies of scale for most business activities. This is a simpler economy to enter but also an economy in which it is easier to fail.
- Advancing computer and telecommunication technology is rendering mass production and distribution obsolete. It is possible today to turn out, and deliver, short runs of highly varied, even customized, products at costs approaching those of mass production and distribution.
- Flexibility is becoming increasingly important. Turbulence in the economy from factors such as unstable currencies can hurt any firm, big or small. Smaller firms, however, are inherently more flexible than bigger firms and often more resilient in riding the waves.
- The move towards a service-based economy is a characteristic of all developed economies. Small firms are typically more prevalent in service industries than larger firms.
- The removal of anti-competitive regulation has spawned shoals of minnows in industries like airlines and telecommunications. These minnows are, on the other hand, often quickly eaten by bigger fish.
- Technological change and increasingly open economies raise the level of international competition. Many business functions spill

over national boundaries, sometimes integrating activities of small units in many nations into a network of a single productive effort.
- More women in the workforce have created an ample supply of people to create or staff small firms, often part-time.

A few statistics:

- In the early 1980s, approximately 4 per cent of the British labour force was self-employed; by the late 1990s this had increased to about 15 per cent (Scase, 2000, p. 43).
- During the 1990s, large corporations in the United States cut jobs by more than 6 million, yet unemployment fell to record low levels, mainly as a result of new companies started by entrepreneurs (Baron and Shane, 2005, p. 6).
- In the United States (US Department of Labor, 2005) in 2004, small and medium-sized companies (companies employing fewer than 500 people):
    Represented more than 99.7 per cent of all employers.
    Employed more than half of the total number employed in the private sector.
    Paid 44.5 per cent of total private salaries in the United States.
    Generated approximately 60–80 per cent of all new jobs (net) per year.
    Generated more than 50 per cent of total GNP in the United States (outside the agricultural sector).
- In Sweden in 2004 (*Statistiska centralbyrån*, 2005), small and medium-sized companies (again, those with fewer than 500 employees):
    Represented approximately 99.9 per cent of all employers.
    Employed approximately 80 per cent of those employed in the business sector.
    Constituted more than 98 per cent of exporting companies in the country (2003).

Small businesses seem to have an advantage – at least in some industries. Innovative ability seems to be inversely related to the size of the company. Big companies have problems being innovative for several reasons (Bjerke, 1989):

- *Industrial leaders cannot afford to assimilate radical innovations.* There is a difference between 'improving' and 'path-breaking' technologies. Big companies have a problem with the latter.

- *Their structure and cultures work against the introduction of new ideas.* Radical innovations demand dramatic shifts in production skills and in distribution as well as in customer relationships. These shifts can threaten the status quo and lead to disorder in hierarchical and social systems that have contributed to the success of the company. The cultures in most big companies function as powerful stabilizing brake-blocks. To exploit and commercialize radical new ideas, especially if they threaten the established order, destabilizes the company.
- *They are too dependent on internal research and development.* The big companies are good at process development but not at product development.
- *Big companies do not attract and do not keep radical innovators.* Innovators tend to be high achievers and are attracted by an environment where they can get direct feedback and have individual responsibility for their own results. Such an environment is rarely offered by the big companies.

Stevenson (1995, p. 51) expressed this extremely well: 'Why is it so easy [for small companies] to compete against giant corporations? Because while they [the giants] are studying the consequences, [entrepreneurs] are changing the world'.

The *Global Entrepreneurship Monitor* is an annual study which began in the late 1990s and looks at the proportion of the population between 18 and 64 years of age in various countries that are in the process of starting a business. Its results published in 2002 are illustrated in Figure 1.5. This figure shows that approximately 4 per cent were in the process of starting a business in Sweden (twenty-first position of 27 countries studied). The equivalent figure in the United States was approximately 11 per cent and in China approximately 12–13 per cent. Thailand had the larger number of start-ups, at approximately 18 per cent; and Japan had the fewest, with approximately 2 per cent.

As far as entrepreneurial activities among people between 18 and 64 years of age are concerned the world can be divided into six regions (Figure 1.6): Developing Asia (Thailand, India, Korea and China), approximately 16 per cent; Latin America (Chile, Argentina, Brazil and Mexico), approximately 14 per cent; the anglophone world (New Zealand, the United States, Canada, Australia and South Africa), approximately 10 per cent; the first 11 EU countries plus Iceland, Norway, Switzerland and Israel, approximately 6 per cent; Eastern Europe (Hungary, Slovenia, Poland, Croatia and Russia), approximately 4 per cent; developed Asia (Singapore, Taiwan, Hong Kong and Japan), approximately 3.5 per cent.

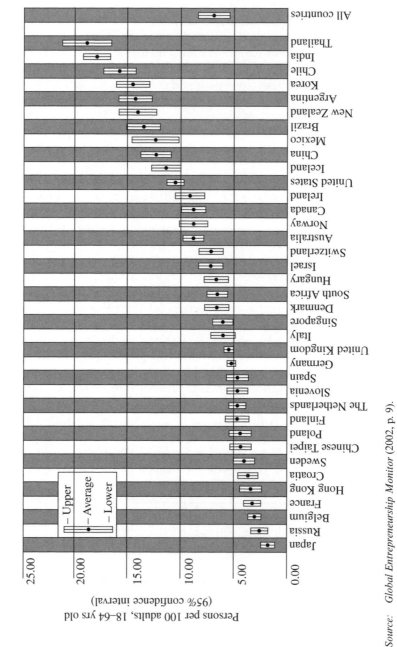

Source: *Global Entrepreneurship Monitor* (2002, p. 9).

Figure 1.5 Entrepreneurial activity in different countries

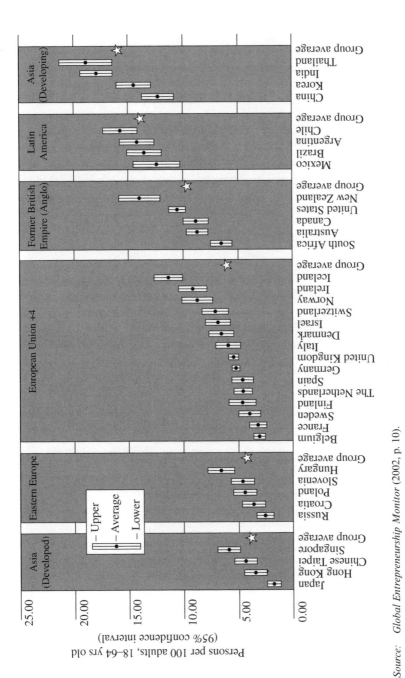

Source: Global Entrepreneurship Monitor (2002, p. 10).

Figure 1.6 Entrepreneurial activity in different global regions

25

A Country Diagnosis

I made a diagnosis of Sweden more than 15 years ago (Bjerke, 1989). An updated version might be like this:

- Explanations of its problems, if they exist, are presented in simplistic terms, for instance, that it is in a recession, that it has a frustrating legal system and high taxes, that it has a complicated and inhibiting bureaucracy and that the power of its labour unions is too restrictive.
- Blame is laid on external circumstances, for instance, Brussels or its immigrants.
- Solutions are presented in traditional terms, for instance, reforming the tax system, reducing bureaucracy, giving more support and subsidies to struggling firms and industries, investing more in research and following 'good' examples from other countries.

Arbnor's diagnosis (2004) is in line with the above, even if expressed in more vivid terms:

- Its model has been clockwork for too long, that is, regular order and harmony. It became a master of interpreting the mission of building a modern society instrumentally.
- Swedes have only used more of the same old instrumentalism, knowledge orientation and outlook on life in their project of building a nation.
- An instrumental description is trivializing life. Swedes suffer from exact stupidity.
- Swedes should visualize the premises on which their thoughts are based and keep up a genuine dialogue on values.
- Better artistic than statistic, better vivid than morbid, better whole-icipating than part-icipating.
- It is not very well-advised to follow the same thought premises which have led to a problem when trying to solve it.
- Imaginative creation of knowledge is the latest and most important production factor. The point is to try to deliver what is possible out of what is factual.

THE MODERN CORPORATION

The modern corporation came into being around 1870 and was built on the following five basic points (*The Economist*, 2001, p. 16):

1. The corporation is the 'master'; the employees are the 'servants'.
2. The great majority of employees work full-time for the corporation.
3. The most efficient way to produce anything is to bring together under one management as many as possible of the activities needed to turn out the product.
4. Suppliers and especially manufacturers have market power because they have information about a product or a service that the customer does not and cannot have, and does not need if he can trust the brand.
5. To one particular technology pertains one and only one industry, and conversely, to any one particular industry pertains one and only one technology.

All of these points are being questioned today.

CONCLUDING COMMENTS

Hedberg and Sjöstrand observed 25 years ago (1979) that the obstacle to action in society depends more on inertia of thought than on inertia to action. This is more valid in our new entrepreneurial society than ever. A leading topic in this book is the way in which thought and action are related. The latter is impossible without the former.

The future will see an increasingly fast turnover of businesses and working opportunities; but closedown is not failure. We will need institutions and traditions that facilitate renewal, adjustment and development – applied at both local and regional levels (Lans et al., 1997). Day by day innovation will be more important than big steps forward (Bjerke, 1989). We must respect the imaginative power of individuals. The fastest growing group in the workforce are 'knowledge workers' (especially knowledge technologists) and they are the new capitalists (*The Economist*, 2001). The key word is *flexibility*. Corporations will need to break themselves down into small entrepreneurial units and they will have to legitimize themselves as never before. Their management of concepts and language can be their major asset – but also their biggest liability when trying to act.

THE STRUCTURE OF THE BOOK

This first chapter has emphasized the necessity of a new kind of thinking in our entrepreneurial society of today. The rest of the book is about entrepreneurs and the importance of entrepreneurship in this society. Chapter 2 considers two different ways of trying to get a picture of what entrepreneurs

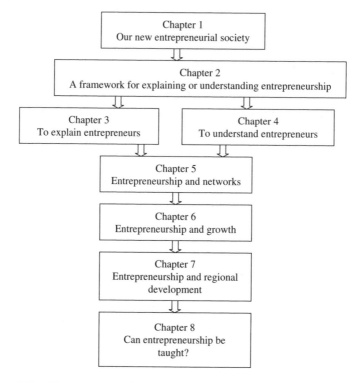

Figure 1.7   The structure of the book

and entrepreneurship means. Traditionally these are called explaining and understanding. Chapter 3 provides a summary of how we have traditionally tried to explain entrepreneurs. In Chapter 4 an equivalent summary is provided in terms of more modern attempts to understand the same subject. In Chapters 5–7, I discuss entrepreneurship in three contemporary situations, that is, in networks, when firms are growing and in regional development. These three chapters contain both explaining and understanding aspects. Finally in Chapter 8, I provide my answer to a question which I often get in my position as professor of entrepreneurship: 'Can entrepreneurship be taught?' The structure of the book is seen in Figure 1.7.

2. A framework for explaining or understanding entrepreneurship

INTRODUCTION

To claim a clear difference between 'explaining' and 'understanding' may seem of little interest to some. However, it has become customary, though by no means universal, to distinguish between trying to get a picture of *events* and trying to get a picture of *acts*. It is suggested that the term 'understanding', in contrast to 'explaining', ought to be reserved for the latter.

Since the inception of the disciplines of social science, lines of controversy have been drawn between those who do and those who do not make a principal distinction between two presumed alternative modes of thought, that is, natural sciences and social sciences. Theorists rejecting any fundamental distinction between those modes have traditionally been called *positivists*. We may call them *explaining-oriented researchers*. They assume that the methods which have proved their unparalleled value in the analysis of the physical world are applicable to the materials of social sciences, and that while these methods may have to be adapted to a special subject matter, the logic of explanation in physical and social sciences is the same. Theorists who draw a distinction between 'understanding' and 'explaining' can be labelled *anti-positivists* or *hermeneuticians*. We may call them *understanding-oriented researchers*. The critical element in anti-positivism is the insistence that the methods of physical sciences, however modified, are intrinsically inadequate to the subject matter of social sciences; in the physical world man's knowledge is external and empirical, while social sciences are concerned with interpretations and with various kinds of experience.

Many methodological and theoretical discourses within social sciences since the late nineteenth century have concerned modes of thought of 'understanding' and 'explaining' (Bottomore and Nisbet, 1979). These discourses reached a high point in the period immediately before World War I, and they have been part of social sciences ever since.

The controversy between explaining and understanding is deeply rooted in western thought. In its most elementary sense it is based on a presumed intrinsic difference between mind and all that is non-mind. The controversy cannot be eliminated by choosing between explaining and understanding, because, basically, they cannot be compared. Most explaining-oriented researchers, for instance, claim that everything, in the natural world as well as in the human world, can be explained, at least in principle; while understanding-oriented researchers claim that understanding is only for humans. Furthermore there is no neutral position where you can choose between explaining and understanding in a businesslike and impartial way. One has to 'choose' at the same time as, by necessity, being positioned in either the explaining or the understanding camp. Which is really no choice at all! Furthermore:

- The purpose of explanations is to depict a factual (objective and/or subjective) reality in order to better predict its course from outside; the purpose of understanding is to develop means in order to better manage human existence from within.
- One explanation can replace another explanation; one understanding can replace another understanding. However, an explanation cannot (according to understanding-oriented researchers) replace an understanding (which it can according to an explaining-oriented researcher). Understanding-oriented researchers (like me) claim that these are two different scientific approaches.

A SHORT HISTORICAL OVERVIEW

According to von Wright (1971) and Apel (1984) the German philosopher of history Johann Gustav Droysen (1808–84) was the first, within science, to introduce the difference between 'to explain' and 'to understand' (in German, *Erklären* and *Verstehen* respectively), to ground historical sciences methodologically and to distinguish them from natural sciences. He did this in *Grundrisse der Historik*, which was published in 1858:

> According to the object and nature of human thought there are three possible scientific methods: the speculative (formulated in philosophy and theology), the mathematical or physical, and the historical. Their respective essences are to know, to explain, and to understand. (Droysen, 1858, p. 13)

Droysen's term, '*Verstehen*', can be traced back to the modern founders of hermeneutics, Friedrich Schleiermacher (1768–1834) and Auguste Boeckh (1785–1867), and was made more generally known through Max Weber (1852–1931). A historically significant form of the debate between understanding and explanation began with Wilhelm Dilthey (1833–1911). He utilized the dichotomy between understanding and explanation as the terminological foundation for distinguishing between natural sciences and *Geisteswissenschaften* (the humanities) as a whole. Initially, understanding gained a psychological character, which explanations lacked. This psychological element was emphasized by several of the nineteenth-century anti-positivist methodologists, perhaps above all by Georg Simmel (1858–1918), who thought that understanding as a method characteristic of the humanities is a form of *empathy* (von Wright, 1971). But empathy is not a modern way of separating understanding from explanation. Understanding can today be associated with *intentionality*, for instance, in a way which explanation cannot. We will come back to this concept a little later.

Generally we can say that natural sciences require concepts which permit the formation of testable laws and theories. Other issues, for instance, those deriving from ordinary language, are of less interest. But in the social sciences another set of considerations exists as well: the concepts used to describe, explain and/or understand human activity must be drawn at least in part from the social life being studied, not only from the scientists' theories (Fay, 1996). Scientific concepts then bear a fundamentally different relationship to social phenomena from that which they bear to natural phenomena. In social sciences, concepts partially constitute the reality being studied; this is opposite to natural phenomena where concepts merely serve to describe and explain (ibid.).

> It is possible to explain human behaviour. We do not try to understand an area of low pressure because it has no meaning. On the other hand we try to understand human beings because they are of the same kind as we are. (Liedman, 2002, p. 280; my translation)

POSITIVISM

Although the term 'positivism' was coined by his teacher Henri Saint-Simon (1760–1825), it was the Frenchman Auguste Comte (1789–1857) who popularized the term. Comte's contemporaries, the utilitarians Jeremy Bentham (1748–1832) and James Mill (1773–1836), presented with equal force, although more modestly, the fundamental requirements of positivism. Between the two world wars in the 1900s, positivism had a revival in the so-called Vienna circle. Leading figures were Rudolf Carnap (1891–1970) and Otto Neurath (1882–1945). The preferred term then was logical positivism (later logical empiricism). The purpose of positivism is to systematize data in our experience.

Even if hardly anybody calls themselves a positivist or logical empiricist today, positivist thinking nonetheless dominates the way we look at society (exceptions are most of the fine arts and imaginative literature). There are still many commentators who claim that explanations – the basic aims of positivists/logical empiricists – are the exact and true ambition of science and that understanding is something else – fuzzier and less scientific.

The positivist movement can be characterized by the three following statements relating to social sciences (Bjerke, 1989):

1. Explanations produced by social sciences should be of the same type as natural science explanations, that is, statements of conformity to law expressed in the form 'A causes B'.
2. Social sciences should, as far as possible, use the same type of methods as natural sciences as far as constructing and testing these explanations are concerned.
3. Ideologies, myths and metaphysics have an extra-scientific content.

Critiques exist against positivism from non-positivists (as well as defence and critique back, of course).
Positivism/logical empiricism is based on the following assumptions:

*   Social reality, like physical reality, can be frozen into a kind of structured immobility such that an objective form of measurement can take place.
*   Human beings, like elements in physical sciences, can be reduced to atoms and molecules which are subject to more or less deterministic and controllable external forces.
*   The social scientist can reveal the nature of the world by examining lawful relationships which are assumed to exist between its elements. These elements can be extracted from their context.

However, according to non-positivists these assumptions ignore a number of factors which are 'natural' among human beings:

a. *Uniqueness* The assumptions do not cater to individual differences between the subjects under study. Human beings possess unique thought processes and perceptions. The use of statistical and mathematical analysis conceals these individual differences by averaging across the subjects under investigation.
b. *Instability* Social reality, as distinct from physical reality, is made up of individuals who are not only influenced by the environment but may also contribute towards it based on their perceptions of reality. As such, the phenomena under study are transitory. This is because not only will the 'facts' of the social events change as perceived by the

subjects but the subjects themselves change and influence the environment over time. As such, no clear-cut, static relationships may exist, nor can any easy dichotomy be made between independent and dependent variables in social sciences.

c. *Sensitivity* The positivistic/logical empiricism approach assumes that researchers and subjects alike are able to behave 'objectively' ('object-like'). This is erroneous because subjects may become 'irrational' or behave 'differently' under research conditions.

d. *Lack of realism* Some opponents of the positivism/logical empiricism believe that this perspective lacks realism because it is not possible to simulate all variables in an organization under 'scientific' conditions. Manipulating and controlling for variables changes the phenomena under study. As such, these studies lack external validity and generalizations of the phenomena under study may be invalid since they may differ from their real-world counterparts.

e. *Epistemological differences* Natural science researchers possess assumptions which are fundamentally different from those possessed by social science researchers. Physical science research usually concentrates on cause–effect relationships. In social science research this leads to the assumption that society has a concrete and factual existence which allows the researcher to remain 'objective' and value-free. However, social reality is not divorced from the context of the environment and the unique social systems in which events occur. In brief, the ontological assumption set and the perception of reality, existence and meaning differ between social and natural sciences which should, according to some researchers, lead to different ways of research.

The person who has argued the hardest against a pure positivism is probably Max Weber (1852–1931). He relied heavily on the concept of *Verstehen*, but he did not mean by this what we normally mean, that is, understanding in general. Alfred Schutz, a social phenomenologist (a topic to which we will return) who bases much of his thinking on Weber, formulates this as follows:

> The critics of understanding call it subjective, because they hold that understanding the motives of another man's action depends upon the private, uncontrollable and unverifiable intuition of the observer or refers to his private value system. The social scientists, such as Max Weber, however, call *Verstehen* subjective because its goal is to find out what the actor 'means' in his action, in contrast to the meaning which this action has for the actor's partner or a neutral observer. (Schutz, 1962, pp. 56–7)

Weber provided an alternative to the positivist ideal of causal explanations (more about this concept later). By *Verstehen* he meant something like

interpretative understanding. Weber insisted that what we have to understand as social scientists is the subjective meaning attached by an individual to his or her behaviour. There is, then, no question of imposing any
framework of explanation on the situation, a framework which the agent
would not accept (Trigg, 1985). As Schutz observes:

> We cannot deal with phenomena in the social world as we do with phenomena
> belonging to the natural sphere. In the latter, we collect facts and regularities
> which are not understandable to us, but which we can refer only to certain fun-
> damental assumptions about the world. We shall never understand why the
> mercury in the thermometer rises if the sun shines on it. We can only interpret
> this phenomenon as compatible with the laws we have deduced from some basic
> assumptions about the physical world. We want, on the contrary, to understand
> social phenomena, and we cannot understand them apart from their placement
> within the scheme of human motives, human means and ends, human planning
> – in short – within the categories of human action. (Schutz, 1964, p. 85)

The consequences are that it could be difficult to develop meaningful
average or typical (most common) pictures of human beings. It is, however,
possible and useful, according to Weber, to construct ideal types
(typifications) – mental constructions developed by the researcher – in
order to discuss some social phenomena, without demanding that these
ideal types must have strict empirical equivalents.

Of course, non-positivistic perspectives also have their critics. Arguments
brought forward include (Bjerke, 1989):

- Non-positivists use metaphors extensively. These are ways to reflect
  social reality, which, however, could be very unrealistic and
  abstracted from the context of the subjects under study.
- Non-positivists introduce and legitimize bias in their studies. Non-
  positivistic perspectives do not rest on a set of given and tested techniques as positivistic perspectives do.
- Results developed through non-positivistic perspectives lack gener-
  ality. Researchers are primarily interested in individuals' perceptions
  of reality, without exploring the way in which such perceptions may
  be verified or translated to attain a reflection of the world as perceived by others.
- There are problems which are more suited to a positivistic approach.

Andersson (1979) has compiled a list of differences between positivism and
hermeneutics (see Table 2.1).

As will be evident by now, we are dealing here with questions and issues
which can be hard to grasp and which remain highly controversial. There

Table 2.1   Positivism and hermeneutics

Positivism	Hermeneutics
Natural science research ideals	Social science research ideals
Unity between physical and social phenomena	Difference between physical and social phenomena
Explanation	Understanding
Matter	Socio-matter
Generality	Totality
Abstraction	Concretion
Simplification	Problematization
Depicting	Interpreting
Differences between facts and values	Unity between facts and values
Differences between feeling and reason	Unity between feeling and reason
Distance	Involvement
Partiality	Non-partiality
Forecast	Change
Differences between science and personality	Unity between science and personality
Differences between scientific and extra-scientific knowledge	Unity between scientific and extra-scientific knowledge

Source: Andersson (1979).

are decisive differences of opinion concerning suitable methods for research, perceptions of reality and the appropriate aims of research. According to Wenneberg (2001) some lack of clarity arises from failure to establish *which* reality is in focus. His viewpoints really concern social constructionism (a concept we will be back to), but they are valid for positivistic and non-positivist perspectives as a whole. First of all, a researcher needs to clarify which of three possible realities the discussion is about:

- natural, physical reality
- social reality
- subjective reality.

Second, he or she has to distinguish between two aspects of reality:

- knowledge of reality
- reality in itself.

MY VIEW ON EXPLAINING AND ON UNDERSTANDING

No one today claims that only natural sciences should aim for explanations and that only social sciences should aim for understanding. In practice, attempts at both are made in both areas. Researchers are also conscious of the differences between the two approaches, although in everyday usage it is harder to distinguish between what is meant by 'explain' and 'understand'. While it seems relatively clear that 'explain' means, by and large, to figure out the external circumstances around what has happened or what is happening, there is, however, a wide variety of opinions as to what we could mean by 'understand'.

- 'To understand' means to find out more details.
- 'To understand' means to get access to subjective opinions.
- 'To understand' means to get a picture of the larger context in which a phenomenon is placed.
- 'To understand' means to get a picture of relevant circumstances which have taken place earlier in a specific situation.

To me, none of these equates to understanding; they are each just more detailed, more circumstantial or deeper aspects of explanation. As I see it, the crucial difference between explaining and understanding is that explanation sees language as *depicting* reality and understanding sees language as *constituting* reality!

Thus, explaining-oriented researchers:

- look for factual (objective and/or subjective) data and use a depicting language
- want to find cause–effect relationships
- build models.

While understanding-oriented researchers:

- deny that factual and depicting data exist (at least in the human world)
- want to look for actors' view on meaning, importance and significance and use a constituting and forming (even performing) language
- come up with interpretations.

In this, *models* are deliberately simplified pictures of factual reality; and *interpretations* are deliberately problematized pictures of socially constructed

Table 2.2   Explanation and understanding

Explanation	Understanding
Is using a depicting language	Is using a constituting language
Believes in a circumstantial world	Believes in a meaningful world
Sees reacting human beings	Sees acting human beings
Aims to depict a naturally complicated reality in models, that is, to come up with patterns in the law-bound reality by finding the most crucial circumstances in a situation and neglect those circumstances which are of less importance	Aims to problematize a socially constructed reality by using interpretations, that is, to construct pictures (maybe as metaphors) which can contain that meaning and those significances which are experienced in a situation, which, furthermore, provide openings for further construction of the social reality

reality. It is natural for explaining-oriented researchers to build models and for understanding-oriented researchers to come up with interpretations! (Table 2.2 offers a summary.)

Further on Explanations

In *Human Knowledge* (1948, p. 18) Bertrand Russell observed that 'the practical utility of science depends on its ability to foretell the future'. Forecasts presuppose cause–effect relationships and require regularities (Liedman, 2002). Explaining-oriented researchers are therefore looking for regularities.

There are three kinds of explanations which can be viewed under two headings (von Wright, 1971, Apel, 1984):

- Explanations which are provided by the model which is constructed in order to provide an explanation:
  1. Cause–effect explanations ('This happened *because* that has taken place')
  2. Purposeful explanations ('That happened *in order for this* to take place').
- Explanations which have to be looked for outside of the explanatory-seeking model:
  3. Further explanation ('This happened *due to circumstances* which must be looked for at another place or at another time').

The philosopher who has most thoroughly discussed cause–effect relations is David Hume (1711–76). He claimed that 'the relation between cause and effect is a regular sequence in time of (instantiations of) generic phenomena' (von Wright, 1971, p. 34). It is in this context necessary to make a distinction between *intrinsic, logical* and *causal (extrinsic)* relations. For example:

1. He started a business venture because he is an entrepreneur!
2. He started a business venture because he wanted to change his life!
3. He started a business venture because he wanted to make more money!

Only the third of these demonstrates a causal relation. (1) shows an intrinsic relation. To 'start a new business venture' is so to say part of the very definition of what it means to be an 'entrepreneur'! (2) shows a logical relation because it is difficult to think of an 'entrepreneur' who does not 'want to change his life'!

Von Wright claims that 'action' can never be part of a cause–effect relation:

> The connection between an action and its result is intrinsic, logical and not causal (extrinsic). If the result does not materialize, the action simply has not been performed. It result is as essential 'part' of the action. It is a *bad* mistake to think of the act(ion) itself as a cause of its result. (von Wright, 1971, pp. 67–8)

There are three requirements for a relation to be called causal, that is, for us to be able to say that one variable is the cause and another variable is an effect:

1. One variable we call cause and another variable we call effect seem related to each other.
2. The cause variable does not come after the effect variable in time.
3. No alternative background or intervening variable can better explain the effect variable in question.

A cause variable can be called *stronger* the more effect variables it can explain (Latour, 1998, p. 62–3).

Further on Understanding

Understanding-oriented researchers see some problems with explanatory knowledge:

- Data never speak for themselves. They have to be interpreted by the researcher.
- So-called 'facts' are always theory-laden (Alvesson and Sköldberg, 2000, p. 1).

- Human beings (including researchers) are never objective but are members of a culture. They may even be seen as constituting a culture.
- Explanations of phenomena can lack depth.

However, understanding is only of interest:

- when studying human beings
- between human beings.

Bauman (1978) distinguishes between various kinds of understanding according to the theoretical ground on which it rests:

- Understanding as the work of history (Karl Marx, Max Weber, Karl Mannheim).
- Understanding as the work of reason (Edmund Husserl, Talcott Parsons).
- Understanding as the work of life (Martin Heidegger, from Alfred Schutz to ethnomethodology).

Understanding (in a modern epistemological sense) calls for accepting that human beings are *intentional*. This is a concept which was developed by the founder of modern phenomenology, the German philosopher Edmund Husserl (1859–1938), who picked the concept up from one of his teachers, the German-Austrian philosopher and psychologist Franz Brentano (1838–1917). Like Brentano, Husserl claimed that all acts are intentional, that is, they are directed at an object and they are always performed in a context. Our consciousness is permeated by our intentionality. We are always stretching ourselves, shaping what we perceive by using our intentionality (Bjerke, 1989).

A further distinction between understanding-oriented researchers and explaining-oriented researchers, is that the former see no particular virtue in quantitative measures; they claim indeed that *meaning cannot be quantified*!

The interpretation of the meanings of actions, practices, and cultural objects is an extremely difficult and complicated enterprise. In order to know the meaning of certain overt movements interpreters must understand the beliefs, desires, and intentions of the particular people involved. But in order to understand these, they must know the vocabulary in terms of which they are expressed, and this in turn requires that they know the social rules and conventions which specify what a certain movement or object counts as. Moreover, in order to grasp these particular rules, they also have to know the set of institutional practices of which they are a part, and how these are related to other practices of the society.

Nor can interpreters stop here. The conventions and institutions of a social group presuppose a set of fundamental conceptualizations or basic assumptions regarding humanity, nature, and society. These basic conceptualizations might be called the 'constitutive meanings of a firm of life,' for they are the basic ideas or notions in terms of which the meanings of specific practices and schemes of activity must be analyzed. (Fay, 1996, p. 115)

But Bauman (1978) asks how much one really has to interpret in order to understand. He claims that one can say, for instance, that there is a difference in kind between laws governing the objects of nature and the rules influencing human beings. Rules are norms, they are standards of behaviour, perhaps with mechanisms attached which cause the actual conduct to approximate the standard, but a standard it is all the same. The actual behaviour may come up to it, but then it may not. We are sometimes told that this is the essential difference between rule-governed human action and the monotonous, law-subordinated behaviour of natural phenomena.

So far the difference between rules and laws looks like one of degree rather than of kind. Human behaviour should be less repetitive and monotonous and, therefore, less amenable to prediction than natural phenomena. But this 'less' makes sense only if related to a somewhat dated notion of scientific laws. Few natural scientists today would agree that the laws they formulate are as free of exceptions as social scientists seem to believe. Laws of natural science are mostly statistical, and they can specify only the degree of probability that a given phenomenon will occur in one instance, rather than any certainty of its occurrence. The existence of a rule, presumably, indicates a similar statistical probability. It would make little sense to speak of a rule in the case of behaviour which occurs only occasionally.

Can we say, then, that we place rules in a category by themselves because *their implementation can only take place through conscious decisions of men*? They must be 'applied' in order to become real and 'known' in order to be applied. The distinctive character of rules should then be grounded in certain psychical events which take place in the minds of people; nothing of a similar nature can be predicated upon natural phenomena.

This, indeed, seems like a valid argument, and one for which we are prepared by the whole of our daily thinking and acting. Whenever we do not grasp 'directly' the meaning of other people's behaviour, whenever we need to interpret behaviour, we rely on concepts such as 'he wants to imply', 'he intends', 'he wants me to believe that' and so on – all referring the meaning of what has been said or done to mental processes of one kind or another. This we do only in the case of human behaviour. We would certainly object to an attempt to describe the function of a machine in the same terms.

However, two very different things are confused here (ibid.). One is a statement of fact: no machine can write a book of Nobel Prize quality. The second, however, is a statement of interpretation: it is possible for a human being to write a book of Nobel Prize quality *because* of thoughts and emotions felt. Human behaviour is unique because of the ability to make suppositions, to interpret the behaviour, of other humans via these suppositions, and to question the behaviour and actions of others on the same basis. 'Understanding' other humans' behaviour, as against merely 'explaining' the conduct of inanimate objects, means ultimately extrapolating the method we use to account for our own action on to our accounts of the behaviour of other objects whom we recognize as human. Recognizing them as humans, and extrapolating the method, mean in fact the same thing. Thus perceiving an object as human boils down to assuming that the object has its own 'inner reality' structured in the same way as ours.

But now comes the crucial question: Do we really need to know what is going on in somebody else's head in order to understand them?

> Do we in fact need insight into the psychical process in the mind of the actor in order to *understand* his behaviour? Do we actually reconstruct this mental process when engaged in the effort of understanding? It is true that we normally refer to such mental processes when accounting for our *interpretation*. We articulate our version of other people's conduct in terms like 'he thinks that', 'he does not like it', 'he does not wish', 'he wanted to', 'what he meant was', etc., all implying that we have penetrated the 'inside' of our partner's mind and found the meaning of his behaviour there. The question is, however, whether these are only the terms which we use to couch our interpretation, or whether they are a true expression of what we have actually done.
>
> As a matter of fact we do not know what '*they*' think', 'intend', 'mean'. Or, at least, we do not know it in the same way as we know our own thinking, intending, meaning. What we know is only their action, the sentences they utter, the prosodic features which accompany their speech, the 'paralinguistic' aspects of their behaviour. All these refer to what we can see or hear. When we speak of their thinking, intending, meaning, we do not refer to what we see or hear, but to the manner in which we interpret what we see or hear. This common-sense-grounded manner of speech is regrettable, as it beclouds rather than reveals the true nature of understanding. It suggests that the activity of understanding needs what in actual fact it can well (and must) do without – knowing something which is essentially 'unknowable'. (Bauman, 1978, pp. 213–14)

So, when we interpret and try to understand other human beings we do not need to have extrasensory, insightful or emphatic characteristics. It is enough to understand how to recognize oneself, that is, to have some cultural aspect in common with the other person (otherwise an understanding would not be possible at all). Furthermore, in order to understand what the other person means when he or she makes a specific remark, we do not need to enter the other person's consciousness. We 'only' need to agree with the other person about where and how this remark can be used, to know the game so to say (compare Wittgenstein's concept of a 'language game', to which we will return).

The concept of intentionality, then, does not refer to any particular psychological process but is related to the (inevitable) mental disposition of a human being in any situation.

According to Norén (1995) an interpretative researcher has three central choices:

- whether to work with a functionalistically-based or non-functionalistically-based, interpretative research;
- whether to lead an interpretative discussion which stresses the unitary or the postmodern fragmentary aspects of society;
- whether to use an interpretative approach close to the researcher or close to the other actors.

He claims that there are three different interpretative approaches:

- *A metaphoric approach*, that is, to construct pictures, which not only catch what seems to be going on, but also open possibilities for new angles of interpretation.
- *An actors' approach*, that is, to construct pictures which stress the actors' own experiences and their points of view.
- *A social constructionist approach*, that is, to construct pictures which stress the researcher's way of understanding how a collective of actors produce and reproduce their own social reality.

As the reader will discover, I think it is possible to combine the last two, or to put it another way, to subordinate the actors' approach to the social constructionist approach. Norén also admits (1995, p. 18) that it is very difficult to separate the two in practice; he considers them separately only for pedagogical purposes.

Explaining-oriented researchers try to find patterns, either as structures or as processes. Understanding-oriented researchers try to gain insights, either through language or through culture. When trying to explain it is quite possible to combine structures and processes (processes might in fact be described as structures over time). When trying to understand it is quite possible to combine language and culture (one may even claim that these two are inseparable). However, I would maintain that it is not possible to combine explaining and understanding in the same research effort (I will be back to this). My interest in understanding could be expressed as 'an interpretative understanding', where I see understanding as the researcher's goal and interpretation as the means.

As we have seen, the meaning of explanation is relatively unambiguous, while what constitutes understanding remains contested. In order to provide a clearer background to the rest of the book, therefore, I want to discuss this area further and look at those philosophical conceptions which have been of special importance to the development of my attitude to this issue of understanding. These are: Ludwig Wittgenstein, hermeneutics, phenomenology, ethnomethodology, social constructionism/sensemaking and social phenomenology.

Ludwig Wittgenstein

Ludwig Wittgenstein (1889–1951) was one of the most influential and most widely-discussed philosophers of the twentieth century. One of the rare human beings who radically differs from the mainstream, but still remains relevant and of his time, he is also rare in another sense. He really knows the meaning of a paradigmatic shift. He made one himself.

Wittgenstein was a language philosopher and professor at the University of Cambridge from 1939 to 1947. It is common to speak of his two periods. The first preceded his doctoral thesis *Tractatus Logico-Philosophicus*. The second began around 1930 and continued to his death. In this period he rejected practically every aspect of his view of language as presented in his thesis. It is these later radical views on how to learn a language, on meaning in language and on language itself which are of interest here.

How can one go about understanding a meaningful act? How can one grasp the meaning of human action or its linguistic symbols if (as discussed above) there is little hope that this can be achieved by empathy, by discovering what has actually happened 'in the head' of the actor? Wittgenstein describes the task of finding the meaning of an act (he speaks more specifically of the meaning of a word rather than of an act, but at the same time he looks at speech as an act – a *speech act*) as that of discovering 'without which it would have no meaning'. In other words, the task is not one of empirical observation and the recording of events, but of the analysis of necessary conditions of meaningfulness: what *has to happen* for an act, like a speech act, to have meaning.

To understand the meaning of an act is not the same thing as being able to provide further details, to define it or to present the motives behind the act in question. Wittgenstein says:

> Try not to think of understanding as a 'mental process' at all. For *that* is the expression which confuses you. But ask yourself: in what sort of case, in what kind of circumstances, do we say: 'Now I know how to go on'? (Wittgenstein, 1953, p. 61)

To understand meaning, according to Wittgenstein, is to know how to go on in the presence of a word, an act or other objects whose meaning we understand. To understand the act 'to read', for instance, is to evoke those circumstances under which the act of reading is possible. To understand is not an emphatic act, it is an analytical act.

Meaning is therefore not a hypothetical entity here, an entity which *precedes* the experience of an act. Meaning is, instead, constituted *in retrospect*, in the course of subsequent analysis, when the memories or the image of experience, and not the experience itself, is dissected and reorganized according to some 'reference schema' external to the experience. This applies to the understanding-oriented professional researcher in the same degree as it applies to the ordinary member of society in those situations, where he or she reflects (Bauman, 1978).

All meaning, according to this point of view, results from interpretation. It is something to be constructed, not discovered. And, according to Wittgenstein, meaning and signification exist in our language practice. Meaning is not a matter of rules at all, but of language regularities (Ziff, 1960).

According to Wittgenstein, language is something we do. To understand a language is not a matter of grasping some inner essence of meaning, but rather of knowing how to do certain things. The emphasis falls on the 'functions' of words rather than their 'meanings'. Wittgenstein refers to this as *language games*.

Wittgenstein stresses the diversity of the language games we play to show what is wrong with the traditional assumption (formerly shared by him) that the essential function of language is to make assertions about matters of fact. In this view, the meaning of a word is what it stands for in the world, and the function of language is primarily to express assertions of the world. Wittgenstein shows this view of meaning to be false, and that this view of language is correspondingly inadequate and misleading. The significance of this shift is impossible to convey in summary form, but we can point to a few of the consequences of Wittgenstein's position (Pitkin, 1972).

If language is seen as human activity rather than a collection of labels for categories of phenomena, then we will not be surprised to find systematic inconsistencies in it – not as a fault or as problems, but as essential to its function. Further, if language is seen as human activity, that activity may be carried out in quite different ways, depending on what the talking human beings are up to. Furthermore, if words need not be used for referring and their meaning is not their reference, and if concepts may be internally inconsistent, then many of our traditional and common-sense assumptions about the relationship between language and reality are called into question. One could, according to Wittgenstein, say that the essential language function is *not to comment on factual circumstances but to be together*.

In *The Blue and Brown Book*, Wittgenstein calls the regularities of our grammar, which bind diverse phenomena together into a single concept, 'conventions'. In his later writings, though he still considers grammar conventional, he has largely replaced this term with the expression 'forms of life'. That notion is never explicitly defined, but its significance is relatively clear (Pitkin, 1972): human life as we live and observe it is not just a random, continuous flow, but displays recurrent patterns, regularities, characteristic ways of doing and being, of feeling and acting, of speaking and interacting. Because they are patterns, regularities, configurations, Wittgenstein calls them 'forms', and because they are patterns in the fabric of human existence and activity on earth, he describes them as 'of life'. The idea is clearly related to the idea of language games, and more generally to Wittgenstein's action-oriented view of language (ibid.). 'The *speaking* of language', he says, 'is a part of an activity, or a form of life' (Wittgenstein, 1953, p. 23).

Let me finish this section with a quotation which shows how deeply and how inevitably we are tied up with our words:

> A word never – well, hardly ever – shakes off its etymology and its formation. In spite of all changes in and extensions of and additions to its meanings, and indeed rather pervading and governing these, there will still persist the old idea. (Austin, 1965, p. 149)

Hermeneutics

Hermeneutics, like most attempts to understand, for instance phenomenology, is ambiguous. Its starting point is that there are many different ways to understand reality. It is sometimes translated as *interpretative science*. Hermeneutics comes from the Greek word *hermeneutikos*, which means interpretation. In the classical context the term referred to interpretation of texts, especially biblical, but also philosophical. Employing mostly philological methods, hermeneutics occupied itself with critical scrutiny of contending texts, with establishment of the authentic version – the 'true meaning' of the document – as its ultimate objective. At that stage of the development of hermeneutics, recovering the true meaning was seen as identical with demonstrating the authenticity of the text (Bauman, 1978).

At the end of the sixteenth century a crucial shift in the purpose of hermeneutics took place. Above all through the works of Friedrich Schleiermacher hermeneutics moved beyond the mere critique of texts left by other writers: it became the question of how a member of one culture struggles to grasp the experience of another, a denizen of one historical era tries to embrace another era's practice of everyday life. The interest in texts, however, is there at the bottom, even if extensions can be seen in two directions:

1. Not so much concern with written and finished texts as such, as interest in the *world as language*. This language world, however, can be studied as texts.
2. A broader interest in interpreting *cultural manifestations in general* (Ricoeur, 1971). The concept 'text' is, however, sometimes used to cover that aspect of phenomena of the world as well (ibid.).

The interest in texts in hermeneutics can be related to the idea that language is an analogue to the constitution of social reality. This idea was presented by, among others, Hans-Georg Gadamer (1900–2002), who is regarded as one of the great authorities in hermeneutics. He claimed that our world is created by language; he also asserted that we can constantly enlarge this world by broadening our horizons. His argument was that this is possible because we can translate between different languages.

Gadamer was of the opinion that 'the world' is in language, rather than constituting its foundation. As a consequence he rejected all notions of a 'world in itself' against which different views of the world can be positioned. Understanding can only be developed by using our own concepts to interpret some manifestation by another culture, for instance a text. At first we may feel that we do not properly understand this particular text, and this may be because we are bringing to bear the assumptions of our own society and failing to make allowances for the social context in which the text was originally written. A proper interpretation has to allow for a mutual interplay between the assumptions in the interpreter's own cultural situation and the context in which the text was written. Gadamer refers to this as a *fusion of horizons*.

As interpreters we operate in a specific context. According to hermeneutics there is therefore no understanding without pre-understanding. The relationship between understanding and pre-understanding is related to *the hermeneutic circle*, sometimes called *the hermeneutic spiral*. When trying to understand we constantly shift between what is specific and what is general. Searching for lost connections, in our attempts to understand what originally seems like completely strange cultural manifestations, we never stop. But we can move from what is specific to what is general and back again in ever wider circles (Figure 2.1).

Phenomenology
Edmund Husserl (1859–1938) popularized the concept of phenomenology in the early twentieth century, since which time it has grown to describe a

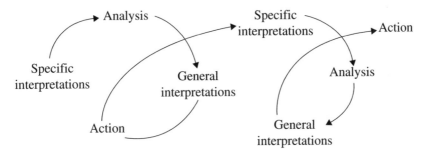

Figure 2.1   The hermeneutic spiral

way to philosophize – by using the phenomenological method. The term, however, is older than that. It comes from the Greek words *phainomenon* ('appearance') and *logos* ('knowledge of'). Generally, phenomenology is a philosophical approach centred on analysis of the phenomena which are part of man's awareness. The term was introduced by the German philosopher Johann Heinrich Lambert (1728–1771), who took 'phenomenon' to refer to the illusory features of human experience. Consequently, he defined phenomenology as 'the theory of illusion'. Kant used the term 'phenomenology' only twice, but he gave a new and broader sense to 'phenomenon' that, in turn, resulted in a redefinition of 'phenomenology'. Kant distinguished objects and events as they appear in our experience from objects and events as they appear in themselves, independently of the forms imposed on them by our cognitive abilities. The former he called 'phenomena'; the latter, 'things-in-themselves'. All we can ever know, Kant thought, are phenomena.

The next generation of philosophers, especially Hegel, tried to show that this was a mistake. Hegel saw Spirit (or Mind) developing through various stages in which it apprehends itself as phenomenon, to the point of full development where it is aware of itself as it is in itself. Phenomenology became to him the science in which we come to know mind as it is in itself through the study of the ways in which it appears to us.

Phenomenology, in the spirit of Husserl, was critical of modern science, which was seen to distance itself too much from man's everyday world, what he called *Lebenswelt* ('life-world'). Instead, according to Husserl and his successors, interest should be focused on the subjective experience in this world.

Central for Husserl was intentionality, a concept which we have met before, which means, as we have seen, that our conscience is not fed by passive impressions but instead is always actively directed at interpreting things around us, trying to make them meaningful; we are not referring here to objects as things in the outer world by themselves, but to things intended.

One of Husserl's successors, Alfred Schutz (1899–1959), suggested that our experience of the world is directed by *the natural attitude*, where we take for granted that the world is built up by assumptions about groups of events in our language, so-called *typifications*, assumptions that we rarely question.

If we compare hermeneutics and phenomenology, we can say the following:

- In relation to pre-understanding, a hermeneutician attempts to fuse pre-understanding (his or her tradition) with the structures of meaning which are in the studied text (or a cultural manifestation in general) which come from another tradition. A phenomenologist tries to reduce his or her pre-understanding in order to better understand the actors.
- The interpretation of a hermeneutic tradition is about the relationship between researcher and text (cultural manifestation). The interpretation in a phenomenological tradition is about trying to understand what the actors see as meaningful in their life-world.

Common to both, however, is that in no case is there a reduction to studying subjects or objects by themselves.

Ethnomethodology

Ethnomethodology can be seen as a branch of phenomenology. Its leading proponent is Harold Garfinkel (1917–). As in phenomenology in general the development and the maintenance of the life-world is studied here. Criticism of traditional social science is strong.

Ethnomethodology is concerned with unconsidered and unquestioned background expectations and implicit rules that govern action in the quotidian world. Its method is to focus on micro processes which make it possible for the life-world to develop and to be maintained. Ethnomethodology has been criticized for studying the consequences of our everyday conventions, while ignoring the sources of these conventions:

[E]thnomethodology never asks the central question: which are the supraindividual structures that shape the actors' behavioural dispositions? (Alvesson and Sköldberg, 2000, p. 43)

Ethnomethodologists forget to bring into their analysis the fact that ambiguity in human societies is partly eliminated by a whole range of tools, rules, walls and things of which they just analyse some. (Latour, 1998, pp. 18–19; my translation)

Ethnomethodology has, however, been called 'the science of sensemaking' (Gephart, 1993).

Social constructionism/sensemaking

According to Wenneberg (2001) there are three philosophical and scientific historical sources of inspiration underlying social constructionism:

1. Kuhn's concept of paradigm.
2. Wittgenstein's language philosophy.
3. Garfinkels' ethnomethodology.

This research orientation is called both *constructivism* and *constructionism*. I prefer the latter. For one thing, constructivism is a branch of mathematics (Hacking, 1999), and for another – and for me this is more important:

> Many researchers use the concepts 'constructivism' and 'constructionism' as if they were interchangeable. There is, however, a basic difference. For constructivists the process of world construction is psychological; it takes place 'in the head'. In contrast, for social constructionists what we take to be real is an outcome of social relationships. (Gergen, 1999, p. 237)

There are a number of variations of social constructionism (Sandberg, 1999). They include social phenomenology (Berger and Luckmann, 1981), ethnomethodology (Garfinkel, 1967), symbolic interactionism (Mead, 1934), discourse approaches (Foucault, 1972), post-structuralism (Derrida, 1998), cultural approaches (Geertz, 1973; Alvesson, 1993) and gender approaches (Keller, 1985; Harding, 1986).

There are, however, a number of similarities among all social constructionist approaches (Wenneberg, 2001; Devins and Gold, 2002):

*   person and reality are inseparable
*   language produces and reproduces reality instead of being a result of reality
*   knowledge is socially constructed, not objectively given.

There are four basic working assumptions among social constructionism researchers (Gergen, 1999):

1. *Those terms by which we understand our world and our self are neither required nor demanded by 'what there is'*   This has to do with the failure of language to map or picture an independent world. Another way of stating this assumption is to say that there are a potentially unlimited

number of possible descriptions of 'the situation in question' – and none of these descriptions can be ruled superior in terms of its capacity to map, picture or capture its features.

2. *Our modes of description, explanation and/or representation are derived from relationship* Language and all other forms of representation are meaningful only in their relationships with people. Meaning and significances are born of coordination between individuals – agreements, negotiations, affirmations. Nothing exists for us as intelligible people before there are relationships.

3. *As we describe or otherwise represent our reality, so do we fashion our future* Language is a major ingredient of our worlds of actions and therefore a part of building futures either as continuations of what already exists or as part of what will be new.

4. *Reflection on our forms of understanding is vital to our future well-being* What shall we save, what shall we resist and destroy, what shall we create? There are no universal answers, only socially constructed ones.

There are many simplistic views held on social constructionism, for instance, those that argue that this research approach denies the values of our basic social mechanisms and orientations, that social constructionists claim that sound decisions are really impossible, that anybody can claim that he or she is right, that there are no firm grounds to stand on at all, and that the answer to all questions can be formulated as 'It depends'. However, 'It is not that social constructionist ideas annihilate self, truth, objectivity, science, and morality. Rather, it is the way in which we have understood and practiced them that is thrown into question' (Gergen, 1999, p. 33).

An interesting discussion of the scientific position of social constructionism is led by Wenneberg (2001). He claims that one can apply social constructionism with a higher or lower degree of radicality. Of the following four levels the last is the most radical:

- *As a critical perspective* Everything in human existence can be questioned. Man is by nature more plastic and malleable than we normally think.
- *As a theory for the development, maintenance and modification of consciousness* This can be called social phenomenology and we will be back to it.
- *As an epistemological position* This position claims that knowledge of reality is exclusively determined by social factors.
- *As an ontological* position This position claims that reality *in itself* is socially constructed.

There are seven questions that are commonly brought up in relation to social constructionism. Let us take them one by one and look at possible answers, all according to Gergen (1999):

1. *What status do the physical world and its very real problems have in constructionism?* Constructionists do not deny air pollution, poverty or death. Constructionists do not try to rule on what is and what is not fundamentally real or not. However, the moment we enter a discussion about what there is, we enter the world of discourses, that is, a tradition, a way of life and a set of value preferences. To claim what is true, what has really happened and so on, closes the door on further discussions.

2. *Does constructionism deny the importance of personal experience and other mental states?* Constructionism does not attempt to eradicate the use of mental terms, either in personal, political or in scientific discussions. From a constructionist's perspective it is not a matter of asking whether these vocabularies are true or not. The important question is what are the consequences on cultural life of the use of these terms.

3. *Is constructionism, as a form of scepticism, logically incoherent?* Constructionism does not seek to be the last word but tries to promote discussion which will avoid that outcome. 'Truth', as a criterion, is simply rendered irrelevant to the acceptance or rejection of constructionist propositions. Constructionism does not ask for acceptance because it is true. Rather, constructionism invites collaboration between people in giving sense and significance to the world and moves towards a more inclusive future world. Alternative 'truths' are not rejected; they are invited as participants in the dialogue.

4. *Does constructionism have a moral or political position, or does it advocate moral relativism?* While constructionist arguments do invite moral and political deliberation, they do not champion one ideal over another. Constructionism is relativistic; all positions may possess legitimacy. However, one should not make the error here of believing that constructionism espouses relativism. There is no relativist position in terms of a transcendent standpoint from which we can rule on the relative merits of various contenders without espousing any values. Constructionism may invite a posture of continuing reflection, but each element of reflection will inevitably be value-saturated. There is nothing in constructionism arguing against having values. However, they must not lead to eliminating voices antithetical to one's own. That would mean the end of conversation, dialogue and negotiation – or, in effect, the death of meaning itself.

5. If all that we take to be real and good is constructed, what is worth doing? It is within relationships that we acquire the sense of the real and the good, the sense of value, justice and joy. This is when we understand our commitments as situated within culture and history, as expressions of traditions, so that we may be less inclined to eradicate the other. It is in this reflexive moment that we are able to appreciate the limitations of our commitments and the potential quality of alternatives. In this sense the constructionist alternative does not invite us to 'give up and do nothing', but rather to open oneself to the enormous potential of human relationships.

6. *Are constructionist dialogues in danger of dogmatic insularity?* First of all, constructionism makes no claim to foundations; it offers no means to justify itself. Second, because alternative orientations are also imbedded in traditions or ways of life, constructionism invites interest in their positive potentials. Constructionists claim that meaning is always negotiable; no arrangement of words is self-sustaining in the sense of possessing a single meaning.

7. *What account can constructionists give of the obvious gains made by the natural sciences?* Nobody, not even the constructionists, can doubt that the natural sciences have generated a harvest of resources for human benefits. However, we must carefully consider what we mean by 'progress'. There is, according to constructionism, little sense to be made to the view that scientific research moves us ever closer to 'the truth'. We simply move from one domain of meaning to another.

Sensemaking is often associated with Karl Weick who presented his theories in a book titled *Sensemaking in Organizations* (1995). Weick's ideas can be summarized in the following points:

- Most of sensemaking is concerned with recreating and confirming those opinions we already have about our social reality (for this reason I talk about 'sense-making' instead of 'sense-creating', which is a possible alternative).
- Sometimes, however, we stop and ask ourselves the question: 'How can this make sense?' This takes place above all when we want to make new and unknown situations meaningful.
- This can be done by retrospectively selecting those aspects of these situations which suit our opinion about what a reality is and should be. We may construct a *narrative* (I will be back to this concept later).
- In this way we *enact* another aspect of our socially constructed reality.
- This could explain why two persons may experience the same situation so differently.

- Enactment could be important when people actively try to generate alternatives to solve problems.

My opinion of Weick's sensemaking is that it is interesting, but also that it by and large only fits those rare situations when we stop and think about the meaning of what we are doing and what is going on. As we have already noted, individuals generally handle their normal days with a fairly low degree of conscious thinking. It seems sometimes as though non-reflected *cognitive manuscripts* are controlling our acts instead (Ifvarsson, 2000, p. 66). The basic idea of Weick's sensemaking is that cognition lies in the path of action. Action precedes cognition and focuses cognition (Weick, 1988). Nonaka and Takeuchi (1995) have pointed out that Weick's retrospective 'view is still passive and lacks a proactive view of organization which includes a nation of creative chaos' (p. 40). Sensemaking, some claim, may also take place proactively (Gioia and Thomas, 1996).

The consequence of this – as we have already observed in this chapter – is that sensemaking in research is a reflective act, which always takes place in retrospective attempts to understand the situation under study.

Social phenomenology

Social phenomenology has its basis in the discussion by Berger and Luckmann (1981) about everyday reality as a reality which is collective, but is produced and reproduced by individual actors. The focus is not primarily on autonomous actors but on how social reality is developed and confirmed interactively (Norén, 1995). Reality is not 'objective' in the sense of constituting an entity independent of man as a subject. Instead it is 'objectified', that is, is seen and treated as objective, even though it is not.

Reality is developed and sustained according to Berger and Luckmann by means of a number of processes, which are intimately interconnected (Arbnor and Bjerke, 1997). That process by which we create our own experiences is called *subjectification*. This process is intentionally directed and leads to the idea that *humans are a subjective reality*.

When we, mostly through language, make these experiences available to others, we talk about *externalization*. Through this we construct the surrounding reality. One could therefore say that *society is a human product*.

That process by which an externalized human act eventually gains an objective character is called *objectification*. Through objectification, externalization loses its subjective meaning and becomes a *typification*, that is, a denotation of a meaning, which in the future is treated as if it were objective. This objective meaning is confirmed in different *institutions* and through different kinds of *legitimization*. By this we can say that *society is an objective reality*.

Another one of the basic processes participating in construction of the social reality is called *internalization*. This represents our connection to the world in which others already live. We become members of society through internalization. This takes place through *primary and secondary socialization*. Finally, therefore, we can say that *humans are a social product*.

These are four different sub-processes in the total dialectical process which constitutes our social reality. It is important to remember that these sub-processes operate simultaneously at all levels in the social order. In order to get a fuller understanding of social contexts it is important to consider them all contemporaneously.

SUBJECTIFICATION →   Humans are a subjective reality.
EXTERNALIZATION →   Society is a human product.
OBJECTIFICATION   →   Society is an objective reality.
INTERNALIZATION →   Humans are a social product.

The whole process is illustrated in Figure 2.2.

In the same way as the social construction of reality has here been described at the societal level, it is also possible to describe the social construction of reality in organizations, for instance, a company. Social phenomenology contains, in a way, two kinds of construction of reality (Wenneberg, 2001, p. 74):

- Construction of social reality – habits, externalization, roles, institutions and objectification together create social reality.
- Construction of the subjective experience of social reality – the social world with all its norms internalized during socialization.

In the development process being described, individuals within society construct pictures of reality which simultaneously reflect subjective (individual) and objective (common) aspects of life. What overlaps, when the pictures of reality from all individuals are aggregated in a society, a company or organization, constitutes its objectified reality. This is the reality in which we live our lives. The content will vary for family life, working life or social and leisure groupings, to mention only a few contexts. But it is always there and its overall constitution is never in doubt, only parts of it will change depending on circumstances. This objectified reality is what we call our life-world or everyday reality (Figure 2.3).

Within the social phenomenological perspective, language plays a crucial role in our social construction of reality (Sandberg, 1999). But at the same time, language is seen as a social construction in itself, sometimes as the most basic social construction aspect of reality of all (Searle, 1995). From

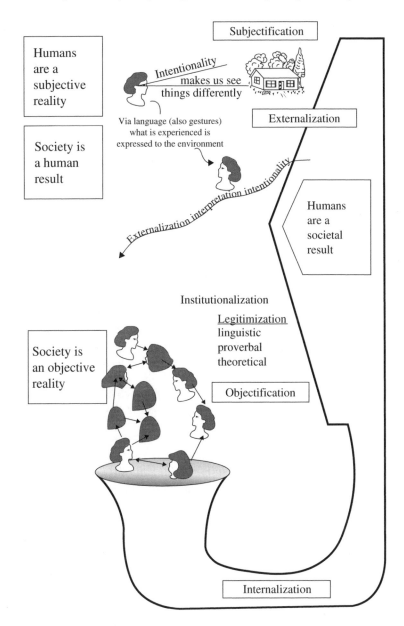

Source: Arbnor and Bjerke (1997, p. 182).

Figure 2.2   Social construction of reality

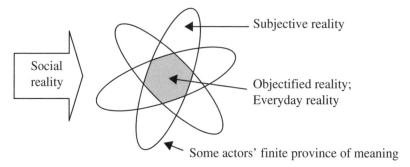

Subjective reality

Social reality

Objectified reality; Everyday reality

Some actors' finite province of meaning

Source: Arbnor and Bjerke (1997, p. 183).

Figure 2.3 Social dialectics and everyday reality

a social phenomenological perspective, language plays the following roles (Berger and Luckmann, 1981; Bourdieu, 1990; Giddens, 1984; Searle, 1995):

1. Language objectifies experiences by categorizing and organizing them in meaningful wholes.
2. Language functions as an interpretive schemata of reality because our experiences are objectified through it.
3. Through the objectification of experiences language also functions as a means for storing collected experience.
4. Language is the primary medium through which collected experience is transferred between human beings and generations, that is, between subjectified and objectified reality.

Language is often seen as operating in common themes and modes of speech between human beings as well as in media and in different kinds of education. These can be described as *discourses* (Potter and Whetherell, 1987). A discourse is then understood as a specific set of linguistic expressions, statements and concepts which organize meaning within a specific area or aspect of reality (Sandberg, 1999).

WHAT DOES REALITY REALLY LOOK LIKE?

One can hold different philosophical opinions about reality and about how to manage learning and research; for instance *realism* (all reality is in its essence or basically material, independent of human consciousness), *idealism* (external matters do not own any independent reality: they are a result of human consciousness), *nominalism* (terms are only sounds or names) or *dualism* (there exists a researching subject as well as an object to be researched). Those dichotomies which are commonly positioned against each other have, in my opinion, limited possibilities in terms of guidance in our role as researchers or to the world which we are researching, and can often cause confusion. Perhaps this is because 'reality' and 'non-reality' may be defined in three different ways, and because the arguments for or against different positions can be based on different assumptions, which may not be obvious in the immediate debate of which to choose (Parker, 1998, pp. 22–3):

1. Reality (as truth) versus untruth.
2. Reality (as material) versus illusion.
3. Reality (as essence) versus construction.

The only position of interest in this book is the third one, as the constructionist approach is sometimes used. Other discussions, such as that between the realist's claim of a factual, independent reality and the relativist's claim that such a reality does not exist, are of no importance here.

Some Points on Language

The relationship between language and reality can be envisaged as occupying three levels with an increasing degree of radicality:

1. Language and reality are related.
2. Language and reality are dialectically constructing each other.
3. Language and reality are one.

As I see it, language is not just a way of dressing our thoughts but their very embodiment (Bjerke, 1989). Our perception of reality, reality in itself, consists in a strict meaning of concepts. According to Gergen (1999, p. 221) Descartes' famous slogan *Cogito ergo sum* ('I think, therefore I am') can be exchanged with *Communicatus ergo sum* ('We are related to each other, therefore I am').

Some researchers claim, however, that the *full* content of meaning can be seen and understood only in action and in further action. There may be an implicit – a tacit – kind of knowledge which is related to action (Molander, 1996). No purely 'theoretical' meaning, completely unrelated to action, would then be possible.

An interesting thought, which follows from the relationship between language, thought and innovation is that:

> A kind of *root knowledge* exists, which is necessary for most knowledge of a more detailed kind. Root knowledge is changing as well, additions are made to

it; other aspects already in there are shown to be untenable or rather inadequate; some parts are changing faster, other parts slower. But it is there, some of it is older, some of it is fresher, and it gives every body of knowledge an internal coherence. (Liedman, 2002, p. 17; my translation)

We may perhaps look at it such that root knowledge can change if new *memes* (the building blocks of a language; compare the concept 'genes') continue to evolve: 'Memes have us in their grip, but if we know the mechanisms we can make use of memes to alter ourselves and our predicaments' (Normann, 2001, p. 196).

Sensemaking through narratives
Sensemaking takes place, as mentioned, only when we stop and think – after the event. It may be done by constructing a narrative, that is, by reconstructing experience in a story. The most important and most frequently cited criteria for a well-formulated narrative include (Gergen, 1999, pp. 68–9):

- *A valued endpoint* An acceptable story must first establish a goal, an event to be explained, a state to be reached or avoided, or more informally, a 'point'. This point is normally saturated with value; it is understood as desirable or undesirable.
- *Events related to the endpoint* Once an endpoint has been established it more or less dictates the kinds of events that can figure in the context. An intelligible narrative is one in which events serve to make the goal more or less probable, accessible or vivid.
- *Ordering of events* Once the goal has been established and relevant events selected, the events are usually placed in an ordered arrangement. The most widely used convention is that of linear time.
- *Causal links* The ideal narrative provides a sense of explanation.

An issue discussed among some social scientists is whether narratives are useful as a tool for researchers to get a new kind of order into what they are studying, or whether reality, as we approach and try to understand it as human beings, means constructing our own narratives in our life-world (Czarniawska, 1998).

Metaphors
A metaphor is a figure of speech in which an expression is used to refer to something that it does not literally denote in order to suggest a similarity. Some of the qualities of the image are thus transferred to the idea or object. By using metaphors, the researcher can gain deeper insights into complex situations:

If one truly wishes to understand an organization it is much wiser to start from the premise that organizations are complex, ambiguous, and paradoxical. Fortunately, the kind of metaphorical analysis developed in earlier chapters provides us with an effective means of dealing with this complexity. For it shows us how we can open our thought processes so that we can read the same situation from multiple perspectives in a critical and informed way. (Morgan, 1986, p. 322)

In *Images of Organizations* (1986), Morgan makes it clear that all our important ways of understanding organizations are metaphorical. They are lived fictions in a world where there is no living beyond fiction (Gergen, 1999, p. 176). Alvesson and Sköldberg (2000) refer to this as *poetic hermeneutics*. The metaphor links two separate occurrences to point out an equivalence between different phenomena; so long as the comparison stands the more unexpected the image, the better is the metaphor.

Morgan (1986) points out that metaphors can be used to elucidate key aspects of complex organizational realities. But researchers do not need to devise their own metaphors, they can use actor based metaphoric thinking which is recommended by Deetz (1986), among others; he is interested in how actors use metaphors to mould their organizational experiences.

Some Points on Culture

Explaining and understanding research approaches are based of different views of what culture is. An explaining-oriented researcher looks at culture as a variable alongside other variables such as strategy and structure, while an understanding-oriented researcher can see it as a root metaphor, that is, the whole organization in envisaged *as* culture (Smircich, 1983).

Culture can be seen as a continuous construction of common meaning (Devins and Gold, 2002, p. 113), a web of significance spun by man himself (Geertz, 1973, p. 5). In its widest sense one can say that culture is everything not given by nature (Liedman, 2002, p. 170). But as with the previous discussion of the interpretation of language, one can also see culture as something that exists only between human beings, something which is triggered when people meet, not something stored in people's memories. Culture needs memory but:

> What we remember are not small casts of what we have once seen or learnt. Nor do we carry around miniature pictures of people we know in the brain. Memory is rather a kind of disposition which exists in the brain. Every time we remember something, we are reconstructing what we remember. It is not like the computer, where all documents are retrieved exactly the same as they were once stored, or like the book, which once again is picked out of the bookshelf containing the same text and the same pictures as before. The brain must create anew every time. (Liedman, 2002, pp. 168–9; my translation)

Further views on culture can be picked up from Geertz (1973). Geertz is oriented towards understanding in his research:

- There is a difference between 'thin' and 'thick' descriptions. In the former case we can read what an actor is doing, in the latter case we can read what meaning underlies the action. The latter is the object of ethnography.
- Culture is public because meaning is. The cognitivist fallacy – that culture consists of mental phenomena which can be analysed by formal methods similar to those of mathematics and logic – is as destructive for an effective use of the concept as are the behaviourist and idealist fallacies to which it is a 'misdrawn correction'.
- A human being not influenced by his or her environment does not exist, has never existed, and most important, could not in the very nature of the case exist.
- To draw a line between what is natural, universal and constant in man and what is conventional, local and variable is extraordinarily difficult. To draw such a line may even be seen as falsifying the human situation.
- Language and culture are intimately related. One can say that they mirror each other.

My Position on the Issue of Understanding

I want to see myself as a social phenomenologist and I am influenced by Gadamer's hermeneutics, Wittgenstein's theory of language and Geertz's opinion of culture. In this book, according to Wenneberg's categorization of increasing radicality of social constructionism, I adopt social constructionism as a theory of how human consciousness arises and develops, that is, social phenomenology. I am not interested here in epistemological and ontological aspects of social constructionism and there is no need here to position myself in matters such as realism or idealism, realism or nominalism, monism or dualism. As I see it, this has no bearing on the discussions in this book.

A METHODOLOGICAL COMMENT

It is natural that the most important way of collecting data for an explaining-oriented researcher is to conduct interviews and/or to join conversations. In the same fashion dialogue is the most important tool for the understanding-oriented researcher (Table 2.3).

Table 2.3   Measurements and criteria for face-to-face research techniques

Interviews and conversations	Dialogues
Main criterion for success	Main criterion for success
To depict factual circumstances with the respondents and their environment	To catch what is meaningful among other actors
Partial criteria	Partial criteria
To be objective	To catch the life-world
To be precise	To gain access to the actors' language pictures
To be relevant/to catch what is general	To catch what is specific
Consistency (between different parts of individual interviews)	Change (as the dialogue proceeds), if it exists
Agreement (between different interviews)	Ambiguity (between dialogues)

Source: Bjerke (forthcoming).

There are several reasons why dialogues are the natural media for understanding. Dialogues are supposed to lead to increased understanding between participating actors – a mutual enrichment and an attempt to understand from deep within the self which goes beyond the habitual patterns and fleeting meetings in life (Buber, 1954). It is 'through dialogue that we accomplish and reaccomplish meaning, and thus bring order to the social world' (Boland, 1987, p. 366). It is in this sense that the dialogue serves as the key organizing metaphor for social constructionist theory (Gergen, 1999, pp. 147–8). One can therefore see dialogue as a *transformative* medium (ibid.).

One important aspect of a dialogue is that it is always open for a continuation, for further rejoinders. A dialogue is therefore, in a way, never a finished project (Molander, 1996, p. 84).

AN ILLUSTRATION

The way I see it, explanation aims at finding patterns, ultimately in order better to control factual reality. Such patterns can take the shape of structures or processes (which can be combined). Understanding, on the other hand, aims at putting pictures of various kinds together (although not as depictions of, or ideal models for, a part of factual reality, the existence of

Table 2.4   A summary of conditions for different research ambitions within the entrepreneurial area

Perspective	What is an entrepreneur?	How are business ventures created?	How to improve the business creation process?
Explain			
Reality as concrete structure independent of us and conformable to law	A person who reacts rationally to certain objective, external circumstances and creates something new	By providing suitable objective, external circumstances to persons who react rationally to them	Introduce more of those stimuli which best explain the effect of the business creation process on rationally reacting people
Reality as concrete determining process	A person who fits in as a component in a goal-directed business creation system	By a well functioning and goal-directed business creation system	Adjust the entrepreneurs and/or the business creation system better to each other
Understand			
Reality as world of language and symbols	A person who looks at creation as a dominating part of his or her world of language and symbols	By language and symbols stressing creation as a natural part of freshly constructed realities	Activate and renew the business creation process language and guiding symbols
Reality as sets of cultural values	A person who looks at creation as an essential cultural act	By creation as an essential cultural act	Influence the culture of the business creation process by acting as living and real-life examples

which understanding-oriented researchers deny), ultimately to advance knowledge in some sense. This can be based on language or culture (these two are intimately related and usually combined). Let us illustrate this, using examples of research from within the entrepreneurial area. The basic situation is summarized in Table 2.4 (compare Bjerke, 1996 and 2000b).

Let us look move closely at some examples of research results in the four perspectives which are presented in column 1 of Table 2.4.

1. To Explain by Structures

The task for a researcher here is to come up with a fixed pattern in factual reality. One approach could be via attempts to list the characteristics and skills that some researchers think are associated with successful entrepreneurs, for instance (Kuratko and Hodgetts, 2004):

- Commitment, determination and perseverance.
- Drive to achieve.
- Opportunity recognition.
- Initiative and responsibility.
- Persistent problem-solving.
- Seeking feedback.
- Internal locus of control.
- Tolerance for ambiguity.
- Calculated risk-taking.
- Integrity and reliability.
- Tolerance for failure.
- High energy level.
- Creativity and innovativeness.
- Vision.
- Self-confidence and optimism.
- Independence.
- Team-building.

Another possible structure might be what some researchers claim to be a good business plan, for instance (Sexton and Bowman-Upton, 1991):

- Summary.
- Table of contents.
- Description of the business.
- Products and services to be offered.
- Survey and analysis of the market.
- Management and organization.
- Financial analysis.

2. To Explain by Processes

The task for a researcher is here is to come up with patterns in factual reality as well, but now over time. An example could be the pattern of a growth process in a company from its inception, where this process is divided into distinct stages (Figure 2.4).

Another example could be those steps perceived by researchers as related

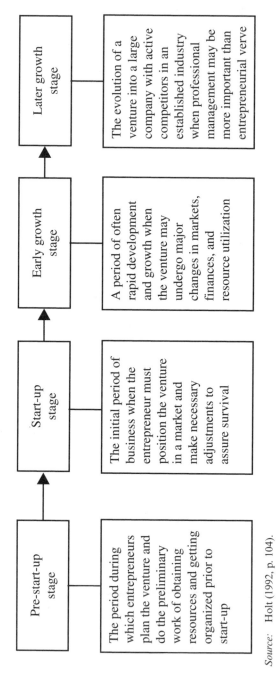

Source: Holt (1992, p. 104).

Figure 2.4 A common picture of the growth of a company

to the promotion of a new business venture within an existing company. This is sometimes referred to as intrapreneurship (Kanter, 1983):

1. Project definition.
2. Coalition forming.
3. Action:
    Manage disturbances.
    Keeping momentum.
    New reformulations.
    External communication.

3. To Understand by Language

Let us, in order to get a view of how it is possible to understand by language, look at some Chinese pronouns (Figure 2.5).

In written Chinese almost all personal pronouns are related to people. 'You' as well as 'he' contain the sign for a human being; 'she' contains the sign for a woman. The Chinese sign for 'I' (or 'me'), however, does not contain a human being but is much more negative in its connotation, even having connections with a symbol for punishment in its original picture (Quanyu et al., 1997, p. 235). Traditional Chinese culture associated self with selfishness. It is therefore not surprising that Chinese society does not perceive people as individuals as we do in the West, but as people whose very existence also comprises relationships to others (Figure 2.6).

One could say that the Western world is built upon individuals, Japanese society is built upon groups and Chinese society is built upon relationships

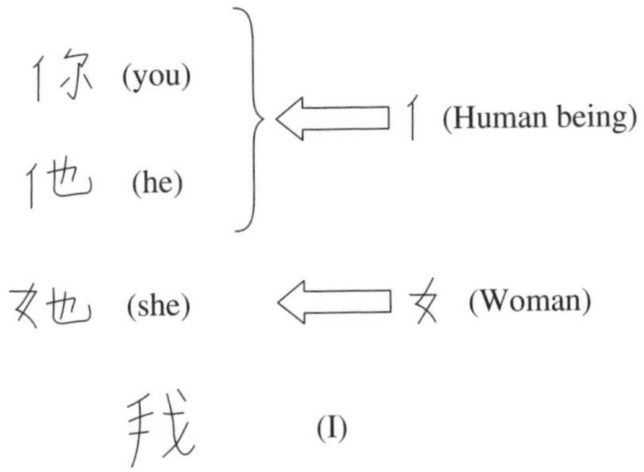

Source: Bjerke (1998).

Figure 2.5 Some pronouns in the Chinese language

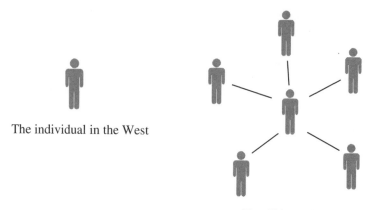

The individual in the West

The Chinese individual

Figure 2.6   'The individual' in two different parts of the world

(Liang, 1974, p. 95). This is, among other things, of importance for any researcher in understanding how Chinese people start new business ventures. They are natural networkers.

An example of the relationship between language and business development was demonstrated to me some years ago when I had a consulting assignment with two different companies in New Zealand (this example is described in more detail in Arbnor and Bjerke, 1997). One of the companies was doing very well, the other company not so well. The two companies differed in almost every respect, including facial expressions and conversation between individuals, even down to the colours and interiors of offices. Relatively quickly I came to 'feel the pulse' of the two companies and thereby device a basis for analysing the two. To everyone I met in the two companies I asked the following question: 'When you talk to each other in this company, which are, in your opinion, the three most common words in your vocabulary?' Using the answers I compiled two 'Top 10' lists of words.

The word which was most common in the company doing badly was ROI ('Return on Investment'). The company was very internally-oriented and everything was seen in terms of money in and out. When, in a meeting in this company, somebody came up with an idea for an innovation the immediate response was of the following kind: 'Can we afford it?', 'Isn't this over the budget limit?' or 'What are the consequences for our ROI?'

The word which was most common in the company doing well was 'service'. This company was very customer and market-oriented. When, in this company, somebody came up with a new idea, the responses were very different: 'Would our customers notice the difference?' or 'How would it influence our image?'

4. To Understand by Culture

An example of the connection between a culture and a business activity, at the level of an individual company, can be taken from another of my consulting assignments (the example is also presented in Bjerke, 1989). In this company, the CEO asked me if I could inspire the employees, 'down to the grassroots', to participate in change and improvements. The company was located in the Pacific. My first visit there was in a meeting with the senior managers, who were all Westerners. They claimed emphatically that I could not influence the climate of the company, the motivation of the employees or their values. Employees (outside the senior management group), who consisted of what were referred to as 'islanders' (from Fiji, Tonga, Samoa and so on), had, according to the senior managers, no interests beyond getting their weekly wages, which were paid on Friday afternoon, going to the pub, staying drunk until far into Saturday night, having a good sleep on Sunday (pubs were closed on Sundays) and starting a new week on Monday. However, I wanted to prove that people can work miracles, so long as they are proud of what they are doing. Pride was not shown and maybe not even permitted in the statement of the senior management group! I introduced, therefore, a number of steps – linguistic, symbolic and cultural – which turned out to have a very dramatic effect on the rate of suggested improvements in the company (several such suggestions led eventually to profitable new products and services). The steps were:

- I started a company magazine. In this magazine, employees could come up with suggestions for improvements in the company. One important aspect was that the suggestions were to be presented in words which could be understood by everybody (not in some kind of business jargon) and which other employees could support because they understood their meaning. These suggestions were numbered from one, but no suggestion was to be seen as minor or major compared with any other suggestion.
- I had the senior management group publicly declare and promise that seven out of every ten suggestions were to be implemented. The choice was made in a committee where all employees were represented.
- The weather was such that outdoor activities were normal, and the company had a long tradition of holding a monthly barbeque, where all employees were offered food, beer and wine. The senior

management group had, so far, never participated. They feared that something would happen to them at those barbeques; feelings could run high when people were influenced by alcohol. The other employees of course saw this as another example of the 'us and them' mentality.

- I built a stage at the spot where the barbeques took place. Furthermore I had the CEO persuade the other members of the senior management group to join him at these parties. The names of the people who had given suggestions which had been presented in the company magazine were called out and they were asked up onto the stage. There they received a medal, which was engraved with the number of their suggestion. (Think about the symbolism of a stage set above the surrounding environment and of the medals as signs of an 'achievement'.)

- Initially those people who came onto the stage had to endure some sneers, but the attitude changed quickly. People started to hang their medals on office doors and on factory machines. It became a kind of a sport to get at least one of these medals. The company started to simmer with different suggestions and activities to achieve improvements.

So, a new company culture was slowly built up.

EXPLAINING OR UNDERSTANDING?

As we have seen, the ambition to explain and the ambition to understand present two distinctly different approaches to research, which cannot be combined in one and the same study. Reality simply cannot be treated simultaneously as objective and objectified, factual and socially constructed. An assertion that explaining and understanding can be combined could only be made if the concepts had meanings other than suggested here. One can certainly talk about 'structures' and 'processes' when trying to understand and 'language' and 'culture' when trying to explain, but these concepts change meaning when they are moved from an explaining context to an understanding context or vice versa.

Because the two views are based on incompatible presumptions, it cannot be claimed that one approach is better than the other. Nevertheless, I would like to see a bit more of an understanding orientation in researching entrepreneurship today, for several reasons:

- We have a new society today which demands different kinds of solutions. Research with an understanding approach possibly provides better solutions to the problems in this society.

- Linguistic, symbolic and cultural research is to a large extent not used in entrepreneurship research and, in my opinion, seems promising.
- Entrepreneurship is a human activity. It could be difficult to appreciate such an activity by trying to explain it.
- I have the impression that the most successful companies today stress language and culture, that is, they have an understanding orientation in a wide sense.

Researching and teaching entrepreneurship guided by an ambition to understand, not to explain, is what I am trying to do. To comprehend the consequences of looking at entrepreneurship from an understanding point of view is a driving force of mine and this force has driven me to write this book.

However, in order to get a proper perspective on entrepreneurship from an understanding point of view, we need to know the content of our knowledge of entrepreneurship from an explaining point of view. So far, most entrepreneurship scholars have tried to explain their subject. The result of their efforts is the topic of the next chapter.

3. To explain entrepreneurs

PREREQUISITES

When trying to explain entrepreneurs (or any other human conditions and events) the following characteristics hold:

- Reality is seen as factual, that is, as consisting of objective and subjective real circumstances.
- The task is to find patterns and regularities in this reality. These patterns and regularities consist of structures and/or processes.
- Above all, it is about finding the most decisive circumstances in these patterns and regularities, that is, the most important causes of a specific effect or course of events. These most decisive circumstances are presented in deliberately simplified pictures of past, present or future reality. Such pictures are called models.

FOUR CLASSIC ENTREPRENEURSHIP THEORISTS

The intention here is not to write a complete history of entrepreneurship as an academic subject, but rather to highlight the work of some individuals who have been particularly influential on the way that we view the subject today, after a history of about three hundred years.

For the first two hundred and fifty years of this period, only economists studied entrepreneurship. Four classical scholars from this period are worth mentioning. They are Richard Cantillon (1680–1734); Jean Baptiste Say (1767–1832); Joseph Schumpeter (1883–1950); and Israel Kirzner (b. 1930).

Richard Cantillon, an Irish banker who mostly worked in Paris, was the first person to give the concept of entrepreneurship an analytical content. In his work *Essai sur la nature du commerce en general*, which was published posthumously in 1755, the entrepreneur was given a recognized role in economic development. Cantillon saw the entrepreneur as a *risk-taker* in the sense that he or she buys at a given price but does not know what demand will be or what the selling price will reach.

Richard Cantillon, as most economists after him, was interested in the entrepreneurial function, not the entrepreneur.

The French economist Jean Baptiste Say distinguished three economic activities (1855): (1) Research generating knowledge; (2) Entrepreneurship applying this knowledge to useful products by combining the means of production in new ways; (3) Workers doing the manufacturing. Say claimed that entrepreneurs bring factors of production together and organize business firms. Say saw entrepreneurs as *business-builders*.

The person often recognized as the most important classical scholar in the theory of entrepreneurship is Joseph Schumpeter. Schumpeter was born in Austria but worked during the last 20 years of his life at the University of Harvard in the United States. To Schumpeter, innovation was the critical function for the entrepreneur – the introduction of new products, processes and organizational units (see, for instance, Schumpeter, 1934). Schumpeter's considerable intellect was wide-ranging – beyond economics he was familiar with classical history, law, history of arts and sociology. Besides seeing the entrepreneur as an *innovator*, he contributed two new ideas to our theory of entrepreneurship:

1. He claimed that the main mechanism for economic development is *creative destruction*, that is, when entrepreneurs disturb existing market mechanisms and market shares.
2. He also claimed that people cease to be entrepreneurs once they have introduced an innovation. The entrepreneurs may then become 'only' small business managers, that is, administrators of former innovations.

To Israel Kirzner entrepreneurs, above all, are *opportunists* (but not in any negative sense), that is, persons who are looking for imbalances in the economic system which can be exploited to coordinate production resources more effectively than before (Kirzner, 1973).

Drawing on the work of these theorists it is common today to define entrepreneurs as risk-takers, business-builders, innovators and/or opportunists.

But Cantillon, Say, Schumpeter and Kirzner are not the only economists to have studied entrepreneurship in the past. Even if entrepreneurship research has never been part of the mainstream of economics, there are many other theories as to the role of an entrepreneur in an economy (Table 3.1).

ENTREPRENEURSHIP THEORIES FROM NON-ECONOMISTS

Since the 1960s entrepreneurship has become a subject for business scholars. Some significant contributions are:

- theories for technology development (Donald Schon, 1930–97)

Table 3.1 Some theories among economists as to the meaning of
entrepreneurs and entrepreneurship

---

1. Economists have referred to entrepreneurial activity as a specific task, like that of a manager or a foreman. Consequently some authors (such as Say and Mill) see entrepreneurial profit as a kind of salary.
2. To many other economists the most important characteristic of the entrepreneur is that of taking on the risk associated with business venturing. These economists include Cantillon.
3. To some economists (such as Smith and Ricardo) the entrepreneur provides financial capital.
4. To others, above all Schumpeter, the most important aspect of entrepreneurship is innovation.
5. Entrepreneurs are sometimes seen as the employer of the production factors.
6. Kirzner, and others, sees the entrepreneur as the person who exploits opportunities.
7. Entrepreneurs have also been seen as:
    *   industrial leaders,
    *   pure speculators,
    *   negotiators,
    *   a source of information.

---

*   behavioural research (David McClelland, 1917–98)
*   sociology (William Gartner, b. 1953)
*   small business research (David Birch, b. 1937; David Storey, b. 1947).

Donald Schon (for instance, 1983) pointed out the importance of what he referred to as *champions* to all technological development. He came up with the following four conclusions:

1. At the outset new ideas face strong resistance. Schon claimed that a social system's resistance to change can sometimes be extremely forceful. He called this the *dynamic conservatism* of the social system.
2. To overcome this resistance *selling* becomes vital.
3. The people who represent the new idea work mainly through the *informal* rather than the formal organization.
4. Typically, *one person* acts as a champion for the idea.

David McClelland tried to come up with a picture of individual motivation in the context of studies of management and entrepreneurship. According to McClelland, people are motivated by three principal needs: (1) the need to achieve, (2) the need for power and (3) the need for belonging. The relative importance of these three needs varies between different people. McClelland claimed that entrepreneurs are primarily driven by a *need for achievement*.

McClelland also stated that societies where the need for achievement is a norm are developing more dynamically than other societies. He wrote a classic book on this theme, *The Achieving Society*, which was published in 1961.

William Gartner, who is a sociologist, claimed in a seminal article (1988) that it is fruitless to ask who the entrepreneur is. According to Gartner, the important question is: How are new organizations created? He even defines entrepreneurship as the creation and establishing of new organizations.

David Birch presented pioneering work about the importance of small businesses in *The Job Generation Process* (1979). Birch claimed that in a country like the United States, most new jobs are created by small firms. This conclusion was contrary to the established, taken-for-granted understanding in that country at that time.

David Storey, an Englishman, is contemporary with David Birch. He refers to himself as a small-business researcher, not as an entrepreneurship researcher. He points out, for instance (Storey, 1980) that:

- Whether a small firm is growing or not is very much up to the entrepreneur/founder.
- The government is important for the development of the small-business sector in a society (Great Britain in his case).
- There are major differences between the frequencies of establishment of new firms in different regions of a country.

The development of entrepreneurship research over the years is summarized in Figure 3.1. Those people represented in the figure have greatly influenced how we perceive the subject of entrepreneurship today.

ENTREPRENEURSHIP AS A SUBJECT TODAY

Entrepreneurship is now a multidisciplinary subject (Landström, 2005). It can be seen as a complex of closely related concepts such as change management, innovation, environmental turbulence, product development, individualism and meaningfulness. The phenomenon can be studied from many different points of view, from that of the economist, of the sociologist, of the financial theorist, of the historian, of the psychologist or of the anthropologist, to name only a few. Each discipline approaches the subject with its own concepts and notions.

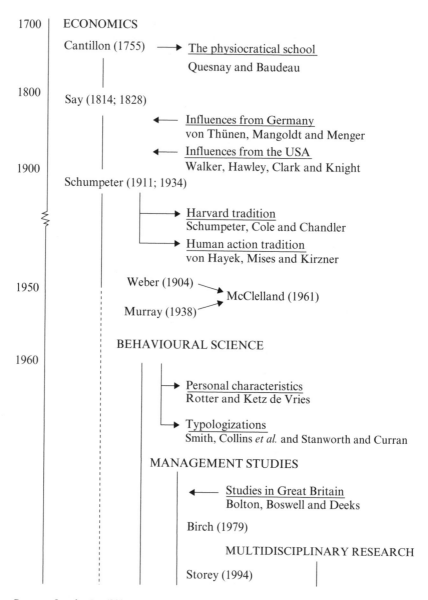

Source: Landström (2005, p. 137).

Figure 3.1 The development of entrepreneurship research

To me it seems clear that even if entrepreneurship has obvious economic consequences, it should not only (or maybe not even primarily) be studied economically, but also (and this is not a comprehensive list) historically, psychologically, sociologically, geographically and politically.

A current debate concerns whether the primary academic interest of entrepreneurship should be focused on:

Alternative 1: The use of chances and opportunities (Shane and Venkataraman, 2000), that is, how, by whom and with what effects chances and opportunities to create future products and services are discovered, evaluated and exploited. Or,

Alternative 2: The process of development of new organizations for doing business (Gartner, 1988).

I believe, as does Davidsson (2003), that these two 'alternatives' could be combined into one, in which case the research field of entrepreneurship (from an explaining point of view) can be defined as covering the process of development of new business ventures, including the ways in which chances and opportunities for such ventures arise and how they are manifested in new organizations.

I see four areas for explaining entrepreneurship research today (Bjerke and Hultman, 2002, p. 57):

- the role which is played by entrepreneurship in society
- the characteristics of entrepreneurs and their thinking
- entrepreneurial environments, including intrapreneurship
- entrepreneurial courses of events.

Opinions about who entrepreneurs are, what they look like and how they behave, vary widely. Such opinions have been influenced by what the information is to be used for, of course. It may sometimes be enough to be clear who *are not* entrepreneurs. In this context, a personal experience is worth mentioning. In the early 1980s I worked as an adviser to a venture capitalist (Bjerke, 1989, p. 517), and one of my tasks was to try to decide which of the hundreds of people we came into contact with should be given financial support and which should not. I learned relatively fast to avoid certain 'types':

1. *The planning fanatic.* A person who presented a project which was planned in detail several years in advance, was lacking in realism as well as flexibility.
2. *The patent genius.* A person who wanted to exploit a patent (possibly filed many years previously), which 'had not been commercialized so

far because of uncomprehending financiers', had often lost contact with reality long ago.

3. *The gambler.* The person who asks for a round sum in order to exploit 'a fantastic opportunity' rarely conveyed confidence.

4. *The over-skilled.* The one-sided, narrow specialist did not normally fit with being an entrepreneur.

5. *The security seeker.* His or her entrepreneurial qualities had been buried long ago.

6. *The egocentric.* Sometimes it is difficult to separate a devoted entrepreneur from an egocentric. I often found, however, that it could be disastrous to put an extreme egocentric on an entrepreneurial job.

One of the reasons why it is so difficult to give a general picture of who is an entrepreneur and of what entrepreneurs do is that so many myths circulate on this topic. Below are a few examples, with my comments (Bjerke, 1989, pp. 526–7; Timmons, 1999, pp. 47–8; Coulter, 2001, pp. 8–9; Kuratko and Hodgetts, 2004, pp. 30–33):

There is no general series of steps or procedures to follow to reach entrepreneurial success Entrepreneurship is far from an objectively rational process. However, it does not take place randomly. Many issues are therefore common from one entrepreneurial case to another, for instance, whether one should start alone or with somebody else, how to get organized, how to assess the business value of one's offer and how to get hold of finance for growth. Many of the risks and trade-offs which are involved are identifiable and manageable; to discover them is an iterative process. To compare oneself with other entrepreneurs and discuss one's problems with those who are backing the business venture could lead to knowledge as well as to development.

Entrepreneurship is something you are born to – either you have the necessary qualities 'from the beginning' or you can forget it This is a much discussed issue. Some commentators claim that entrepreneurship is primarily a matter of inborn qualities. Others claim that entrepreneurship emerges when external circumstances, such as cultural, family and business conditions are right. My opinion is that entrepreneurial qualities (whatever they are – and we are far from agreement about this) cannot be compared with such inborn talents as a musical ear or strong bones. Over roughly twenty years of involvement with the subject, I have seen entrepreneurship appear under the most improbable circumstances and being realized by the most unexpected people. I am therefore inclined to claim that, in principle, almost anyone can become an entrepreneur.

To start a business is risky and often leads to failure Because entrepreneurship means pursuing something which is, at least partly, new, and because many aspects associated with it by their very nature cannot be planned to any major extent, entrepreneurship is often about taking chances. However, while entrepreneurs might not be afraid to take risks, successful entrepreneurship is more likely to depend on calculated risks than on simple gambling. Furthermore, there are situations where entrepreneurship, in order to succeed, may mean minimizing and even avoiding risks. One can finally say under this point that business ventures sometimes fail, entrepreneurs may not. A mistake can be seen as an opportunity to learn and trigger the entrepreneur to try again.

All entrepreneurs need is a good idea – everything else is secondary A good idea is just one part of the equation for successful entrepreneurship. Understanding the demands of different phases of the entrepreneurial process, taking an organized approach to developing the entrepreneurial venture and coping with challenges are also key ingredients in successful entrepreneurship. But perhaps above all, as is proven again and again, the qualities of the entrepreneur are the most essential components of a business success. It is sometimes said that it is better to have a top quality entrepreneur with a less than top quality idea than the other way round. A good idea is all too easy to spoil, while a skilled entrepreneur can achieve miracles from a less than perfect idea.

All entrepreneurs need is money – everything else is secondary It is true that a venture needs capital to survive, above all for growth; it is also true that a firm may fail to grow due to lack of financial capital, but money is not the primary resource to start a business. Lack of proper financing is often an indication of other problems: managerial incompetence, lack of financial understanding, poor imagination and drive and the like. Money is, in fact, one of the less important ingredients to attaining success in business. Money is to the entrepreneur what the paint and brush are for the painter – a tool which, in the right hand, can create marvels.

Entrepreneurs are lone wolves and cannot work with others The reality is that an entrepreneur in modern times is a leader of some kind, who builds a venture in constructive interaction with customers, colleagues, key suppliers, investors and many others.

Entrepreneurs are always inventors This is an old idea which has stayed on for a long time, perhaps because many large present-day companies started from an invention of some kind related to their founders. Today it is more correct to say that even if many business firms are started by inventors, a complete picture of entrepreneurship requires an understanding of all kinds of innovative behaviour.

Entrepreneurs are academic and social misfits   Sometimes we read or hear that really successful entrepreneurs are people who dropped out of school or failed to hold a job. In some cases, such events have been blown out of proportion in an attempt to 'profile' the typical entrepreneur as somebody very different from the rest of us. It is a fact that, historically, educational and social organizations did not recognize the entrepreneur who was isolated in a world of corporate giants. Business education was also, for a long time, aimed almost exclusively at corporate activity. Today entrepreneurs are considered heroes – socially, economically and academically. They are no longer misfits and they are often very professional.

Entrepreneurship only takes place in small firms   This misconception is so common that it will be addressed further in other sections of this book.

ENTREPRENEURIAL SCHOOLS

There are a number of different schools trying to explain entrepreneurs and entrepreneurship. In order to illustrate variety, let us look at four existing methods of classifying such schools. We will see that these four proposals overlap to a large extent. They are:

1. Macro and micro schools
2. Entrepreneurial description models
3. Supply and demand schools
4. Psychological and behavioural schools.

Macro and Micro Schools

Kuratko and Hodgetts (2004) suggest a classification of entrepreneurial schools in two groups: macro schools (based on factors beyond the control of entrepreneurs) and micro schools (based on factors which the entrepreneur can control).

Macro schools can be broken down into the *environmental school*, which focuses on factors in the socio-political environment which positively or negatively affect the development of the entrepreneur; and the *finance and capital school*, which focuses on opportunities for the entrepreneur to look for and to find venture capital during different phases of the development of a business venture. Furthermore, the *displacement school* is counted as a member of this group; this considers the consequences for the entrepreneur of being outside certain political, cultural or economic situations.

Micro schools consist of the *entrepreneurial trait school*, which aims to identify the personality traits which characterize successful entrepreneurs; the *venture opportunity school*, which focuses on the process of searching for opportunities to exploit a business opportunity; and the *strategic formulation school*, which stresses the planning process for effective business development.

Entrepreneurial Description Models

Different entrepreneurial description models are summarized in Table 3.2.

Table 3.2   Entrepreneurial description models

The entrepre-neurial model	Central focus or purpose	Assumption	Behaviour and skills	Situation
'Great person' school	The entrepreneur has an intuitive ability – a sixth sense – and traits and instincts with which he or she is born	Without this 'inborn' intuition, the individual would be like the rest of us mortals, who 'lack what it takes'	Intuition, vigour, energy, persistence, and self-esteem	Start-up
Psychological characteristics school	Entrepreneurs have unique values, attitudes, and needs that drive them	People behave in accordance with their values; behaviour results from attempts to satisfy needs	Personal values, risk-taking, need for achievement and others	Start-up
Classical school	The central characteristic of entrepreneurial behaviour is innovation	The critical aspect of entrepreneurship is in the process of doing rather than owning	Innovation, creativity and discovery	Start-up and early growth
Management school	Entrepreneurs are organizers of an economic venture; they are	Entrepreneurs can be developed or trained in the	Production planning, people organizing,	Early growth and maturity

Table 3.2   (continued)

The entrepre-neurial model	Central focus or purpose	Assumption	Behaviour and skills	Situation
	people who organize, own and assume the risk	technical function of management	capitalization and budgeting	
Leadership school	Entrepreneurs are leaders of people; they have the ability to adapt their style to the needs of people	An entrepreneur cannot accomplish his or her goals alone, but depends on others	Motivating, directing and leading	Early growth and maturity
Intrapreneur-ship school	Entrepreneurial skills can be useful in complex organizations; intrapreneurship is the development of independent units to create, market and expand service	Organizations need to adapt to survive; entrepreneurial activity leads to organization-building and entrepreneurs becoming managers	Alertness to opportunities, maximizing decisions	Maturity and change

Source: Cunningham and Lischeron (1991, p. 47).

Supply and Demand Schools

A relatively common ground for classification is to divide studies of entre-preneurship into *supply schools* focusing on the availability of suitable indi-viduals to occupy entrepreneurial roles, and *demand schools*, where focus is on the number and nature of entrepreneurial roles which need to be filled (Thornton, 1999, pp. 20ff.).

Factors influencing the supply of entrepreneurship can in turn be divided (Bridge et al., 2003) into:

- *Population growth and density.* Expanding population and growing population density in some regions can mean that more people are considering self-employment as a means of securing an income.

- *Age structure*. Entrepreneurial attitudes, skills and resources are acquired over time and consequently age can have an impact on entrepreneurship.
- *Immigration*. Immigrants need work like everybody else, but may have problems in accessing existing jobs. Starting their own businesses could be an alternative.
- *Participation*. Increased participation in the labour market, especially among women, increases the number of people who are prepared to consider self-employment.
- *Income levels and unemployment*. High income levels can mean that a person has too much to lose by leaving a permanent job. Unemployment, on the other hand, increases interest in starting on one's own.

Similarly factors that influence the demand for entrepreneurship can be divided into (ibid.):

- *Economic development*. Economic development can affect the interest in starting new companies. In developed countries, high salaries may discourage people from trying self-employment. However, in developing countries, low per capita income may have a positive impact on the self-employment rate.
- *Technological development*. In recent years the speed of technological development, which reduces the advantages of scale, has created new opportunities for small business start-ups.
- *Globalization*. Globalization makes people more aware of the diverse range of opportunities which do in fact exist; this may stimulate phenomena such as ethnic restaurants.
- *Industrial structure and clustering*. The break-up of monopolies and the reduction of protectionism has offered more opportunities for small business start-ups as have trends such as localization in clusters.

Psychological and Behavioural Schools

These could be subdivided into the *personality school*, the *social demographic school*, the *cognitive school* and the *behavioural school*.

The personality school
The task of the explaining-oriented researcher, as mentioned before, is to find patterns and regularities – not strict deterministic, sufficient and necessary relationships, which would be unrealistic in social sciences, but at least those that could be seen as average or typical (most common). The

ultimate ambition for such a researcher would be to get a clear picture of
the true entrepreneur, for instance, in terms of personality. Personality can,
in turn, be defined in terms of patterns and regularities in action, feelings
and thoughts that are characteristics of the individual (Snyder and Cantor,
1998). Some personality traits which by tradition have been identified with
entrepreneurs (Bridge et al., 2003) are:

- *Achievement motivation.* When individuals accomplish something
  which they consider as worthwhile, their self-esteem is enhanced
  and they are encouraged to take on other demanding assignments. Enterprising people are constantly on the look-out for
  challenges.
- *Risk-taking propensity.* Proactive achievers break new ground, but
  their behaviour is risky. The outcomes of enterprising undertakings
  are less certain than conservative ones and enterprising individuals
  must have the capacity to tolerate risk and the psychological make-
  up and mental resources to cope with failure.
- *Locus of control.* Enterprising people believe that they themselves
  make things happen in a given situation and they underplay the
  importance of luck and fate. They make things happen; things do not
  just happen to them. In essence they feel that they exercise considerable control over events in their everyday world.
- *Need for autonomy.* This may follow from a feeling of being in
  control, but it is not the same thing. Enterprising people have a strong
  desire to go it alone. In interviews with enterprising people they
  repeatedly refer to the need to control their own lives.
- *Determination.* Enterprising people also possess determination. They
  normally complete their projects and a certain degree of persistence
  is necessary for success.
- *Initiative.* A person may have a strong need for achievement, may
  possess determination, may welcome the chance to do his or her own
  things and to exercise control over his or her environment when pursuing as assigned project and may, when presented with an opening,
  exercise many enterprising qualities. If, however, he or she does not
  actively take the initiative and seek openings and opportunities, the
  enterprise will be limited in its results.
- *Creativity.* The ability to come up with something new is not evenly
  distributed in a population. Some people tend to have more origi-
  nality than others and to have the ability to come up with solutions
  that fly in the face of established knowledge. They are also inclined
  to be more adaptable and prepared to consider a larger range of
  alternative approaches.

- *Self-confidence and trust.* It is most unlikely that enterprising people lack self-confidence. Proactivity, creativity and achievement are not accomplished without changes, sometimes major ones. Along with self-confidence goes trust. In reality, successful enterprise requires the coordination of disparate inputs, and a degree of trust in those who contribute.

Other personality traits which are often associated with entrepreneurs (Timmons, 1999; Delmar, 2000; Zimmerer and Scarborough, 2002; Allen, 2003) are:

- *Responsibility.* Entrepreneurs feel a deep sense of personal responsibility for the outcome of the venture they start. They prefer to be in control of their resources and use those resources to achieve self-determined goals.
- *Opportunity obsession.* Successful entrepreneurs are obsessed with opportunity. Their obsession with opportunity is what guides the entrepreneurs when dealing with important issues.
- *Desire for immediate feedback.* Entrepreneurs enjoy running their businesses, but they like to know how they are doing and are constantly looking for feedback.
- *Future orientation.* Entrepreneurs have a sense of constantly searching for opportunities. They look ahead and are less worried about what was done yesterday than with what should be done tomorrow. Entrepreneurs see an opportunity where other people only see problems if anything at all, a characteristic that often makes them the object of ridicule (at least until they succeed).
- *Tolerance of ambiguity.* The start-up process is by its very nature dynamic, uncertain, complex and ambiguous. Entrepreneurs, however, seem to work well in this type of environment, possibly because it is challenging and exciting and offers more opportunity than a structured environment.
- *Over-optimism.* Over-optimism is closely related to the feeling of being in control, because both are related to the expectation of success. When entrepreneurs are asked about their chances for succeeding, they tend to be extremely optimistic.
- *High commitment.* An extraordinary level of commitment is commonly required from entrepreneurial ventures. Entrepreneurs often live under high and constant pressures – first for their firms to survive start-up, then for them to stay alive and finally for them to grow. They have to be the top priority for the entrepreneur's time, emotions and loyalty.

- *Leadership.* Entrepreneurs are patient leaders, partly to be first with a tangible vision and managing for the longer haul, partly to be a model for their team and to motivate its members.

Much has been said over the years about entrepreneurs as risk-takers beyond the ordinary run, and this is worth a few comments in the context of our new entrepreneurial society. Traditionally it is assumed that entrepreneurs run four kinds of risks in their endeavour (Kuratko and Hodgetts, 2004): (1) financial risk – putting one's financial savings, maybe even house and property, at stake in an entrepreneurial effort; (2) career risk – not being able to go back to one's old job if the venture should fail; (3) family and social risk – neglecting family and friends because a new entrepreneurial effort uses much of the entrepreneur's time and energy; and (4) psychic risk – risking one's own well-being.

However, how does the risk of undertaking something compare with the risk of not doing so? Is it not so in our new entrepreneurial society that the quickest way to go under is *not* to do something? I can see great risks – financially, in terms of career, family and social life and, perhaps above all, psychologically – in sitting still in the belief that the future will simply be a repetition of today. The concept of 'risk' gets a new meaning in our new entrepreneurial society!

The personality school has endured much criticism. It has been unable to differentiate clearly between entrepreneurial small-business owners and equally successful professional executives in more established organizations (Carson et al., 1995). Most of those factors believed to be entrepreneurial have not been found to be unique to entrepreneurs but common to many successful individuals (Boyd and Vozikis, 1994). Most entrepreneurs do not possess all the enterprise traits identified, and many of the traits are also possessed by those who could hardly be described as entrepreneurs (Bridge et al., 2003). To use only the personality school approach may even lead to problems in identifying those aspects of a person which are *not* specifically entrepreneurial. One example is a large and very careful study of 11 400 persons in the UK (the cohort contained 1300 entrepreneurs) who were born the first week of March 1958. When compared with the rest of the cohort the entrepreneurs did not turn out to be either more persistent, self-motivated or risk-taking. Almost the only factor that distinguished the entrepreneurs from the others was that those who became entrepreneurs were more likely to have received an economic gift or an inheritance which could be turned into money (*The Economist*, 1998).

There are theoretical as well as methodological problems associated with an approach based on the personality school (Delmar, 2000). The school does not recognize that entrepreneurship is a dynamic, constantly changing process. A person is not always an entrepreneur. Different entrepreneurial qualities may also be needed in different phases of an entrepreneurial venture (Carson et al., 1995). The personality trait approach can easily lead to the conclusion that the entrepreneur springs from the cradle with all faculties, drives and qualities pre-formed, needing only the opportunity to exploit them (ibid.).

Part of the problem with trait approaches arises from how the entrepreneur and entrepreneurship are defined. In the first instance a focus only on the individual who establishes a new venture is arguably too narrow. It fails to recognise sufficiently the entrepreneurial potential of people who work to develop and grow established enterprises. In addition, there is the difficulty raised by the fact that entrepreneurs are not an easily identifiable, homogeneous group. Entrepreneurs, it appears, come in all shapes and sizes, from different backgrounds, with varying motivations and aspirations. They are variously represented and addressed in the literature as opportunists or craftworkers, technical entrepreneurs or so-called intrapreneurs. (Carson et al., 1995, pp. 51–2)

Perhaps it would be better in an explanatory context to place less emphasis on entrepreneurial qualities and speak, like Gibb (1998), of 'entrepreneurial skills'. These may be seen as:

- synonymous with basic interpersonal skills, core skills or transferable skills, such as communication, planning and presentation (Rajan et al., 1997).
- those skills associated with personal 'enterprising' behaviours which may be exhibited in a range of contexts, not purely business (Gibb, 1993).
- strongly associated with setting up and running an independent owner-managed business (Coffield, 1990; Gavron et al., 1997).
- associated with managing dynamic growing businesses, businesses with a high risk of failure (Churchill, 1991) or those businesses exhibiting high rates of innovation (Stevenson, 1983).
- associated, at least in part, with business skills development in the broad management sense of being 'qualified', for example, in marketing, financial management, production management and human resource management (OECD, 1989).
- synonymous with attaining greater insight into the business world or with an appreciation of industry. In this interpretation, developed entrepreneurial skills are about the same as work experience and business appreciation. This is a perception that may particularly hold in the higher and vocational education sector (Watts and Hawthorn, 1991).

The social demographical school

Socio-demographic circumstances can explain entrepreneurs to some extent.

- Some regions or communities encourage entrepreneurship more than others because they have institutions ready to help small firms (Curran and Blackburn, 1991). Such localities could be said to be more favourably disposed to the notion of entrepreneurship (Bridge et al., 2003, p. 75).
- People who have self-employed parents are over-represented among those who are self-employed themselves (Shapero and Sokol, 1982; Delmar and Davidsson, 2000).
- Education and work experience influence entrepreneurship. Two groups are over-represented among those who start a business (Delmar and Davidsson, 2000, p. 4): (1) individuals previously self-employed trying to start a new business and (2) unemployed individuals trying to start a business as a way of earning a living. As regards education most studies indicate a positive effect on self-employment, at least for low versus intermediate levels of education.
- Ethnicity: self-employment is often suggested as a way for new immigrants to establish themselves in a new society. However, the interest in self-employment differs widely between different categories of immigrants.
- Those people who find themselves in an in-between situation in life seem to be more inclined to seek entrepreneurial outlets than those who are in 'the middle of things' (Dollinger, 2003, p. 43). Examples of such situations, apart from immigration, are between military and civilian life, between student life and career, and between prison and freedom.

However, no socio-demographic (or other individual level) variables have turned out to be particularly strong predictors of self-employment (Delmar and Davidsson, 2000, p. 2).

In this context it might be pertinent to ask why, in the Western world, about twice as many men as women start a business. First, female entrepreneurship has not been on the agenda for long (Carter, 2000; Holmquist and Sundin, 2002). Second, differences have been detected in motives between men and women business starters. Men more often want to make money and to expand their business; women are more likely than men to work part-time and to combine family with work (Coulter, 2000; Holmquist and Sundin, 2002).

Some research results show that women experience obstacles to starting a business. They feel financially discriminated against, they perceive themselves hampered by lack of previous business training and they underestimate what it actually costs to start and to run a business (Carter, 2000). It has long been recognized that women also feel discriminated against because they are not always taken seriously in the business world (Hisrich and Brush, 1986). This has been confirmed in later studies (Bridge et al., 2003). Women start-ups and female managers tend to experience more obstacles to success than their male equivalents (Chell, 2001).

Nonetheless, increasing numbers of women are discovering that the best way to break the 'glass ceiling' is to start their own companies (Zimmerer and Scarborough, 2002). The rate at which women are starting businesses in the United States is twice as high as the national average (Kroll, 1998). This means that their share of businesses will gradually increase (Carter, 2000). The percentage of women starting businesses in Sweden increased from 19 per cent to 30 per cent during the 1990s (Holmquist and Sundin, 2002).

The cognitive school
Theories which try to explain behaviour by how people perceive and comprehend information surrounding them are called *cognitive theories* (Delmar, 2000, p. 138). Some general results within this area of interest to entrepreneurship (Baron, 1998) are:

- Many entrepreneurs seem to think contrary to those facts that exist.
- Many entrepreneurs live more in the present and the future than in the past.
- Many entrepreneurs become very involved when making decisions and evaluating things.
- Many entrepreneurs underestimate costs as well as time required to succeed.

When modelling people, psychologists tend to make a distinction between *distal* and *proximal* factors affecting behaviour (Ackerman and Humpreys, 1990). A distal factor explains general behaviours (such as eating, sleeping or having sex). A proximal factor defines the more concrete situation in which the individual finds him or herself. Actual behaviour is better explained by proximal factors (task characteristics) than by distal factors (traits and needs). Traits are, mostly, distal factors and they may therefore have little success in explaining actual behaviour, even less business performance (Delmar, 2000).

Delmar (2000) divides more specific models for entrepreneurial behaviour into: (1) Attitude-based models and (2) Models for motivation in achievement contexts. *Attitudes* are tendencies or dispositions to behave in generally favourable or unfavourable ways toward the object of the attitude. Attitudes are proximal factors and they can provide some basis for explanation. They may influence a person's choice but they say very little about the level of effort and persistence employed (Locke, 1991). In order to do this a more *planned behaviour* is needed (Ajzen, 1991).

Two proximal factors discussed in models in achievement contexts, according to Delmar (2000), are *perceived self-efficacy* (Boyd and Vozikis, 1994) and *perceived intrinsic motivation*. Intrinsic motivation can be seen both as an antecedent to and as a consequence of high self-efficacy (Bandura, 1995).

To understanding-oriented researchers of entrepreneurship who are not using these types of models the explaining-oriented results can seem somewhat self-explanatory. Who can deny, for instance, that a person who experiences positive attitudes towards starting a business and who feels that he or she is efficient and motivated enough to make it, has a higher chance of succeeding than others? The models in question should not, however, according to their advocates be seen in this way. They are attempts to come up with constructs such as 'planned behaviour', 'perceived self-efficacy' and 'intrinsic motivation' which should provide the grounds for the establishment of tests, which through quantitative analysis are to be used as better instruments for forecasting who will be an entrepreneur and who will start a business. This is a natural and respected aim if you are an explaining-oriented researcher.

The behavioural school
The aim is here to look at a larger complex of behaviour and how elements within it are related to supporting entrepreneurship. Examples of variables that may be contained in such complex are:

- ability to make judgements and decisions
- goal-oriented behaviour
- planning behaviour
- taking on responsibility
- creativity
- technical skills
- networking ability
- knowledge of project management.

An example of the type of model that is used in the behavioural school is shown in Figure 3.2.

We have seen in this chapter several models suggested by explaining-oriented researchers as attempts to establish links between the ways in

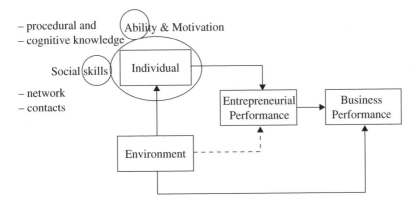

Source: Levander and Raccuia (2001, p. 40).

Figure 3.2   General model of entrepreneurial and business performance

which circumstantial factors and variables may lead to entrepreneurship and entrepreneurial behaviour. However, we have seen very little of entrepreneurial effects, that is, how entrepreneurship may explain the development of a business firm, a region, a nation. There is, as we have seen earlier, some evidence that entrepreneurship may improve economic factors such as employment and growth, but this is far from straightforward.

1. There are problems in establishing strict causal links in the human world in general. Human free will may 'distort' any belief we may have about causes and effects in this world.
2. It is probably even harder to come up with causal relationships when human 'action' is considered as a cause. Remember von Wright's warning, which we met in Chapter 2, that 'the connection between an action and its results is intrinsic, logical and not causal (extrinsic). If the result does not materialize, the action simply has not been performed' (1971, pp. 67–8). Perhaps the same thing could be said about entrepreneurship, which is a very action-oriented behaviour. Referring to Figure 3.2, for instance, can 'Entrepreneurial performance' exist without 'Business performance'? Is the latter not part of the former?
3. And again referring to Figure 3.2, does 'Environment' exist independently of 'Individual'? We know by now, of course, that the answer to this question is one of the major differences between 'explaining' and 'understanding', the discussion on which this whole book is based.

Back to more explaining models!

INTRAPRENEURSHIP

When established large corporations develop new products and services which are closely related to existing products and services, this is *not* intrapreneurship. If technical innovations are used to solve old problems in a more efficient or effective manner, this is also *not* intrapreneurship.

Intrapreneurship according to Dollinger (2003, p. 333) is:

- entrepreneurship within an existing business
- the development within a corporation of more or less autonomous business units that produce goods, services or technologies in an (at least partly) unique way
- an opportunity for corporate managers to take initiative and try new ideas
- an internally initiated diversification.

Intrapreneurship can start *generally*, that is, by developing a climate for new business ventures, *formally*, by, for instance, establishing autonomous units in the organization to develop new products and/or services, or *informally*, that is, through trying to encourage employees to take their own initiatives to innovate (Jones-Evans, 2000).

It is not difficult to understand the need for intrapreneurship in our new entrepreneurial society. It provides the corporation with the ability (Dollinger, 2003, p. 334) to:

- adapt quickly to changes in the macro-environment
- diversify from the core business
- conduct market experiments
- train new managers and leaders
- establish new channels of distribution
- invest and profit from new venture creation.

But how is intrapreneurship done? Pinchot, who coined the term, wrote (1985) that intrapreneurship, when initiated by the employees, runs through several phases:

1. *The solo phase.* Intrapreneurs generally build up the initial vision alone.
2. *The network phase.* Once the basic idea seems clear, intrapreneurs start to share it with a few friends in their company and some few trusted customers. From their reactions they can learn about the strengths and the weaknesses of the concept. It may be surprisingly easy to get others to contribute their know-how to an intraprise. The

fact that you have singled them out means, after all, that you look upon them as experts of some kind.

3. *The bootleg phase.* As the network phase proceeds, some people close to the intrapreneur start to help with more than helpful words and useful facts. A team starts to develop, although it still works unofficially, maybe at the intrapreneur's home or at a neutral place.

4. *The formal team phase.* Increasingly, what is needed for the intrapreneurial venture to succeed is more than an idea supported by somebody who thinks and many who act. A formal intrapreneurial team is started, which is functionally complete and which acts autonomously and stays together at the commercialization stage and beyond.

Kanter (1983) provides a similar model of the stages of the same process:

1. *Project definition.* To get access to and to apply the information to proceed with a manageable, saleable project within the firm.

2. *Coalition building.* To develop a network of those who agree to provide resources and support.

3. *Action.* Applying resources, information and support for the project and mobilizing a team.

THE CONSEQUENCES OF STARTING A BUSINESS

Much has been written about the positive consequences for entrepreneurs of starting a business; some examples follow (Coulter, 2001; Zimmerer and Scarborough, 2002; Bjerke and Hultman, 2002). These are:

- to tackle opportunities
- the opportunity to create one's own future, to achieve and to mean something
- to be able to use one's own abilities and talents fully
- to have a high degree of independence, to make one's own decisions without restrictions
- to be responsible only to oneself
- to gain financial advantages
- to have the chance to have fun
- to follow in the family footsteps.

The same authors (Coulter, 2001; Zimmerer and Scarborough, 2002; Bjerke and Hultman, 2002) have of course something to say about the negative consequences for entrepreneurs of starting a business:

- change and uncertainty
- a multitude of sometimes contradictory decisions to make
- being forced to make economic choices
- risk
- uncertain financial flows
- much work
- the possibility of failure.

THE ENTREPRENEURIAL PROCESS, BUSINESS OPPORTUNITIES AND BUSINESS CONCEPTS

It is not easy to provide a general picture of the entrepreneurial process. Partly this is because the process (Bjerke and Hultman, 2002):

- is initiated by a process of human willpower
- involves a state of change
- involves a discontinuity
- is a holistic process
- is a dynamic process
- is unique
- involves a huge number of variables
- is extremely dependent on the input values of these variables.

A model which describes and partly explains the start-up of a new business is provided by Deakins and Whittam (2000) (Figure 3.3).

The start-up of a new business may uncover or even create a further business opportunity. This opportunity is the result of a number of factors (Figure 3.4).

Most ideas behind new businesses are fairly ordinary. Those that survive tend to be based on improved versions of what is going on already in the market. According to Coulter (2001, p. 68) there are a number of misconceptions related to 'great ideas' (Table 3.3).

According to Baron and Shane (2005, pp. 72–4), it is possible to increase one's opportunity recognition:

- *Build a broad and rich knowledge base.* The capacity to recognize opportunities, like creativity, depends in large measure on how much information you have. The larger the knowledge base that you have, the more likely you are to recognize the connections and patterns that constitute opportunities before somebody else does. Learn

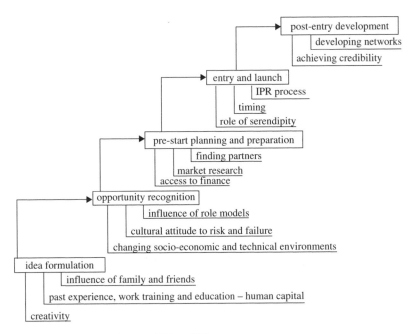

Source: Deakins and Whittam (2000, p. 121).

Figure 3.3 A possible model to start up a business

everything you can, whenever you can; the result will be an enhanced capacity to recognize opportunities.

- *Organize your knowledge.* Knowledge that is organized is more useful than knowledge that is not. This means that as you acquire new information, you should actively try to relate it to what you already know so that the connections between existing and new information come clearly into focus. Information that is connected and organized is easier to remember – and to use – than information that is not.

- *Increase your access to information.* The more information that is potentially related to opportunities and that you receive on a regular basis, the more likely you are to recognize opportunities when they emerge. You may enlarge your information by holding a job which provides opportunities for acquiring information, by building an extensive social network or by having a rich life.

- *Create connections between the knowledge you have.* The more richly connected knowledge structures are, the more readily the information in them can be combined into new patterns. One way in which

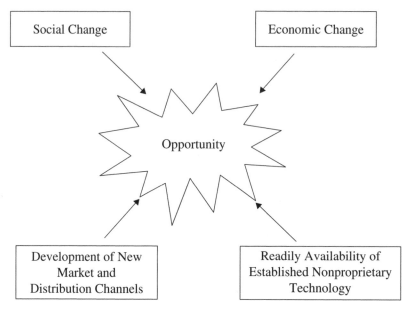

Source: Baron and Shane (2000, p. 10).

Figure 3.4   Business opportunity comes from a number of factors

Table 3.3   Some misconceptions around 'great ideas'

Misconception	Truth
Ideas just appear out of nowhere	The most successful idea generators do so in a structured, systemic way
There are no stupid ideas	The most powerful ideas often are resoundingly bad, at first glance
Customers will tell you what to do if you'll only listen	Although customers can help identify unmet needs, there's much more involved with making an idea workable
We can generate all the ideas we'll ever need if we just sit down at a meeting	Great ideas are best shaped through an ongoing dialogue
Getting ideas isn't the problem; implementing them is	The problem is not carefully screening the ideas that are generated

Source: Coulter (2001, p. 68).

such connections can be formed is to think about what you know and how different parts of what you know might be related.

- *Build your practical intelligence*. Try, as often you can, to think of new and better ways to handle practical problems. This may increase your own practical intelligence – and hence your ability to recognize opportunities.
- *Mix your eagerness for hits with wariness of false alarm*. If you want to be successful as an entrepreneur and in recognizing genuine opportunities, you should fight against your natural tendencies to be optimistic by at the same time considering negative factors as well. Doing so may go against your personal inclinations, but the result may be that you avoid one of the most dangerous pitfalls lying in wait for unsuspecting entrepreneurs: the quicksand of illusory opportunities.

DIFFERENT KINDS OF NEW BUSINESS VENTURES AND ENTREPRENEURS

It is common to distinguish between *lifestyle firms* and *growth firms* when talking about business start-ups (Burns, 2001). Lifestyle firms are set up primarily to undertake an activity that the owner-manager enjoys while also providing an adequate income, for example craft-based businesses. Expansion is not an issue, and once a level of activity that provides a reasonable income is reached, management becomes routine. Growth firms are set up with the intention of expansion, which normally requires exceptional entrepreneurial qualities of their starters. We will be back to growth problems in Chapter 6.

There are, of course, entrepreneurs of many different kinds, and many imaginative categories are suggested, for instance, technopreneurs, E-entrepreneurs, academic entrepreneurs and team entrepreneurs. One classification that I suggested in an earlier book (Bjerke, 1989) is as follows:

- First a distinction between *independent entrepreneurs*, that is, entrepreneurs who start businesses on their own and become their owners, and *intrapreneurs*, that is, entrepreneurs who start new business ventures for their employers.
- Independent entrepreneurs can then be classified into:

  Extrapreneurs, that is, people who leave their employment taking along ideas that have come up in the course of employment and start their own venture;

  Novopreneurs, that is, people who get an idea which does not compete with the activities of their employer and start a new venture to exploit their creative potential;

Interpreneurs, that is, people who connect ideas, resources and possibilities from different sources and start a venture based on this; *Renovateurs*, that is, people who save businesses in trouble and start a new venture based on the best pieces of the old one.

I have come to the following conclusions through studying the above entrepreneurial types over the years:

- extrapreneurs and renovateurs are common in critical situations,
- the majority of new business ventures are started by extrapreneurs,
- most countries have some kind of government institution supporting novopreneurs and their innovations,
- renovateurs seem to have become more common,
- novopreneurs seem to have become more rare.

4. To understand entrepreneurs

PREREQUISITES

When trying to understand entrepreneurs (or any other human conditions and events) the following, as mentioned before, must be borne in mind:

- Reality is seen as (socially) constructed. There is nothing, from the social science point of view, worth knowing beyond this reality.
- The task is to come up with an interpretation which is based on language/culture.
- Those interpretations which are most fruitful are those which advance the understanding of the researcher as well as other actors in some important way.
- An interpretation is not a deliberately simplified picture of past, present or future reality (which is the case with a model) but an image which, at least partly, constitutes a new reality.

Entrepreneurship is an increasingly popular research topic, and as we have seen most of this research is of an explaining type. There is consequently much material to choose from when attempting to summarize the results from explaining-oriented entrepreneurship research (as in Chapter 3). The results from understanding-oriented entrepreneurship research, on the other hand, are generally much more recent, more sporadic and, by the nature of the approach, more subjective. This chapter, therefore, contains more of my own views as an understanding-oriented researcher. One could say that while Chapter 3 is mostly about what other researchers have done, Chapter 4 is more about what I have done as a researcher myself.

ENTREPRENEURIAL LANGUAGE AND THINKING

Entrepreneur comes from the French. It consists of *entre* (the English word 'inter'), that is, to place oneself between (perhaps by placing oneself between resources and implementation or between potentiality and reality) and *prendre* (to take) which is related to grab, to catch (Chia, 1995). It *could* mean to be a contractor, that is, to undertake a task for a negotiated price in order to implement some kind of (often public) activity. Of more interest, however, for the development of the subject in theory as well as in practice, is to look at entrepreneurship as some kind of creative process, as grabbing an opportunity or exploiting a possibility. The point is to be *venturesome*, to be ahead of the game, or simply to be active, to forestall or to be seen. To be venturesome might mean to do something with somebody else, or that you do it alone. It is related to 'adventure'.

In German, one speaks of an *Unternehmer* and previously in English of an *undertaker* (now generally only a funeral director). This is related to taking something on, that is, to sign (*under*). Here the sense of adventure is missing.

In terms of entrepreneurial language and related thinking, it is interesting to set management against entrepreneurship – *managerialism* against *entrepreneurialism* (Hjorth and Johannisson, 1998). These are essentially opposites and each should be seen as ideal types of conceptualizations in Weber's sense (compare the distinction I made earlier between definitions = delimitations and conceptualizations = summaries; see p. 17). Table 4.1 presents a few aspects of a management approach and an entrepreneurial approach from an organizational point of view.

The management approach and the entrepreneurial approach can be seen in Table 4.1 as the difference between *behaviour* and *action* (Hjorth and Johannisson, 1998). Managerial behaviour may, for instance, represent instinctive subordination to existing circumstances, thereby contributing to preserving the status quo. Managers try to clarify existing structures via controlling behaviour and one-way communication. The manager needs to be economically rational in the hierarchy in which he or

Table 4.1   Organizing for management versus entrepreneurship

Aspects of the organizing process	Organizing at management approach	Organizing at entrepreneurship approach
Point of acting	Administration	Renewal
Acting clarifies	Existing structures	New processes
Interpersonal communication	Monologic	Dialogic
Driving force	(Economic) rationality	Passion for creating meaning
Success is achieved through	Role-defined hierarchies	Personal networks
Time focus	The present	The future
Context creating meaning	Institutional rules being given to the managers	All possible arenas

Source: Hjorth and Johannisson (1998, p. 95; my translation).

she is operating and where behaviour is regulated by relatively clear institutional rules.

Entrepreneurs, on the other hand, act, they take action. The ambition is renewal, which demands new processes. This must take place through dialogues in personal networks. The focus is not on what is, but on what will be, in creative arenas. These places, however, are never completely given, even less permanent.

Research results may also be based on other language pictures – consciously or not. Various assumptions are contained in the following suggested alternatives:

- *homo traditionalis*
- *homo oeconomicus*
- *homo administrativus*
- *homo ludens*
- *homo risens*
- *homo communicatus.*

The first three pictures are clearly related to the explaining perspective on entrepreneurship; the last three pictures are equally clearly related to the understanding perspective of entrepreneurship.

Homo traditionalis ('traditional man'), *homo oeconomicus* ('economic man') and *homo administrativus* ('administrative man') together provide an image of man which fits well with the rational, calculating, forecasting and planning view of an entrepreneur which is gained from an explaining approach and which we considered in the last chapter.

A different view, an understanding view, will be gained if we base it on *homo ludens* ('playing man'), *homo risens* ('laughing/humorous man') and *homo communicatus* ('communicating man'). The varieties of ideas which are generated by these pictures challenge us, even as authors, to become more entrepreneurial (Hjorth et al., 2003). This is because these pictures are close to everyday life for us, stressing our communicating, cultural, passionate, playing and laughing sides.

In his book *Homo Ludens*, Johan Huizinga (1971) argues very convincingly that human culture in all its richness is a result of our human ability to 'play' ('play' can be read here as playing a game as well as playing with existence). Man, unlike animals, seems to have an unlimited ability to play, to experiment, to try. If you give a dog a carton, the dog will start chewing at it. If you give a child a carton, it can be transformed into a dolls' house, a castle, a toy chest, a place to put soft toys, a car or a boat.

Similarly with the human values of humour and laughter. The myth that working and being serious is more important than playing and laughing is widely circulated. To work and to be serious, to play and to laugh are, however, very intimately related; these are mutually supporting and they are often aspects of the same activity. To make the comparison with animals again, we can say that we share seriousness with them, but in laughter we are alone.

Koestler (1964) presents a simple but brilliant recipe for how to be innovative (and thereby also be entrepreneurial). He claims that three experiences are necessary to be creative (say them aloud):

AH   = the aesthetic experience
AHA   = the intellectual experience
HAHA = the humoristic experience.

Another way to phrase the last of these three could be to say: To be a successful entrepreneur, it is necessary to have fun!

Finally, to really have fun and to get something out of a game it is necessary to play and laugh with other people, with whom we communicate and co-create reality.

A REMINDER

To help the reader understand the rest of this chapter, remember that:

- socially constructed reality consists of socio-matter
- the study focus is on significances and meaning
- to find symbols and meaning is to understand, not to explain
- we must interpret, not depict
- given and developed problems cannot be taken for granted, reality must always be problematized
- we cannot be impartial but have to admit that we, by necessity, are co-actors even as we are researchers
- one important task for the researcher is to participate in further dialogues – the questions might be more important than the answers.

FOUR WAYS OF UNDERSTANDING ENTREPRENEURS

This section will consider four ways of understanding entrepreneurs. They are:

- Entrepreneurs as sense-makers
- Entrepreneurs as language-makers

- Entrepreneurs as culture-makers
- Entrepreneurs as history-makers.

Why these four? I mentioned earlier that my basis for understanding is language and culture, so it is quite natural that language-makers and culture-makers are in there. Another, very general, aspect of understanding others is to look at the meaning they attach to what they do, that is, how they are able to make sense of their everyday reality; therefore, sense-makers are in there. Finally, a more specific, but nevertheless very interesting, theory has developed in the field of trying to understand entrepreneurs. This is presented by Spinosa et al. (1997) who look at entrepreneurs as history-makers. This nicely supplements the other three.

Common to these, as I see it, is that they are all varieties of social constructionism (which is, as we have seen, one pillar of my ambition as an understanding researcher of entrepreneurship).

The reason why I use the term 'maker' instead of 'creator' is, as was mentioned in Chapter 1, that I see most of entrepreneuring as building on 'given' elements of construction; in other words, that most entrepreneurs base their construction on factors that are perceived as already in place. So the entrepreneur as sense-maker uses what is perceived as meaning and sense as elements to construct his or her venture; the entrepreneur as language-maker uses the memes of his or her language; the entrepreneur as culture-maker uses fundamental values in his or her culture; and the entrepreneur as history-maker uses lifestyles that surround him or her (compare professions such as saddle-makers or shoe-makers, where most of the time the design and the idea behind their efforts are given). There are, as we know, cases of very radical and innovative entrepreneurship, where what we may call super-entrepreneurs are in action, but these are exceptions rather than types. In these cases, it may be justified to speak of entrepreneurs more as 'creators' than as 'makers'. The borderline between creating and making is certainly very vague.

To see an entrepreneur as a sense-maker is to understand how entrepreneurs function as sense-makers and to try and understand the differences between entrepreneurs and non-entrepreneurs as sense-makers (which we all are). Similarly, to see an entrepreneur as a language-maker is to understand how entrepreneurs function as language-makers and to try and understand the differences between entrepreneurs and non-entrepreneurs as language-makers (which we all are), and to see an entrepreneur as a culture-maker is to understand how entrepreneurs function as culture-makers and to try and understand the differences between entrepreneurs and non-entrepreneurs as culture-makers (which we all are).

To see an entrepreneur as a history-maker is, according to Spinosa et al. (1997), different from the other three views above. These authors see entrepreneurs alone as history-makers. For instance, entrepreneurs have a particular ability to interpret the implicit style of their time, to understand what is in the air so to say, and out of this, they are able to disclose a space which others can use.

These four kinds of makers are intimately related. Which one to focus on as a researcher is often a matter of preference. The choice will depend, for instance, on which part of people's social construction of their reality is in focus and what the researcher wants to use the results for, perhaps language development or cultural comparison. Researchers as well as entrepreneurs depend not only on time, physical and financial resources, but also on the intellectual ability to come up with adequate pictures and to generate purposeful cognitive processes (Suchman et al., 2001, p. 351). This can also influence and is influenced by which of the four makers a researcher is interested in.

One interesting question here – a question which is difficult to answer in general terms – is whether a researcher and a writer can adequately consider reality-making only in theory, neglecting it in action. Molander (1996, p. 139) believes that this has serious flaws. He talks about 'knowledge in action'. This book is, however, based on the assumption that a discussion of theories of constructing reality may have great value in itself. We do not always have to do it to understand it.

Entrepreneurs as Sense-makers

As we have seen in Chapter 2, my version of sense-making is a social phenomenological one. This means:

- The interesting world is the life-world: everyday life, that reality which is the constructed and experienced everyday reality, not the scientific world.
- The life-world is socially constructed but individually based (Sanner, 1997, p. 39).
- Sense-making takes place in a continuous process which is characterized by dialogues and communicative exchanges between people.
- This approach, which is based on phenomenology as presented originally by Edmund Husserl, has clear dialectic undertones.

This approach was described as *the actors' approach* (Arbnor and Bjerke, 1997).

The social phenomenology idea is based on four dialectically interrelated processes for sense-making (Arbnor and Andersson, 1977):

1. *Subjectification.* Consciousness of self is an important part of the consciousness of an individual. To be conscious means here that an individual has interpreted his or her situation, that he or she knows what has been interpreted and has an opinion of what it means. A subjectification means for an entrepreneur, for instance, that he or she starts to understand the business situation and its organizational form.
2. *Externalization.* In our life-world there are continuous externalizations between people. People meet people. We interpret each other. We act against or with each other. We show ourselves. An entrepreneur, in various language games, uses language to describe and transfer various meanings, for instance, what is the meaning of his or her business.
3. *Objectification.* An interpretation or an act is manifested through externalization and positioned as 'objective' through objectification. Externalization and objectification can take place simultaneously and may therefore be difficult to separate.

   Externalizing new knowledge perceived by other people can be the beginning of objectification. But externalizations can also be influenced by previous objectifications and thereby confirm partly existing knowledge. An objectification by an entrepreneur means, for instance, that his or her venture becomes more accepted and established. This takes place, above all, if the entrepreneur seems to be successful.
4. *Internalization.* This is the process by which earlier objectifications influence coming subjectifications and externalizations, that is, the historical influence which the socially constructed reality may have on subjectification and externalization of the individual. Internalization for the entrepreneur can mean, for instance, taking on the generally established understanding of business venturing in his or her own situation.

These four processes need to be *institutionalized* and *legitimized* to function in the long term (Arbnor and Andersson, 1977):

- *Institutionalization.* Socially constructed reality has more or less fixed forms and is taken more or less for granted. Institutionalizations such as rules of law, organizational diagrams and business (including entrepreneurial) educational programmes can have a dominant influence on any situation, where an entrepreneur perceives him or herself to be.
- *Legitimization.* This is often seen as important in establishing oneself as a new business venturer, the sense that one has something to provide and to get acceptance for trying to do so.

All acts, including entrepreneurial ones, take place in a context. We may call such context, after Hjorth and Johannisson (1998), the *organizing* context. This context is institutionalized as well as constituting a potential and a possibility. It may support entrepreneurship at the same time as embedding an entrepreneur in a social context (Winnicott, 1971; Stacey, 1996). For an entrepreneur it is possible to see three contexts (Sanner, 1997):

1. *The commercial context.* This context concerns production, distribution and exchange in a market for goods and services. The entrepreneur is rewarded there if his/her offer is satisfactory. Those who, in the end, will judge what is 'good' or not are the users of the outcome of the entrepreneurial efforts.
2. *The institutional context.* This context is characterized by rules and requirements which the entrepreneur must follow in his or her sense-making to gain support and legitimacy. The entrepreneur and other actors of interest to his or her venture are participating in this sense-making effort, taking into account its rules and requirements.
3. *The personal context.* Family and friends are often important to the entrepreneur's attempt to realize his or her ambitions (more of this in Chapter 5).

It is important here to separate three ways of looking at 'reality', that is, reality as objective, as perceived or as sense-made (Smircich and Stubbart, 1985). In the first case, reality is seen as something 'out there', a reality to discover and to depict. Reality is then seen as full of contexts and as *objective*. In the second case, reality is seen as very complex. Human ability to generate more holistic and encompassing pictures of such a reality is limited. We can only look at one part of such a reality at a time. Reality can then be seen as *perceived.*

The third case offers a different way of looking at reality. In this case, reality is not believed to be full of contexts, of which we, limited as we are as human beings, can see only a part. Instead it is assumed, consciously or unconsciously, to be controlled by our intentionality, we enact a reality which we have *made sense of*, a reality which means something to us. If this reality exists as such, or if it does not, is of less importance, as it is of no interest whether our perception is right or wrong. People act here *as if* reality were this way.

I will illustrate this by considering my own office. *Objectively* it consists of more than one thousand books and, God knows, how many papers and reports. *Subjectively*, I think I should categorize the content of that place more often than I do. But, then, how to do this – really? There are places in that office, where reports and books *make more sense to me than to any other person*.

Sense-making can be conceptualized as the reciprocal interaction of information-seeking and meaning-construction with action. Created meaning influences action. Reciprocally, action influences the meaning you give to an action. One may conceptualize action as meaningful behaviour (Sanner, 1997, p. 38).

Sense-making can provide special insights into uncertain and ambiguous situations, for instance, when taking on a new and innovative activity related to an entrepreneurial venture. It is important for an entrepreneur to pursue opportunities without being restricted by any fixed ideas or definitions of what the business is all about. The environment can be acted upon in order to widen the opportunities for the business venture and in order to include other actors. A broad network widens the environment through social constructions and then enlarges the room to act. Developing a problem into an opportunity can be achieved through entrepreneurial sense-making of reality (Sanner, 1997).

Sense-making concerns the future but tends to be retrospective. Planning future actions involves imagining that they have already occurred and anticipating and making sense of their consequences (Gartner et al., 1992). One could say that we use the meaning we place on the experience of our everyday life (Schutz, 1967, p. 73) as an interpretative scheme for our actions. We could also say that we, often unconsciously, act according to or enact a narrative. The narrative might indicate 'I will present myself as an unconcerned person' or as 'incredibly experienced in relating to the opposite sex'. An entrepreneur might enact the narrative 'I have been around before' or 'I know what I am doing'.

Interpretative schemes, which we often take for granted (although without being able to tell somebody else their full content), make it possible for us to 'recognize', interpret and 'negotiate' even strange and unanticipated situations and thus to continue confirming and reconfirming meaning in the course of interaction with others (Ranson et al., 1980). But these schemes may also work as blinkers in a situation which should be seen as new.

Sense-making, however, is more than a process of recalling existing interpretative schemes or playing out old narratives. If that were true, no new learning could take place (Gioia, 1986). Instead, sense-making and construction of meaning involve associating new experience with existing knowledge, sometimes modifying existing schemes and narratives to incorporate new knowledge and also, even if infrequently, dramatically restructuring existing knowledge or creating new knowledge by using intuition and revelation (Bartunek, 1984).

Arbnor et al. (1980) defined 11 basic foundational pieces of what they refer to as the actors' theory, which is related to what Arbnor and Bjerke (1997) call the actors' approach. Among these pieces are:

- Practise what you preach but also learn by looking at your own practice.
- Mobilize social courage.
- Look for the potential crisis in a situation.
- Development means excitement – discharge – excitement.
- We become together, not alone – if we behave, authentically.
- You have to understand the way your own language constructs your reality.
- Dialectics is not a tool but a way to see.
- Reality is a social construction.

Baumol (1993) thinks that since entrepreneurs change the world we live in, no level of description can fully capture what they do. But I think, as do Spinosa et al. (1997, p. 65), that describing entrepreneurs as changing backgrounds and showing how they make such changes amounts to a description that points beyond the empirical at the same time as it provides an understanding of the limitations of theoretical rationalizations.

Entrepreneurs as Language-makers

Think about language as reality. To work symbolically through language and thereby transcend our biological limits is a hallmark of humanity and can even be counted as the most significant feature of a human being. Our acts are not only controlled by our intentions, but acts as well as intentions are controlled by the language we use. Genuinely new problems require genuinely new solutions. We do not find these genuinely new solutions if we do not have the appropriate language (Bjerke, 1989, p. 135).

There are many examples of the magic and importance of language in our everyday life:

- Companies try to make the concept of 'employee' or 'worker' more humane by talking about, say, 'member of the crew' or 'associate'.
- In some organizations it is important to be called 'partner' rather than 'member', even if one does not have any economic responsibility. On the other hand, one is a 'member' of American Express, not just a 'holder of a credit card'.
- 'Restructuring' or 'downsizing' are euphemisms used in some companies when they cut down. They refuse to say that they 'fire' anybody.

- How many times have we heard empty phrases in top-heavy bureaucracies, where the mode of presentation is what is most important and the medium is the message? When we listen to these people we often ask ourselves: 'What did they say – really?'
- Why, in some countries, are they changing the term 'public sector' to 'common sector'?

Language has certainly entered the theory and practice of business in the past 20–30 years:

- A company is defined by its language. The symbols, concepts, visions and focus of the senior managers offer a better understanding of the company in question than either its plans or decisions.
- Every moment is a symbolic moment. Even to ignore this as a business leader is symbolic. Are you accessible? Is your door open? Who is invited to your meetings? Who is not? Are you present at the Christmas party?
- The vocabulary of a company can be an important asset, but it can also be a major liability. Is the vocabulary of your company based on terms like 'efficiency', 'productivity', 'growth' and 'return' or is it based on terms like 'feeling', 'commitment', 'pleasure' and 'creativity'?
- To renew a company it may be necessary to identify those who hold to relics of its old language (Arbnor et al., 1980). The point is to clarify the original ideas underlying the language being used in a company in order to reveal those who are still living in an outdated world.
- To renew a company may also require changing the central building blocks of its language, that is, its memes. Think about mapping the genuine phenomenological language of starting a business used by an entrepreneur, that is, a personal language in an individual life-world!

The language philosopher John L. Austin (1911–60) introduced the concept *speech act* for those acts which are performed when a speaker has made a statement and the listener has understood it. However, more fundamentally, the great language philosopher, Ludwig Wittgenstein, coined the brilliant concept *language game*. This concept serves several purposes. First, Wittgenstein wanted to stress that language is used and functions in many different ways beyond the trivial sense of, for instance, pointing something out, asking questions or giving commands. Language is used one way when we tell a story, another when we participate in a debate and still another when we do mathematics. Here we can really talk about different language games. Second, Wittgenstein wanted to draw attention to the fact that the meaning of a linguistic expression is determined by its use *within* that language game to which it belongs. Third, the concept accentuates the fact that speech acts are related to other social acts. Fourth, 'game' indicates an activity which can be done for its own sake; there is no specific purpose to which all use of language is subordinated. In this context, Wittgenstein stresses the concept *life form*, where a language game takes place in a natural way contrary to a purposeful activity. Fifth, one is reminded by the concept of language game that the use of language is an activity governed by rules.

If we follow Wittgenstein we must deny that understanding in the life-world consists of something special, a mental process in particular. Instead we should ask ourselves what is the situation in which we use the concept 'understanding' in a language game. Furthermore, there are no generally valid or exact conditions for somebody to say that he or she thinks or understands. If that were the case it would be meaningful to ask for the moment when somebody thought or understood for the first time. This would naturally lead to the idea of mental processes. Such questions, however, are not asked in the games using this concept in everyday life. There, understanding is something which takes place between people (compare the corresponding discussion about 'culture' in the next section).

This provides us with a basis for discussing how to use language in order better to understand entrepreneurship, language which enables entrepreneurs to become the free and creative human beings they deserve to be (see, for instance, Hjorth and Johannisson, 1998 and 2000). Concepts from everyday life, such as interplay, passion, vision, initiative and responsibility could be utilized to stimulate entrepreneurial acts. Ambiguous concepts could be used to compare different understandings of entrepreneurship, action and behaviour, problems with possibilities or circumstances with meaning. Vocabulary could be re-established by, for instance, talking about becoming rather than being, or using terms from arts and theatre such as inspiration, creativity and spontaneity. Ingrained concepts such as coordinating or understanding could be reinterpreted. The use of verbs could be increased and the use of nouns decreased; organizing instead of organization, or why not 'entrepreneuring' instead of entrepreneurship? Finally new words could be constructed in order to enliven old ideas, such as 'cre-activity' for what entrepreneurs are doing and 'observ-actor' to denote the person who studies the phenomenon (from an understanding point of view).

Let us look at two different business development situations in which a company may want to progress, by using sets of words that belong to those two situations. We call the two situations business development in order to grow ('more of the same thing' – growth) and business development in

Table 4.2   Two different vocabularies

Growth	Innovation
Planning	Learning
Totalization	Simplification
Unity	Variety
Systems	Social units
Structure	Process
Components	Actors
Business concepts	Visions
We are	We become
Efficiency	Commitment
Fit	Excitement
Marketing	Networking
Economies of scale	Small is beautiful
Standardization	Surprises
Capital	Entrepreneurs
Managers	Leaders
Education	Culture
Models	Creative language

order to innovate ('something genuinely new' – innovation). It is clearly possible to see two different vocabularies applicable to the two situations (Table 4.2).

The lists could have been longer, but they are long enough to convey an important message. The two business development situations are definitely different. Different language is used in the two situations – and the idea is to act accordingly.

- *Business development in order to grow* means to plan total, united systems, where every component in the system structure is seen as a part of the whole thing. The background consists of different business concepts, where every part efficiently fits the others. Marketing and economies of scale in production are standardized. The essential resource is capital. The members of the organization, above all the senior managers, have the right education and the right attitude, which means that they also are living models for each other.
- *Business development in order to innovate* means to learn to understand the fundamental logic that every possible business is based on, but at the same time to tolerate a variety of working groups which are unstructured (in a process orientation) and which are run by their actors. Each such group is led by visions, against which the businesses

emerge. All members feel committed to creating excitement and contributing to small, but beautiful, networks. Surprises are wanted and seen as opportunities for learning. The most important resource are the entrepreneurs, above all those that can take on leadership positions. A strong culture is developing in these groups, part of which is a truly creative language.

Let me briefly comment on some of the words presented in Table 4.2, some of which may seem odd to the reader, before I discuss five selected pairs of words in more detail. The concept *structure* has been used for a long time to describe stable (or at least forecastable) behaviour in an organization against which change can be explained. One common saying is, for instance, that a company can move from one stable structure to another through a period of change.

In a situation where business development is necessary, change is the natural state. Factors to consider are not static. They *become* all the time. They will never be complete. When new orientations are needed, structures can be obstacles. Procedures can take over. What we can hope for then is to start a *process* in a more hopeful direction. It is difficult to implement a successful innovation without taking radical steps on the way; one may even have to completely redefine one's concept.

Marketing is a must at growth which needs to optimize its whole range. It is then a question of choosing a specific environment (market) and trying to adapt to this environment by using a number of tools in the marketing mix. There is, however, another way to perceive reality 'out there' which seems more suitable for business development in order to innovate. One concept in this context is *networking*. Consequences of this concept include seeing actors in the market as being at the same level as the company, seeing consumers as participants in an extended value-adding process, listening, learning from the environment, establishing contacts and creating new patterns (more of this in Chapter 5).

Figure 4.1 shows an ordinary growth curve for a given business venture (or maybe a group of ventures).

Figure 4.1 specifically shows the beginning and the mature phases of a venture, as opposed to the growing one, that is, those situations where one cannot continue as before. In the beginning phase there are no historical data to build on and in the mature phase it is normal to actively try to establish a new trend, hopefully in an upward direction. These phases of development share an important similarity, which is that business development in order to innovate is the only alternative. Between these two phases one can say that business development in order to grow takes place. Let us discuss business development in order to grow and in order to innovate

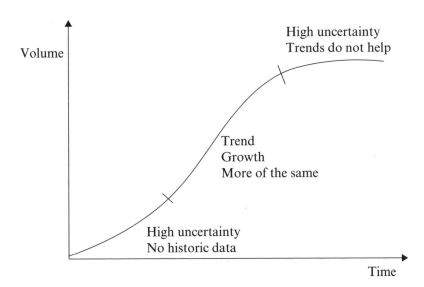

Figure 4.1 A growth curve

Table 4.3 Five conceptual pairs in two different business development situations

Business development in order to grow	Business development in order to innovate
Planning	Learning
Systems	Social units
Capital	Entrepreneurs
Managers	Leaders
Models	Creative language

further by selecting five conceptual pairs from the list presented in Table 4.2 and studying those pairs in more detail (Table 4.3).

Planning versus learning

The conceptual pair 'planning' and 'learning' is fundamental to understanding the differences between business development in order to grow and in order to innovate. The necessary foundation for the future is often seen as planning. This can be acceptable in a situation where we can foresee a clear possibility for growth. But if we cannot see such a possibility and still need to go forward the reality is very different. The situation contains genuine uncertainty, which can only partly be reduced by analysis.

At one time it was believed that carefully planned business development could always substitute for the disorder of passionate entrepreneurs. But study after study has proven this false. Innovation rarely takes place in established organizations without an individual or a small group refusing to waver in their conviction that they can start such a renewal. 'Planning' as we normally understand the term is in a way incompatible with an entrepreneurial situation. Renewal must, almost by definition, be uncontrollable and specific. It should start small, tentative, prepared for surprises. Opportunities for innovation are found, on the whole, in the detail and close to events. Possibilities for renewal are not found among the massive aggregates with which the planner by necessity deals and which cannot contain their own deviations – the unexpected. By the time the deviation becomes 'statistically significant' it may be too late. Innovative opportunities do not come with the tempest but with the rustling of the breeze.

Larger companies tend to make too sophisticated analyses of new projects. However, there is always a high degree of uncertainty in new things which cannot be planned away. Despite apparent rationality in retrospect, innovation never takes place as planned, simply because nothing *really new* can be planned in full. The earlier stages of such processes consist of grouping around a vision, making progress by learning from mistakes and figuring out the way that works.

Too much planning can be dangerous. Guided by an understanding approach, an organization constructed by man is a vehicle which keeps on going. It consists of continuous movements and stability does not exist in any statistical sense. During the course of an organization's development, there is a risk that too much of its social energy will be devoted to planning and too little left for reorientation, when such a reorientation is needed. This latter necessity is more common in the situation of business development in order to innovate than in business development in order to grow.

Good leaders of business development in order to innovate are not sticklers for return-on-investment projections carried out to the last decimal place. The time it takes to bring a new product to market – a decade is not unusual – makes such projections absurd. They know that formal business plans can be used as a substitute for forcing the participants to think their projects through, for providing evidence of the scope of the opportunity and for presenting credible scenarios for retrenchment in case they are wrong. Ironically, planning systems in many corporations can stifle strategic thinking because dependency on formalized strategic planning builds a false sense of confidence. At business development in order to innovate considerably less complicated approaches are needed.

Let us compare two alternative business development philosophies applicable to our two situations. Figure 4.2 shows what could be a way to

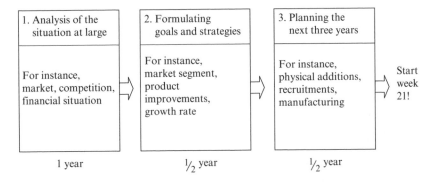

Figure 4.2   Alternative A ('The relay race')

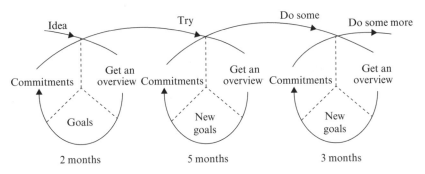

Figure 4.3   Alternative B ('The committed spiral')

start a new office in an existing consulting company looking for *growth*, but probably would not represent the start for the same company at its very beginning. Figure 4.3 shows a road of learning or revitalization, that is, of innovation. A similar distinction is made by Normann (1975), who talks about a goal orientation versus a process orientation (see Table 4.4).

It is fashionable to assume that any forecast is better than no forecast. The reasoning might sound like this: 'Make a guess, call it an assumption, and derive an estimate by subtle calculation. The estimate is then presented as the result of scientific reasoning, something calculated which is far superior to mere guesswork.' Large planning errors may result because this method offers a bogus answer where an entrepreneurial judgement is required. Judging the future is a necessary evil, which should be done as little as possible.

The essential point here is that planning is both more feasible and more important at business development in order to grow and that this should be

Table 4.4   Goal orientation and process orientation

Goal orientation	Process orientation
The decision-maker first formulates goals and then (alternative) plans which are assessed against their degree of goal fulfilment	Planning is a course of learning in which the perspective is constantly shifting between visions and immediate action taken
Man (and management) are seen as rational decision-makers	Man (and management) are seen as learning and knowledge-building units
Useful in well-defined and known planning environments or when one has a superior strength, such that when planning, the environment does not have to be considered	Useful in a complicated planning environment (cause–effect relationships; limitations and possibilities are partly unknown)
Mature stages of the development cycle of the company	Earlier stages of the development cycle of the company
Tensions and mis-fits are not wanted and are eliminated through planning	Tensions and mis-fits are wanted to a large extent and seen as planning resources; sometimes tensions are created deliberately

Source: Normann (1975, p. 67; my translation).

reflected in the language spoken in this situation. At business development in order to innovate the situation is different. There the activities are directed more by visions than by goals, and visions and goals are very different (Normann, 1975). Visions are intuitive images about future states, which can be very different from the present ones and which may exist only as ideas among a small number of insightful and possibly significant actors in the business development context. To have a vision does not mean to be committed to a specific future state or even to any future state which currently seems possible, but rather to use the vision as part of a mechanism to determine which aspects of the present are to be stressed, as a source of inspiration or even as a challenge.

Normann (1975) notes three important purposes of a vision:

1. The vision controls learning by making it possible to derive 'the next step'.
2. Changes in the vision are a measure of learning, as learning from actual steps of the process are checked against the vision, which in turn may be influenced and modified.

3. The vision makes it easier to set priorities and to generate driving forces such as ambition and commitment within the business development group.

Consequently, the vision is an instrument for learning, but it is also an expression of learning and is changed during its course. The vision may be relatively unclear in the beginning, but may gradually become more precise. The vision is flexible – an inflexible vision is a sign of a badly functioning learning process. There is no reason to be ashamed of having changed one's vision.

The problem with committing too early to a vision, that is, turning it into a goal, is that in a situation of genuine reorientation it is often impossible fully to understand the present situation or to know which circumstances will be changed during the course of development.

The vision probably consists, at least in a business context, of some general ideas of which consumer groups and market segments the firm intends to turn to, which types of products are to be offered to the market and which organization and resources will make the vision possible.

Another aspect of business development in order to innovate is that decision-making is seen as a process. The choice itself, that is, the decision, is stressed less than what precedes it. In everyday language, 'decision' usually stands for the moment when the choice is made. From the point of view of an explaining-oriented researcher this moment is stressed as well.

This view of decision-making as a limited act by a person or by a group of persons at a specific point in time is too simplistic and may even be dangerous at business development in order to innovate. The decision as a process which includes the preparation for making a decision, and sometimes even the implementation of the decision, becomes the main interest. The decision itself is less important than the thinking and debate that go into it (Pinchot, 1985). The plan decided upon may soon become obsolete, but what will remain will be a clearer view of the issues and options. As each member of the business development team is stretched and challenged by the attempts at imagining, predicting and deciding the future, he or she develops the mental tools to think more clearly about the business. When changes occur later, once the business venture is under way, earlier discussions and debate become the background for what others will call rapid intuitive decision-making. What happens is that barriers can quickly be overcome by applying solutions imagined long ago in the planning process. This kind of learning has been described as attacking the problem incrementally (Quinn, 1980) and as applying milestone planning (Block and MacMillan, 1985).

At business development in order to innovate it is important to be particularly open to uncertainty. There is no risk-free route into the future, but sometimes we can choose the degree of uncertainty we wish to run with. To accept uncertainty means, among other things, to be less surprised by unexpected events. It also means admitting that renewal and innovation are tricky and do not pretend to resolve once and for all that which is in a perpetual flux.

To be willing to accept uncertainty means feeling free to learn, to err, to adapt, to invent and to go back to the drawing board again and again. Then we can also accept mistakes; even *learn to make them faster*. This has several advantages:

1. The mistakes will be cheaper.
2. The mistakes will be more educative *per money unit*.
3. The mistakes will give us more space to manoeuvre as we have not yet come so far.

We *always* make mistakes when we take on something new. We may even dare to express it such that there are no failures (Ferguson, 1980). An experiment has results. We learn from it, but it adds to our understanding and expertise, so whatever the result we have not lost.

If we give up our need for certainty in terms of control and fixed answers, it does not mean that we have to lose certainty altogether. It can be replaced by another kind of certainty – a feeling of direction. It may also mean that we start to trust our intuitive abilities.

Systems versus social units

The systems approach has dominated the subject of business administration for at least 30 years. It emerged as a planning philosophy at the peak of the period of the large organizations, a period when business development in order to grow was natural and in many industries the only conceivable route. To see business development as a unity, where the point is to coordinate different participating units, is still applicable to this business development situation.

I am old enough to have participated when systems thinking entered business administration. We said in those days: 'What happens if we look at a company, *as if* it behaves like a system?' The systems language was taken from the biological and the technical sciences (a few examples of such terms are 'equilibrium', 'fitness', 'components', 'feedback', 'niche' and 'survival'). This language has today become self-sufficient. We have forgotten 'as if'. We do no longer look at the approach as a language besides other languages, but claim that reality *is* constructed systems-wise. This approach has influenced our thinking (and actions) to such a degree that it is even possible to hear statements of the following type: 'I cannot do anything

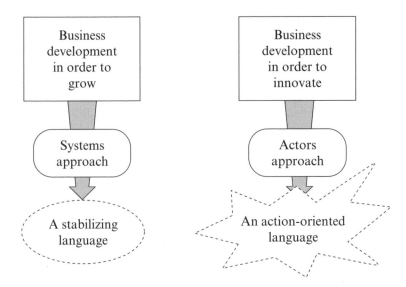

Figure 4.4   Language for stability or action

about it. I am just part of the system!' The systems language is, by and large, stabilizing rather than innovative.

At business development in order to innovate we need another language, an action-oriented language, where people feel they are part of living social units in which individual contributions are possible as well as welcome. We can pick several terms from the right side of the vocabularies in Table 4.2, which are natural to such a language, for instance, 'learning', 'variety', 'actors', 'visions', 'networking', 'leaders' and 'culture' (Figure 4.4).

Capital versus entrepreneurs

In a situation of growth, the most strategic resource is capital, in a situation of innovation, it is entrepreneurs. To put it in simple terms, we can say that 'predictability' is almost an antonym for 'entrepreneurship'. Because unpredictability is one of its essential features, entrepreneurship is inherently difficult to take into account in a systematic analysis, which may not be attainable if there are no stable patterns or repeated behaviour. This view also stresses further our almost intuitive opinion of entrepreneurs at business development in order to innovate. If they are not given room to act, stagnation will spread very quickly.

In grasping opportunities, some institutions with vast resources (such as public institutions, larger non-profit oriented organizations and major corporations) are tempted to commit resources heavily, to go 'first class' all the way. In this way, the rationale goes, the chances of failure are reduced and the eventual returns are increased.

However, there are compelling forces toward the gradual commitment of resources – reflecting the entrepreneurial end of our conceptual pair – which are in many cases external. They include:

Difficulties in predicting resource needs   Given the rapid and erratic pace of change in our new entrepreneurial society, it is necessary to assume that corrections will be necessary as the business development process goes on. Rapid advancements have also made technological forecasting hazardous, and projections of consumer preferences, inflation rates and market responses have been equally difficult. To commit oneself one stage at a time allows responsiveness; a one-time commitment creates unnecessary risk.

Limits to external control   Companies can no longer say that they own the forest and therefore do as they like with it; environmental considerations must be taken into account. Similarly, strict zoning and environmental division can affect the companies' control of real estate. International access to resources is no longer guaranteed, as the oil crises in the 1970s made very clear. Corporate executives must be flexible in this respect.

Social needs   The idea that 'small is beautiful' and the argument that too large a gulf separates producers and consumers are very persuasive. Gradual commitment of resources allows managers to determine the most appropriate level of investment for a particular task.

The opposing pressures felt by large organizations toward a single, heavy commitment of resources (reflecting the 'capitalistic' end of our conceptual pair) include the following:

Need to reduce risk   Managers limit the risk they face by throwing all the resources they can muster at an opportunity from the outset, even if it means waste. Such a commitment is seen to increase the likelihood of an earlier success and to reduce the likelihood of an eventual failure. To stress concentrated, heavy inputs of resources fosters the belief that the resources themselves bring power and success.

Sensitive positions of senior business managers   In companies where executives are either promoted every two years or exiled to corporate Siberia, they need quick, measurable results. Cash and earnings gained in each period must surpass the last. One must here achieve quick, visible results or the job is in danger.

Focus on incentive compensation To concentrate resources up-front yields quick returns and measurable results, which can be easily translated into a manager's bonus compensation. Small-scale strategic experiments, however, often show very little immediate results on the bottom line while consuming scarce managerial time.

Single-minded capital allocation systems These assume that the consequences of future uncertainty can be measured now or at least that uncertainty one year from now will be no less than it is now. Thus a single decision point seems appropriate. Many capital budget systems make it difficult to get two bites of an apple.

Bureaucratic planning systems A project can win the support of 99 people and be scuttled by one rejection. An entrepreneur, however, can be rejected 99 times but go ahead if one crucial person gives approval.

We can summarize the first steps at business development in order to grow and business development in order to innovate (somewhat simplified) as steps in opposing directions (Figure 4.5).

Managers versus leaders

'Manager' has become a negative and belittling word in some camps (Jay, 1970). It can connote an individual put in by a business owner to keep things going while he or she is not there. 'Director' has a ring of opulence, 'worker' has an unpretentious dignity, but 'manager' can sound like a euphemism for dogsbody. Neither a thinker nor a doer, but just a manager. This dates back to a time when a manager really was just a manager: the mill owner or the mine owner wanted a simple and unvarying process to be continued indefinitely in more places than could be supervised personally, so someone was hired to manage in the owner's absence, someone drawn from the same social class as the workers who would discharge the more disagreeable tasks of the employer.

Of course words can outgrow their base origins, but titles can be used as an excuse for not having to do anything which is radical or new. 'Administrator', for example. The concept has been used in civil service and in corporations for many years to justify leadership-size salaries where no leadership was really exerted. Now there seems to be a danger of people hiding behind 'management' in order to fend off the idea of creativeness. Some managers find it unsatisfactory that the future of a business should rest, as it often does, on such unpredictable and uncontrollable phenomena as 'creativity', 'entrepreneurship' and 'leadership'.

But we can see a clear trend in the development of the terminology around 'management'. More and more voices are raised in the attempt to escape the

Business development
in order to grow

1. Get *capital*	5. Finance *soundly* and *intelligently* (too much capital discourages an entrepreneur from continuing to be creative)
2. Learn the *rules* (e.g., about how the system functions)	4. 'Unlearn' the old rules and get *insight* into the conditions of the new situation
3. Choose an *environment* (e.g., main office or Singapore)	3. Create a *culture* which promoted good ideas to become better
4. Get a *smart idea* (e.g., a patent)	2. Clarify all ideas floating around and formulate them as *visions*
5. Employ a *manager*	1. Identify and develop the *entrepreneurs*

Business development in
order to innovate

Figure 4.5   To develop businesses

concept of a manager as a distant, goal-setting person from the main office. 'Management by exception' has become 'management by walking around' and 'visible management'. 'Management by objectives' is on its way to become 'management by talking around'. It is obvious (and all experience speaks for it) that most of business development (especially business development in order to innovate) requires more leadership than management.

Models versus creative language
To try to come up with simplified pictures of the present or future of complex business realities, that is, models, is the dominating process in business administration today. This can be adequate at business development in order to grow, when it is a question of continuing on a course that is already set in order to extend an existing successful pattern. A continuation of existing cooperation between different forces is what is asked for. Providing information to members of the business development team as to

what is going on and what should be going on could then be done through models. If the point is to continue by building on what is there already, terms such as 'planning', 'systems', 'structure', 'marketing', 'efficiency', 'standardization' and 'economies of scale' are understood. Also, not a great deal of personal commitment is needed.

Again, at business development in order to innovate the situation is different. Then one must set a new course. This can only happen once the members of the business development team are committed. It may then be necessary to problematize instead of simplifying, to interpret instead of depicting. A creative language is needed, a language which really uses the ideas on which this book is based, that is, that language, thought and action are very intimately related. The vocabulary of 'Innovation' in Table 4.2 is part of such a language: 'learning', 'social units', 'actors', 'commitment' and 'surprises'. If the terminology under 'Growth' is a fertilizer, the terminology under 'Innovation' consists of *new seeds*!

A comment

I have been painting in black and white. I am aware of it. I have provided very little space for nuance. What has been said should not be misunderstood. We may, for instance, say that we can never be completely without 'planning', there is room for some 'structures' even if 'processes' are fast, we can build 'systems' of 'social units' and so on. We should understand, however, that the meaning of terms will be different when they are placed in different contexts. What is important is to understand that every language is based on a certain image of reality and the presumptions by which that image is governed. Every terminology answers some questions, neglects others. The terminology which I have presented under business development in order to grow is based on a certain image of reality and certain questions, that terminology which I have presented under business development in order to innovate is based on another image and answers other questions.

It is a matter of priorities. We cannot do everything, cannot be best in everything. Five or six jobs half done do not add up to one good job! We cannot stress everything at the same time. Business development needs to stress one set of actions in order to innovate and another set in order to grow, and this can be done by using different terminology in the two cases.

Below are a few final points on the relationships between language and creating new business ventures, that is, concerning entrepreneurs as language-makers:

- We *can*, as researchers, talk about creating new business ventures without having experienced it. Entrepreneurs cannot do this, however – as entrepreneurs.

- We *cannot create* new business ventures without talking about it.
- We do not understand entrepreneurship *before* we speak its language.
- To be an entrepreneur *always means*, at least partly, modifying one's language.
- A problem is not completely formulated until *it is solved*.
- To renew businesses (and so also language) in a firm it may be necessary that somebody comes in *from outside*.
- A word can only get its *full* meaning in a concrete context and in concrete action.
- If we do not talk about entrepreneurship, it will not take place. *The word can give space to it*.
- Entrepreneurs do not succeed very well *if they do not practise what they preach*.

Entrepreneurs as Culture-makers

Culture is a concept which is used in many different areas of society. In public debate the concept is often taken to mean those human creations which give a higher spiritual experience – fine arts, literature, music and so on. This has given us concepts such as 'cultural heritage', 'cultural debate' and 'our Western culture'.

Of more interest to a business researcher is the cultural anthropologists view. Cultural anthropology traditionally takes a very wide view on culture. Kluckhohn and Kelly (1945, p. 97), for instance, define culture as 'all the historically created designs for living, explicit or implicit, rational, irrational or nonrational, which exist at any given time as potential guides for the behaviour of men'. Culture is 'the man-made part of the environment', says the anthropologist Herskovits (1955, p. 305). There are, however, cultural anthropologists who recommend a more restricted use of the meaning of culture to cover only thinking, not acting. In this case culture could be perceived as the system of meaning which gives order and direction to human life.

Some examples of how culture can be defined in a business setting are:

Organizational culture is that pattern of beliefs and expectations shared by the organization's members which powerfully shape the behaviour of individuals and groups within the organization. (Byars, 1987, p. 48)

As knowledge and belief, culture exists only as thought and is nonmaterial and nonbehavioural (therefore, behaviour is guided by and reflects culture but is not the thing itself). (Dredge, 1985, p. 412)

An organization's culture can be described by its management in terms of the way their tasks are typically handled in the context of key relationships. (Schwartz and Davis, 1981, p. 36)

[Culture is] the way we do things around here. (Deal and Kennedy, 1988, p. 4)

No matter how culture is understood, it is generally seen as being based on the following (Bjerke, 1999):

1. Culture is something which unites a certain group.
2. Culture is something which one learns as a member of a group.
3. Culture is related to values.

> Of those more than 160 definitions of culture analyzed by Kroeber and Kluckhohn, some conceive of culture as separating humans from nonhumans, some define it as communicable knowledge, and some as the sum of historical achievements produced by man's social life. All of the definitions have common elements: culture is learned, shared and transmitted from one generation to the next. Culture is primarily passed from parents to their children but also by social organizations, special interest groups, the government, the schools, and the church. Common ways of thinking and behaving that are developed are then reinforced through social pressure. Culture is also multidimensional, consisting of a number of common elements that are interdependent. Changes occurring in one of the dimensions will affect the others as well. (Czinkota et al., 1994, p. 264)

In spite of this, one can ask how extensive culture is. When business scholars discuss culture, they usually do it along one of two dimensions or both (compare the definitions above):

1. One dimension is to ask whether culture is behaviour, alternatively what is influencing and regulating behaviour, that is, different kinds of values (compare all definitions just given above).
2. Another dimension which is touched upon less often, but which is of great importance in a book like this one, where I make a distinction between explaining and understanding, is to ask oneself whether culture is something one is conscious of or whether it is something deeper, that is, something unconscious.

Based on these two dimensions it is possible to construct Table 4.5 (Bjerke and Al-Meer, 1994, p. 177). Culture (in a business setting) can be seen as represented by one or more of the cells in this table.

1. *Conscious behaviour*. A company might have a procedure to determine the budget which is repeated year after year. Perhaps a first budget meeting takes place at the beginning of September. At this meeting, a budget committee is appointed which is given the task of collecting information from all departmental managers, to find out their expected

Table 4.5   Culture in terms of behaviour and consciousness

Culture as	Something conscious	Something unconscious
Behavioural	(1) E.g.: The budget process	(2) E.g.: Sitting down at a meeting
Non-behavioural (values only)	(3) E.g.: The fewer accidents, the better	(4) E.g.: Planning is good

Source: Bjerke and Al-Meer (1994, p. 176).

costs and revenues during the next budget year. This information is compiled and presented in an executive budget meeting in the middle of December, when the budget for the next year is decided. This recurrent behavioural pattern may be called the *budget culture* of the company.

2. *Unconscious behaviour.* An example which also concerns a behavioural pattern, but where the pattern is now unconscious, could be the way in which people sit down in a meeting in a company. It is perhaps taken for granted that the boss sits at the head of the table, that those who are closest to the boss sit next to him or her and that newcomers sit at the back of the room. This has become an unconscious *meeting culture* in the company.

3. *Conscious values.* If we consider the possibility that culture does not consist of behaviour at all, but instead is concerned with controlling behaviour through various values, assumptions and beliefs, these values and the like can be conscious or unconscious. A conscious value could be represented for instance in posters making the statement that 'the fewer accidents, the better'.

4. *Unconscious values.* When a language is seen from an understanding point of view, it is, above all, not seen as a mechanism for depicting an objective reality but as a performative tool (speech acts and other acts belong together). We have said this before. In Wittgenstein's terminology, with each language game there is also a related life-form. It is 'natural' to behave in a certain way when some concepts are uttered. But this discussion can be brought one step further if we look at culture, language games and life-forms from an understanding point of view. It may not be necessary for a word to be uttered for a specific behaviour to be natural in a cultural situation. It may simply be enough that the situation 'speaks for' a specific behaviour. In a company, for instance, confidence in the value of planning may have been built up.

So, when a situation is seen to invite planning that may be 'the most natural thing in the world' to do, even without being asked. In such a case one could really, in the spirit of Wittgenstein, speak about culture games and life-forms!

The crucial question here is: What does culture consist of and where is it? If we limit the content of culture to consist only of cell (4) in Table 4.5, we could conceptualize culture as basic, mostly unconscious values, assumptions and beliefs which are controlling behaviour (compare Bjerke, 1999). Cells (1)–(3) could then be called cultural manifestations, but not culture itself. And using an understanding approach, culture would, according to our discussions about understanding earlier in this book, exist only *between people*, interactively. Culture would be situated in the coordination that takes place between individuals belonging to a specific cultural group. And in this view of culture (unconscious as well as non-behavioural), one person cannot tell others of its content (it is unconscious) and it cannot be directly observed (it is non-behavioural).

Therefore, if a researcher wants to find out which culture is associated with a specific group of people, he or she must interpret this indirectly through what people in the group are saying and doing in their everyday life. I believe that such an interpretation can be done through a metaphor. However, while all of what could be contained in culture (the whole of Table 4.5) would be too much to function well as a metaphor, if we limit our understanding of culture only to cell (4), there is, in my opinion, one metaphor that can work to interpret culture. This is *value hierarchy* ('hierarchy' does not, of course, have that concrete meaning here which the concept can be given in an explaining orientation).

Let me illustrate the above with a study I conducted between 1994–96 (I lived during this period in Southeast Asia). The mission was to get a picture of the climate for SMEs in Southeast Asia, a region which at that time was (as it still is) a very interesting growth region. To set a manageable limit to the study and at the same time to build on my interest in culture in a business context, I decided to limit the study to overseas Chinese, that is, to try to understand the business culture (and its consequences) of those approximately 50 million Chinese who lived outside mainland China and who were dominating business activities in Indonesia, Singapore, Malaysia, Thailand, Taiwan, Hong Kong and the Philippines.

Methodology-wise the study was governed by an outline which is illustrated in Figure 4.6. The ideas behind the outline were as follows:

1. I visited all seven countries on several occasions and conducted extensive dialogues with different interested parties and holders of political power

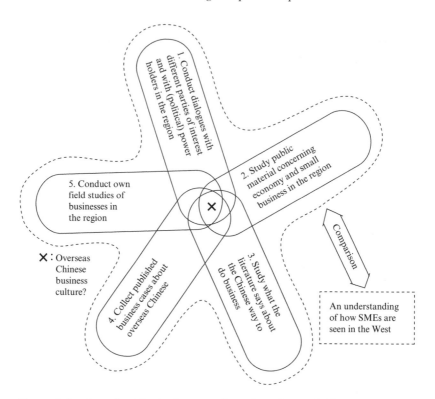

*Figure 4.6   A methodological approach to the culture of Chinese in
Southeast Asia outside mainland China*

in the region. Examples of interested parties were industrial federations
and local commercial unions (for instance, the Chinese Chamber of
Commerce in Singapore and Pusat Data Business Indonesia), universities (for instance, National Cheng-Chi University in Taiwan, the
National University of Singapore, Universiti Pertanian Malaysia and
Bangkok University) and Asia Pacific Economic Cooperation (main
office in Singapore). Examples of holders of political power were senior
people in the Malaysian Industrial Development Authority, the Ministry
of Industry and Trade (Indonesia) and the Department of Industrial
Promotion (Thailand).

2. I studied as much public material I could get hold of and had the
    time to read about the economy of the countries in general (very
    rich material) and their SMEs in particular (surprisingly meagre
    material).

3. I studied about twenty published major works about Chinese business culture and around one hundred articles on the subject, and participated in conversations and discussions about Chinese business culture with different people in all the seven countries.
4. I tried to retrieve published case studies of as many overseas Chinese SMEs as I could. In all I was able to get hold of 43 such practical cases during the two years in which the study was under way (public stories about Chinese business were still very rare at that time).
5. I did my own field studies of around thirty small business managers and their world in the region; sometimes I did them on my own, but most of the time I was working with interpreters.

My idea was that the common denominator from the five different angles above (the central X in Figure 4.6) would give me a picture of overseas Chinese SMEs. The five angles can also all be seen as cultural manifestations and X as culture itself. To get a wider perspective of the subject I made a summary of how we look at SMEs in the West and compared this with what I found in the East. The tables below (Tables 4.6–4.9) summarize a small part of my findings (for more information see Bjerke, 2000a).

Entrepreneurs as History-makers

I have presented three views of mankind which are intimately related to each other and applied them to entrepreneurs. We are all, entrepreneurs or not, sense-makers, language-makers and culture-makers. However, there is a fourth view of interest to the attempt to understand entrepreneurs, the notion devised by Spinosa et al. (1997) that some people are also *history-makers*. Entrepreneurs belong to this category. This section is based on Spinosa et al. (1997) and applied to a study that I conducted recently.

We occasionally experience anomalies or disharmonies in our lives. There are things happening in our socially constructed life which do not seem to fit. Most of us merely note such situations. But there are those, including entrepreneurs, who act when faced with such disharmonies, thus disclosing a new reality for the rest of us. By doing so, they change the way something in society is done – what Spinosa et al. (1997) call the 'style'. This can be done in three different ways:

- *Articulation* is the most familiar type of style change. It occurs when a style, which so far 'is in the air' – only potential – is brought into sharper focus. Entrepreneurs act instinctively. In an articulating change, the style does not alter its core identity, but becomes more recognizable for what it is. There are two forms of articulation. All

Table 4.6   Chinese business culture (as value hierarchy)

- The business owner is definitely proud of belonging to one of the world's oldest, in several respects still intact, cultures.
- He (I met only men, which is normal in this part of the world as far as business is concerned) is half philosopher, worrying much about what is going on, but accepts fate, is very superstitious, intuitive, very risk-willing, but only if circumstances seem to speak for him, does not see much value in strategy, but is very tactical, looks at time as time and money as money.
- He has often started in trading and holds on to trading values – he is transaction- and negotiation-oriented, and holds to product and price as important business parameters. He does not appreciate marketing in the Western sense; sees no value in after-sales activities or service; does not like industries which require advanced knowledge in management and/or marketing.
- He has often taken over the company after his father, as well as his fathers' values.
- He can be satisfied with a very small profit margin as long as it is long term; if he expands he likes to do it by setting up more units, each of which is small enough to be controlled individually.
- He values frugality highly, is persistent and persevering in business (but not privately); he accepts long hours in his business – and expects his employees to do the same.
- He raises funds, if needed, through private sources, but neglect in repaying as agreed is unthinkable; he sees strict financial discipline as a must, plans all costs in detail and never delegates the right to spend.
- He sees contacts as valuable, not to say indispensable; he is part of a number of networks and thinks it is necessary to act within such networks.
- He bases his thinking on the principle that trust in business relationships is an investment which can be used; friendship is a variable for a Chinese and he has problems trusting anybody outside the extended family.
- The firm is run as a family business independent of size – in theory as well as in practice.
- The business owner is very self- and power-centred; he exerts an autocratic and centralized management style; he does not appreciate initiatives taken by the employees; mutual obligations are more important than individual rights; the control of employees is very detailed, but, on the other hand, they expect it and appreciate it.
- All members of the firm have respect for seniority.
- The business owner has a creative attitude to laws and regulations and is very pragmatic in his efforts.
- He is characterized by optimism and a passion to imitate everything that can be of value to his business.
- He has relationships with the outside based on honour, reputation, shame and prestige – in order to gain face not lose it; within the firm, face is more important in horizontal social and business relationships than in other relationships.

Table 4.7 An interpretation of entrepreneurial qualities in the West and in the East

In the West	In the East
Moderate, calculative risk-taker; evaluates carefulness lowly.	Less of a risk-taker, more of an opportunist; more careful.
Creative and innovative.	Less of an innovator, more of an adopter of business concepts existing already elsewhere.
Self-confident and optimistic.	More self-confident and optimistic than in the West, once willing to take the plunge.
Obsessed by opportunities.	Obsessed by opportunities.
Leadership type.	Benevolent autocrat type.
Partners at start are common.	Most starters are members of a family.
Strict line between business life and private life.	No strict line between business life and private life.
The SME stands and falls with the quality of the entrepreneur.	The SME stands and falls with the quality of the entrepreneur.

Table 4.8 An interpretation of the reasons for starting a business in the West and in the East

In the West	In the East
Motivated by personal achievement.	Motivated by social status and prestige of the family.
Dissatisfied with present work situation.	More tolerant with present work situation, even if bad.
Following public role models and given institutional support.	Following family traditions.
Spotting an opportunity.	Spotting an opportunity.
SMEs are often started with spouse to supplement family income.	SMEs are often started with spouse to supplement family income.

articulation makes what is implicit explicit. If what is implicit is vague or confused, then we can speak of *gathering from dispersion*. If what is implicit was once important and has been lost, we can call it *retrieval*. Articulation is the most common form of entrepreneurship.

• *Reconfiguration* is a more substantial way in which a style can change. In this case some marginal aspect of the practices coordinated by a style becomes more dominant. This kind of change is less frequent in everyday life than articulation. In the case of reconfiguration, a greater sense of integrity is generally *not* experienced (as in the case of articulation). Rather, one has the sense of gaining wider horizons.

Table 4.9   An interpretation of type of companies being started in the West and in the East

In the West	In the East
Most new businesses are marginal firms, some are lifestyle firms and a few are high-potential firms.	Similar to the West, except that the definition of 'lifestyle' is not the same.
Most new firms are found in service and the commercial sector.	Differs with development of society.
(The picture is more complicated in the West)	SMEs are often started in light labour-intensive industries, commonly crafts-based, in sub-contracting or in franchising.
SMEs may be discouraged from starting in some sectors, due to major investments required to start there.	SMEs may be crowded out from some sectors, because the government has earmarked the sector for major investments.
No general restrictions to specific economic sectors in terms of management and marketing skills required.	Avoid economic sectors requiring complex management and marketing skills.

- *Cross-appropriation* takes place when one disclosive space takes over a practice from another disclosive space, a practice that it could not have generated on its own but that it finds useful.

Articulation, reconfiguration and cross-appropriation are three different ways in which disclosive skills can work to bring about meaningful historical change of a disclosive space. All of these three changes are called *historical* by Spinosa et al. (1997) because people sense them as a continuation of the past: the practices that become newly important are not unfamiliar. Spinosa et al. (1997) are, therefore, contrasting their notion of historical change with discontinuous change.

One may ask, of course, why it is that our potentialities as history-makers are discovered by so few? Spinosa et al. (1997) assert that there are three ways to understand this. All of them can be seen as aspects of social phenomenology:

- Our common sense works to cover up our role as possible disclosers of new reality. Common sense practices cover the situation that everyday common sense is neither fixed nor rationally justified. The ultimate 'ground' of understanding is simply shared practice – there is no *right* way of doing things.

- Once we have become habituated to a style, it becomes invisible for us. It becomes part of what we take for granted in our everyday reality. If someone behaves in a way that does not fit in with our dominant style, we can fashion his or her behaviour to fit with ours.
- Because we do not cope with the style of, for instance, our culture or our company or our generation directly – we simply express this style when we cope with things and with each other – we have no *direct* way to handle it or come alive to it and transform it. Our practices are designed for dealing with things, but not for dealing with practices for dealing with things, and especially not for dealing with the coordination of practices for dealing with things. We do not normally sense our potential as disclosers, because we are more interested in the things we disclose than in disclosing as such.

Through these three ordinary tendencies to overlook our role as disclosers, we lose sensitivity to occluded, marginal, or neighboring ways of doing things. By definition an occluded, marginal, or neighboring practice is one that we generally pass over, either by not noticing its unusualness when we engage in it or by not engaging at all. Special sensitivity to marginal, neighboring, or occluded practice, however, is precisely at the core of entrepreneurship. This sensitivity generates the art, not science, of invention in business. (Spinosa et al., 1997, p. 30)

Spinosa et al. (1997) claim that three widespread ways of thinking about entrepreneurship right now (entrepreneurship as theory, entrepreneurship as pragmatism and entrepreneurship as driven by cultural values) are not enough for several reasons.

- They are not genuinely innovative; to reduce entrepreneurship to a number of fairly stable and regular procedures places ourselves virtually outside of change.
- They only try to satisfy those needs that exist already or which can be discovered or created without talking about how a person as an entrepreneur is changing the *general* way in which we handle things and people in some domain.
- They are deeply antihistorical.

The authors instead suggest a composite entrepreneurship which:

- has the ability to act on *the links* between innovation and implementation;

- exists to develop a feeling for *the roots* of our way of being;
- creates domains for history-makers by attaching itself to perceived anomalies. The essential issue, according to the authors, is what they call historical, unlike the dominant ways of thinking by developing specific skills, by being pragmatic or by living according to one's culture;
- plays a leading role in determining which needs are important and in making change occur *as it does*;
- brings up and makes central what is only implicitly understood but still moves with its time (articulation), takes up an innovation and, above all through speech acts, turns it into a practice (reconfiguration) or finds other domains for entrepreneurship (cross-appropriation).

Spinosa et al. (1997) claim that entrepreneurship is human activity at its best (p. 66). Let us illustrate this in an area which has come to be called 'social entrepreneurship' (see also Bjerke, 2005; Bjerke and C.-J. Asplund, 2005; and Hjorth and Bjerke, 2006).

The dominant (American) view of the area is as follows. Like every change-oriented activity in a society, social entrepreneurship has not evolved in a vacuum. It has progressed in a rather complex framework from all kinds of forces at all levels of our societies (Johnson, 2000). Some of these forces are global (de Bruin and Dupuis, 2003). In our new society, there is a search for more innovative solutions leading to sustainable improvements and increased openness to experimentation with various methods in the social sector (Dees et al., 2001).

The number of non-profit organizations has increased exponentially. Peter Drucker estimated (without specifying the geographic boundaries) that 800,000 non-profit organizations have been established in the last 30 years (Bornstein, 1998). Cannon (2000) notes a 40 per cent increase in the number of non-profit organizations in the United States during the last decade. The trend is the same in Sweden (Westlund, 2001).

This trend has created a blurring of the boundaries between the public, private and voluntary sectors of society (Johnson, 2003). The concept of the commercial entrepreneur has been broadened to encompass those who work for social innovation through entrepreneurial solutions – the 'social entrepreneurs'. The term was coined by Drayton, founder of Ashoka (Catford, 1998). The hopes for these entrepreneurs are high:

> There are three different types of benefits which social entrepreneurs can bring to communities. In the short term they can help create new buildings, services and jobs which would not otherwise exist, but they can also improve accessibility,

effectiveness and efficiency of existing services. In the medium term they can act as powerful models for reform of the welfare state, and in the longer term they can create and invest social capital. (Catford, 1998, p. 96)

Major differences between social entrepreneurs and business entrepreneurs are, according to Thalbuder (1998), that social entrepreneurs gain strength from collective wisdom and experience, focus on long-term capacity, limit ideas by mission, look at profit as a means and put profit into serving people. Business entrepreneurs, on the other hand, gain strength from personal skills and knowledge, focus on short-term financial gain, see no limit on scope of ideas, look at profit as an end and reinvest profit for further growth. In summary, social enterprises have a social objective towards which they blend social and commercial methods (Dees et al., 2001).

[Social entrepreneurs] share many characteristics with commercial entrepreneurs. They have the same focus on vision and opportunity, and the same ability to convince and empower others to help them turn their ideas into reality – but this is coupled with a desire for social justice. (Catford, 1998, p. 96)

Defining what social entrepreneurship is, and what its boundaries are, is not an easy task. This is partly due to the fact that the concept is inherently complex and partly because the literature in the area is two new for consensus to emerge (Johnson, 2003). In the literature, social entrepreneurship is often seen as encompassing a rather broad range of activities (for example, Thompson, 2002).

Peter Drucker claimed that social entrepreneurs 'change the performance capacity of society' (Gendron, 1997, p. 37). Bornstein (1998, p. 36) characterizes social entrepreneurs as 'pathbreakers with a powerful new idea, who combine visionary and real-world problem-solving capacity, who have a strong ethical fiber, and who are "totally obsessed" by their vision for change'. Schulyer (1998, p. 1) argues that social entrepreneurs are 'individuals who have a vision for social change and who have the financial resources to support their ideas . . . who exhibit all the skills of successful business people as well as a powerful desire for social change'. Boschee (1998, p. 1) presents social entrepreneurs as 'non-profit executives who pay increased attention to market forces without losing sight of their underlying mission'. Thompson et al. (2000, p. 238) describe social entrepreneurs as 'people who realize where there is an opportunity to satisfy unmet need that the welfare system will not or cannot meet, and who gather together the necessary resources (generally people, often volunteers, money and premises) and use these to "make a difference"'.

According to Johnson (2003) one commonality emerges from almost every description of a social entrepreneur: 'the "problem-solving nature" is prominent, and the corresponding emphasis on developing and implementing initiatives that produce measurable results in the form of changed social outcomes and/or impacts' (p. 2).

Various forms of motivation for social entrepreneurship are identified in the literature. As an example, Cannon (2000) presents three general types of people who become social entrepreneurs. The first are individuals who have made a lot of money elsewhere and want to give some of it back to further social goals. The second type are 'recovering social workers' who are looking for a more effective approach than using the existing social support system. The third are a new breed that have left business school or come from a similar educational environment with social enterprise in mind. Thompson et al. (2000) make a distinction between 'vision-oriented' motivations for socially entrepreneurial activities and 'crisis-oriented' ones, and Prabhu (1999) presents an uneasiness with the status quo, a need to be true to one's values, and a need to be socially responsible as other motivations for social entrepreneurship.

This could be summarized as follows:

- The picture that emerges is of individual entrepreneurs.
- The assumptions are very rationalistic. If you are of the right quality as a person and apply the correct set of activities, you will make it as an entrepreneur, social or not.
- Entrepreneurs are presented as super-persons. Only some people can make it as entrepreneurs.
- Along the same lines, entrepreneurship is presented as relating to extraordinary activities not everyday tasks.
- Entrepreneurship should, according to some statements in the literature, use as much as possible of what management stands for. A social entrepreneur is seen as a somewhat different type of entrepreneur, but he or she will succeed best if he or she applies management principles.
- Definitions of a social entrepreneur are either done by stating his or her mental profile or by stating what he or she is doing in decision-making terms, not so much in terms of processes or in terms of specific ways of operating.

Against this picture of what social entrepreneurs stand for and what they do, I would like to set a study which I began in August 2003. I followed six cases of social entrepreneurship in the south of Sweden during a period of 18 months and had people involved in these cases participating in recurrent monthly workshops. The purpose has partly been to assist these six to progress successfully, partly for me to learn what social entrepreneurship can mean in practice. The six cases are:

1. *'The Brewery'*. An unusually successful example of a place where young people in the city of Malmö can meet for different kinds of leisure activities.
2. *The old shipyard park*. Something of a continuation of 'The Brewery'. It is an area of a former shipyard which includes a youth park for skateboarders with Europe's largest outdoor skateboard arena.
3. *Home service consultants*. An attempt to integrate immigrants into Swedish society by providing an opportunity for them to get involved in professional cleaning and maintenance of households and industrial facilities.
4. *SeX-BoX*. A modern programme for progressive sex education for young people.
5. *The Green Room*. An idea to use all the horticultural knowledge and possibilities that exist in south-east Sweden as a relaxing and therapeutic opportunity.
6. *Fair Play*. A progressive programme for expanding opportunities among young people in a soccer team in the city of Lund.

My experience from working with the social entrepreneurs in the above projects is that:

● They have no overall plan for what they are doing.
● They have no real knowledge of or interest in what it means to work in a formal organization.
● They do not apply management (or marketing) skills in any formal sense. They just do what they do naturally. They even have problems afterwards in describing in any detail what they have actually done.
● They are very humble people and see their colleagues as the main contributors to their success.
● They are aware of the fact that their projects are seen as marginal, but are convinced that in a country like Sweden, for different reasons, such projects will be seen, and must be seen, as more and more central.

So, we have two pictures of social entrepreneurship, the dominant one and the one that I have presented. How do these two contrasting pictures, in the terminology of Spinosa et al. (1997), show the participating entrepreneurs as history-makers? The American picture is quite clearly an example of cross-appropriation, claiming that social entrepreneurship should adopt as much as possible of the business entrepreneurs' ideas of what it means to be successful. The Swedish variety, on the other hand, is more a matter of reconfiguration, a vision that some phenomena in society, which have previously been seen as marginal, should be looked at as more central – and in the social entrepreneurs' own terms.

One may then ask whether social entrepreneurship is the appropriate label for these phenomena in the Swedish context. 'Social' entrepreneurship has the ring of social support. The alternatives, 'voluntary' or 'idealistic' entrepreneurship, give an image of something that few people are involved in and which does not concern most of us. Maybe 'public entrepreneurship' would be more appropriate, describing activities, which, according to the original meaning of 'public', concern us all and for which none of us can deny responsibility.

SOME CONCLUDING POINTS

Creating New Business Ventures as a Causal or as a Dialectic Process

I have problems thinking of entrepreneurs as objects responding to various (external) stimuli. Where is creativity in such a view? My experience from new business ventures is rather that some visible, tangible step must be taken in order to start the energy flowing. The process must also be guided by a vision – or at least a direction. It is impossible to say which comes first, the tangible step or the abstract vision. Both must be there and a dialectic relationship must be developed between the two.

To aim at specific goals, to choose means, to realize intentions, to establish rules – none of these typical human actions has the slightest similarity to a response to external forces the way a billiard-ball is set in motion.

Dialectics stresses processes, contradictions and mistakes. When these are made public, something better can start to grow. Something new is created at every moment, and the vision is gradually modified.

Entrepreneurs in Structures or as Actors in Social Constructions

Social theorists have a tendency to get entangled in the problem of the primacy of the individual over society or vice versa. There are those who believe society should reflect the nature and character of the people who make it up; society is, according to this view, properly subordinated to the individual. On the other side are those who believe that individuals must reflect the nature and character of the society of which they are a part; from this perspective the person is properly subordinated to the society.

It seems as though the dominant opinion is that individuals are subordinated to society. How else can we explain the interest in whether a person should be a conformist or not, or understand why those who do not conform attract such attention, are sometimes discredited and often experienced as a threat? To assert oneself is – by definition – an act against society.

The dominant view in business administration is that of the subordinated individual. It is common to see, even if perhaps implicitly, the members of an organization as components in an efficient business system, as cogs in a machine.

This can easily lead to people being isolated within themselves and to a view of society as a concrete external phenomenon. The opposite, which is to see society as a social construction, means that individuals and society become one, and also, in a way, that the social world becomes 'invisible'. To put it another way, the content of social relationships cannot be perceived directly by our senses; it can only be known by learning the meaning of the relationships to the participants. Our language then becomes very important.

Most structural analyses are valid only in a rational world with objectively rational individuals. To understand entrepreneurship, on the other hand, becomes a matter of interpreting activities which are breaking patterns and creating new realities, in short, those circumstances which the structural analysts and the systems theorists must postulate away. It is then also a matter of getting away from causal, holistic and organic theories and instead adopting a more active perspective.

The Rational Creation of New Business Ventures

The term 'rational' has come to have a great influence within both the academic world and the world of everyday affairs. What is a rational person? How did our belief in rationality come to have such massive support? Why do we seek to develop rational educational programmes, build rational organizations and construct rational models of man?

Much of our view of rationality comes from Weber. He asserted that the time was ripe to interpret acts as rational choices given the specific goal of decision rationality. He also saw discussion in terms of ideal types as purposeful for the social researcher. But Weber also discussed another type of rationality, that is, consistency. To be true to a specific pattern of behaviour means that rationality can be expressed differently in different parts of human life, for instance, it can look different to the researcher in his or her study and in everyday reality.

Whichever view of rationality one holds, it is not possible, as I see it, to be rational beyond a certain level when creating new business ventures. One has to take action, to experiment and to try. One has to move on in the hermeneutic spiral (compare Figure 2.1).

The Creation of New Business Ventures as Everyday Reality

Husserl presented the concept of 'everyday reality' and made a clear distinction between this reality and the known scientific reality of the time. Today, social researchers of everyday reality have several theoretical perspectives to chose from, for instance, symbolic interactionism, phenomenology, existentialism and ethnomethodology. The aim of these researchers is to understand how actors denote and give meaning to their existence and how they construct and maintain their everyday reality.

Everyday reality contains that which is constant as well as that which is changing. The latter is only revealed, however, when everyday reality, in a wider sense, is perceived as problematic, when something is not in order, when we face an anomaly. The borderline between these two parts is, of course, fluid, movable and very individual.

'The problem' with everyday reality is precisely that it is everyday reality. When people are questioned about their everyday activities, they are unable to describe what differentiates these activities from those that are not everyday. The paradox of everyday reality is that actors feel that their activities are unproblematic there, although they can be extremely hard to describe. We cannot come to grips with familiar and ordinary behaviour by asking the persons involved in it to tell us about it. They are too immersed in the familiar to be able to recognize it or articulate it. Somehow, the imagination of the actors and the events with which they are involved become a single, reasonable happening. They are able to take whatever is there and transform it into something that 'makes sense'. But, more significantly, it can make so much sense that there is little point in discussing the matter. It simply happens.

How is it possible for a researcher to study and to understand what is happening at a point where imagination and reality unite to create acceptable social behaviour, for instance, an entrepreneurial act? There are many answers to this question, but what is important is to move beyond the obvious and apparent features of such activity. It is necessary to question that which few people normally do, to become, in a way, a stranger in a familiar land.

There are two decisive reasons why common, ordinary, day-to-day events are particularly significant for advancing our understanding of human social action, including entrepreneurship. In the first place, most human action is of an ordinary variety (we could call this behaviour unreflecting action). Even people who at times deserve the label extraordinary (like some entrepreneurs) spend most of their time in commonplace activities in everyday life. If we ignore the commonplace, we bypass most of what is going on among human beings, including most entrepreneurs. It seems as difficult for people engaged in creative activities, such as new business ventures, to talk about what they do as for people engaged in everyday activities.

In the second place, the study of the taken-for-granted character of everyday reality is important because of the special power it has over us. There seems to be something in this everyday reality that is a key to 'higher' moments of our lives. It might be culture. In that case culture is the key – and language is the master key.

Entrepreneurs and the Natural Attitude

Another phenomenological concept is 'the natural attitude', the non-reflecting state of man in everyday reality. It was our silent natural attitude that interested phenomenologists in their philosophical activities.

Talking of the natural attitude (as well as everyday reality), we have to distinguish a problematic part of it. This problematic situation exposes the nature of familiarity. Any object is 'simply there' when experience is typical. When a problem emerges, it is put up against existing perspectives and possibilities, which readjusts the individual and his or her world. Individuals assume, then, two basic attitudes. In the attitude of *immediate experience* the environment is not noticed in any deeper meaning; in the attitude of *reflective analysis* knowledge is created. Even if the former attitude is more 'natural', the world is always potentially problematic. It can, however, appear as such only in so far as a non-problematic world is there of which it is a part, and can serve as the touchstone of its reality. A problem does not arise except over against that which is not problematic.

But consciousness and 'the world out there' are not independent partners; the natural attitude is also determined by language and its typifications. A distinction between the actual and the possible, between us and others is therefore artificial.

As an understanding-oriented constructionist with social phenomenology as a ground, one obviously has to learn how the reality of everyday business development is constructed and how an attitude emerges which accepts change as something natural. If all actions are to be seen as based on intentionality, that is, as directed, one way to direct them towards new business ventures could be to create (or maybe just stress) tension, to make what is seen as natural more problematic.

BEFORE WE GO ON

We have now gone through the basis of this book, that is, we have clarified two alternative ways of doing research, the explaining and the understanding ones, and seen how one can look at entrepreneurs in our new society using either of these two approaches.

The book contains four more chapters. These concern applications, that is, entrepreneurs in networks, growth, regional development and education.

These chapters have explaining as well as understanding elements. Most of the time, it should be clear to the reader which of the two is intended by the individual or individuals who constructed the theory being discussed. If that is not the case, the reader will have to ask questions of the following types: 'In this section, is "network" seen as a factual (objective or subjective) reality with an existence of its own or is it seen as a typification and a social construction which exists only as long as we talk about it?' 'In this section, is language used to depict something real, or is it a language meant to be performative, that is, meant to transfer activities of thinking and relationships to other activities?' We should keep in mind that which of the two alternatives that is 'valid' does not, in a sense, depend on the text itself but on the reader of it. The spectacles that you wear determine the way in which you see what you read!

5.   Entrepreneurship and networks

WHAT IS NEW ABOUT NETWORKS?

The network metaphor appeared in the study of business as early as the 1970s. It is, however, widely accepted that networks are more popular today because they represent an integrated and natural part of our new entrepreneurial society. Whether the reason for this greater popularity is because networks have increased in numbers or because the type of thinking which is associated with the network metaphor has turned out to be more important is a matter for debate. For example:

> Networks have existed in all economic systems. What is different now is that networks, improved and multiplied by technology, have entered our lives so deeply that 'the network' has become the central metaphor around which our thinking and our economy is organized. If we cannot understand the logic characterizing the networks, we cannot exploit the economic change which has now started. (Kelly, 1998, p. 10; my translation)

> The diversity of networks in business and the economy is mind-boggling. There are policy networks, ownership networks, collaboration networks, organizational networks, network marketing – you name it. It would be impossible to integrate these diverse interactions into a single all-encompassing web. Yet no matter what organizational level we look at, the same robust and universal laws that govern nature's webs seem to greet us. The challenge is for economic and network research alike to put these laws into practice. (Barabási, 2002, p. 217)

Storey (2002) sees a natural development of organizational structures and forms into our new entrepreneurial society (Figure 5.1). Figure 5.1 shows that companies have moved towards externalization of relationships and towards diversified activities, performance-based control and the open-market mode of regulation.

THE NETWORK SOCIETY

'Networks are the new socio-morphology of our societies and the diffusion of the logic of networks is, to a large extent, influencing the function and

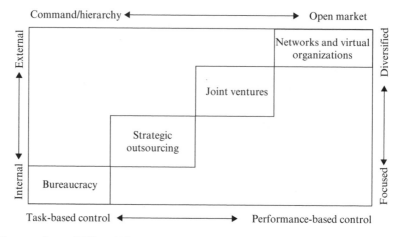

Source: Storey (2002, p. 350).

Figure 5.1   New organizational structures and forms

results of production processes, experiences, power and culture' (Castells, 1998, p. 519; my translation). We could therefore rightly call our new entrepreneurial society *a network society*. It is the first time in history that the economic unit has been other than the individual, for instance as an employee or as a consumer, or the collective, such as the business firm or the public sector. Instead the economic unit is the network, in which subjects and organizations are connected to each other and are constantly being modified and adapted to each other and to supporting environments and structures (Castells, 1998).

The network society is a more open society. A continuous search across the whole economic and technological field is therefore necessary for the business actors of today to keep in touch with events. Through this search, relationships are built and maintained. 'The network economy is based on technology, but can only be built on relationships. It starts with chips and ends with trust' (Kelly, 1998, p. 179; my translation).

Consequently, the study of networks is popular today. However, there is considerable variation in what can be meant by 'network' and 'networking'. Competing definitions and perspectives exist.

Networks have been studied within a number of different disciplines, such as transaction economics, industrial marketing, organization theory, small business management and entrepreneurial marketing. In small business research, SMEs in networks have primarily been seen as part of industrial districts. Networks are also seen as support structures for business start-ups and as existing between owners/entrepreneurs in small firms for development and growth (Shaw and Conway, 2000).

Let us now look at networks at different levels and in different contexts.

NETWORKS AT DIFFERENT LEVELS AND IN DIFFERENT CONTEXTS

A network is a number of connected nodes. A node is the point where a curve is crossing itself. What the node then contains more concretely depends on what kind of network we are talking about. It is the stock exchanges with their centres of advanced support functions in the network of global financial flows. It is ministerial meetings and commissioners in the political network governing the EU. It is poppy and cocaine cultivation, secret laboratories, hidden airfields, street gangs and money-laundering financial institutions in the network of the narcotics trade which is penetrating economies, societies and states across the whole world. It is TV-systems, recording studios for entertainment, workshops for computer graphics, news teams and mobile equipment for generating, transmitting and receiving signals in the global network of new media which are the ground for cultural expressions and general opinion in our information era. (Castells, 1998, p. 520; my translation)

We see some examples of what networks can be in the quotation above. But networks can be much more. Shaw and Conway (2000) indicate five broad categories of networks to which entrepreneurs can be connected.

1. Scientific and technical networks organized around scientific or technological domains.
2. Professional networks, consisting of individuals within a given profession, such as medicine or education, and bound by 'professional ethics of co-operation'.
3. User networks developed with the end-users of a firm's products.
4. Friendship networks, referring to the personal networks of individuals based predominantly on friendship.
5. Recreational networks, particular types of friendship networks whose cohesion arises from the mutual feeling of attachment to some recreational activity, such as sailing, mountaineering or rugby, where the feelings of challenge, achievement and comradeship, through participation, create and maintain personal bonds.

It is possible to distinguish between the *industrial* networks which develop between established (major) companies and the *personal* networks which create and drive small firms (Johannisson, 1996) (Table 5.1).

Table 5.1   Industrial networks and business networks

	Industrial networks	Business networks
Primary frame of reference	Market as action field	Society and market as source of power
Basic challenge	Reduction of uncertainty in a dialogue with others	Handling ambiguity under own responsibility
Interacting subjects	Organizations, represented by individuals	The business owner, representing him- or herself
Characteristics of connection	Mutual adaptation of norms and competencies	Mutual understanding and respect for idiosyncrasies

> Relationship interaction is frequently influenced by other relationships in which the interacting partners are involved. Customer's customers, supplier's suppliers, competing and complementary suppliers, consultants and intermediary firms can all have an influence on the interaction in the customer-supplier relationship. This [may give] rise to the general conclusion that relationships are connected to one another in the sense that the interaction in one has an impact on the other. Thus, each relationship is embedded in a set of connected relationships forming a network structure. It seems that business markets are networks of interconnected business relationships . . . we label such interconnected business relationships *business networks*. (Håkansson and Johanson, 2001, pp. 3–4)

It is possible to classify business networks according to their content (Krackhardt and Hanson, 1993):

- *Advice networks* show the prominent players in an organization on whom others depend to solve problems and to provide technical information.
- *Trust networks* show the pattern of sharing with regard to delicate political information and support in a crisis.
- *Communication networks* show the employees who talk to one another on a regular basis.

Networks may also be classified according to their structure (Varadarajan and Cunningham, 1995):

- *Functional* (linking functional aspects of organizations that result in joint manufacturing, marketing or product development). These networks tend to share knowledge, information and resources.
- *Intra/inter-organizational* (developing relationships either nationally or internationally). These networks share information.

- *Intra/inter-industry* (building relationships through resource pooling). These networks share resources.
- *Motivational* (sharing of marketing and technological know-how). These networks tend only to share knowledge.

One can also classify networks according to their process (Johannisson et al., 2002):

- *Resource-based.* Each firm controls their own unique resources which are combined to strategic advantage.
- *Industrial organization.* In which firms are autonomous entities establishing their own unique market position.
- *Virtual organization.* Independent yet interdependent organizations striving for joint variety using advanced technology.
- *Industrial district.* Small firms characterized by production type, organized for internal co-operation and external competition.

Another proposal to classify networks according to their process comes from Achrol and Kotler (1999):

- *Internal.* Designed to reduce hierarchy and open firms to the environment.
- *Vertical.* Networks that maximize the productivity of serially dependent functions by creating partnerships between independent skill-specialized firms.
- *Intermarket.* Networks that seek to leverage horizontal synergies across industries.
- *Opportunity.* Networks that are organized around customer needs and market opportunities and are designed to seek the best solutions to them.

Finally here, networks can be classified according to power (Dennis, 2000):

- *Dominated networks.* A group of smaller companies dominated by a single larger company.
- *Equal partner networks.* Where there is no governing partner and each relationship is based on reciprocal, preferential, mutually supportive actions.

A more dynamic model for networks at different levels and in different contexts is given in Figure 5.2.

Understanding entrepreneurship

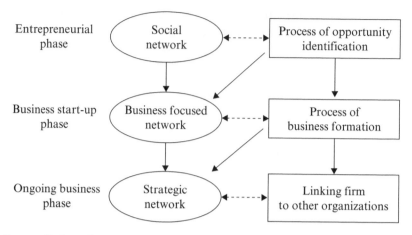

Source: Butler and Hansen (1991, p. 3).

Figure 5.2   Model of entrepreneurial network evolution

In principle, two different types of network models can be identified as having an ambition to explain entrepreneurship (Hoang and Antoncic, 2003):

1. *Networks as a critical independent variable.* The important and varied role that networks play in influencing entrepreneurial processes, such as opportunity recognition, resource mobilization or the creation of an organization, and in getting results, such as the formation or outcome of a new venture, or activities such as going public, acquisitions, mergers or alliances.
2. *Networks as a dependent variable.* Change that networks go through as the business venture develops, such as the content of its relationships or how they are governed.

A Caveat

However, it is not all green lights for the network approach, and not all members of the research community have been converted (Johannisson, 1994). There are those who claim that the use of networks instead of formal contracts and openness to acquire and organize resources may be seen as illegitimate means to gain personal favours (the *moral* challenge). A basic assumption behind the network approach is that of a willingness to interact in the creation of new realities. This is objected to by those social scientists who consider structures to be essential to frame and to restrict personal decisions (the *ontological* challenge). Other social scientists who build their theories on the possibilities of the impersonal market mechanism may feel threatened by the view of the network approach towards cooperation through mutual trust (the *theoretical* challenge). Finally, there are researchers who claim that 'correct' research consists in statistical analysis of data collected through questionnaires and are suspicious of qualitatively oriented research which is what network research tends to use (the *methodological* challenge).

Nevertheless, it may turn out to be difficult to prove any definite relationship between entrepreneurial networking and the success of a particular business venture, for instance in terms of its result and growth (Johannisson, 2000). First, networking may not have as its primary purpose the promotion of business results or the growth of a business. Networking is a normal existential activity for every human being. It may be that through networking an individual finds the opportunity to come out of a marginal position in society and organize a business, but having achieved this such a person may not have any particular interest in the result of the business and its growth. Second, networking is not just an answer to contemporary challenges but also an investment in human and social capital for future use or in reciprocating support received earlier. Third, an entrepreneur may start several business ventures (simultaneously or one after the other), which questions the notion of the single venture as an analytical unit related to the entrepreneur. Fourth, because of their construction, networks contain large elements of randomness and chance from unexpected meetings. This may bring greater opportunities for a business venture than systematically and consciously working in a network in order to promote results and growth. Fifth, networks may also lead to a deteriorating position and even failure because of locked-in situations and narrow views.

CONTENT IN NETWORKS IN MORE DETAIL

It is possible to talk about three important parts of a network (Hoang and Antoncic, 2003): (1) the content of the relationships, (2) the governance of these relationships, (3) the structure or pattern that emerges from the cross-cutting ties.

Relationships (between people and between organizations) are viewed as the media through which actors gain access to a variety of resources held by others. One key resource for an entrepreneur is information and advice. The reliance on networks is not restricted to the start-up stage. Entrepreneurs continue to rely on networks for business information, advice and problem solving, with some contacts providing multiple resources. Relationships can also contain signals or provide the opportunity to justify one's business reputation. In the uncertain and dynamic conditions under which entrepreneurial activity occurs, it is reasonable that resource holders (potential investors and employees) seek information that helps them to gauge the underlying potential of a venture. Entrepreneurs seek legitimacy to reduce this perceived risk by associating with, or by gaining explicit certification from, well-regarded individuals and organizations. Positive perceptions based on a firm's network linkages may in turn lead to subsequent beneficial resource exchanges.

The second construct that researchers have explored is the distinctive governance mechanisms that are thought to undergird and coordinate network exchange. Trust between partners is often cited as a critical element that in turn enhances the quality of the resource flows. Network governance can also be characterized by the reliance on 'implicit and open-ended contracts' that are supported by social mechanisms – such as power and influence or the threat of ostracism and loss of reputation (more about this in the next section) – rather than legal support. These elements of network governance can give cost advantages in comparison to coordination through market or bureaucratic mechanisms.

The third construct is network structure, defined as the pattern of relationships that are engendered from the direct or indirect ties between actors. A general conceptualization guiding the focus on network structure is that differential network positioning has an important impact on resource flows, and hence, on entrepreneurial outcomes. In order to generate a more comprehensive picture of the different positions of entrepreneurs and their ventures in networks, a variety of dimensions and measures can be used. Let us look at some of these.

Network dimensions can be divided into *morphological* and *interactional* dimensions (Shaw, 2001; Shaw and Conway, 2000). Networks are seen as having four morphological dimensions: (1) anchorage, (2) reachability, (3) density and (4) range.

Anchorage refers to the focus at the centre of the network. This can range from the owner-manager in a smaller organization to a major, entrepreneurial company. Most network studies, which as so much else in entrepreneurship research are of an explaining type, seem to perceive the entrepreneur as at the centre. An understanding view, with its constructionist orientation, sees no factual centre in this sense.

Reachability is a measure of how far and easily an anchorage is able to contact other individuals and organizations within the same conceptually distinct network. Reachability can be measured by the number of interactions which have to be made to reach other social actors (see Figure 5.3). The fewer the number of interactions, the greater the reachability of the

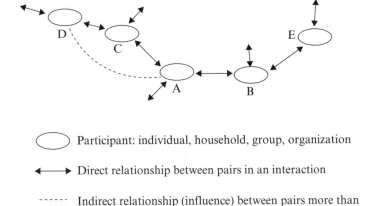

Participant: individual, household, group, organization

Direct relationship between pairs in an interaction

------ Indirect relationship (influence) between pairs more than
one step away from each other

Source: Shaw and Conway (2000, p. 372).

Figure 5.3   Example of a social network map

anchorage. Reachability can assess to what extent relationships far
removed from anchorage have the potential to influence its behaviour. One
can conceive that some of the actors in a social network might operate as
'brokers', linking social actors who do not share a direct relationship.

Density refers to the extent to which social actors in a network are connected to each other through social relationships. One could here distinguish between 'loosely-knit' and 'tight' networks. Such a measure could, for
instance, indicate how easy or how difficult it is for information to travel in
the network and indicate, therefore, the impact that the structure of a social
network can have upon the activities and behaviours of its actors. One
could argue, for instance, that in a dense network the flow of information
is likely to be freer.

Range refers to the number of actors in direct contact with anchorage and
the social heterogeneity of these actors. One could think of an entrepreneur's network as 'narrow' or 'diverse'. The latter is probably often better.

The interactional dimensions in networks are content, intensity, frequency, durability and direction.

Content is the most important dimension of the five. It refers to the meanings which people attach to their relationships and the understandings they
have about how they should behave with regard to different relationships.
This suggests, for instance, that if an entrepreneur defines a relationship
as a 'friendship', he or she should behave like a friend in it. The content of
relationships cannot, of course, be viewed directly by an outsider and an

identification of such content is complicated by the variety which could exist even in one single relationship.

Intensity of a network relationship gives an indication of the influence which relationships can have on actors' behaviour and demonstrate how complicated network relationships can be. So, for instance, where a relationship primarily has an economic and normative content, it can still be influenced by possible friendship relationships that exist between the actors. As the intensity of a relationship can also not be directly observed, durability and frequency are suggested as suitable indicators.

Frequency refers to the amount of time entrepreneurs spend interacting in relationships. A high frequency of interaction might be a sign of an intensive relationship. However, it might not be so simple. A friendship relationship may be intensive at the same time as it has a low level of frequency of interaction. Applied to small firms, measures of intensity and frequency might usefully be employed to more fully understand the relationship between small firms and customer loyalty.

Durability is an indication of the length of time over which a relationship continues and can also provide an indication of the intensity of a relationship. The durability of a relationship is affected not only by its content, but also the extent to which both parties in the relationship perceive it as mutually satisfying. If parties to a relationship perceive that they give and receive what they hope for from a relationship, it is more likely to continue.

Direction gives an indication of the direction of the power in a relationship. For example, where organizations share a partnering relationship, the orientation of the relationship may be such that the smaller of the firms holds a more vulnerable position.

SOCIAL AND COMMERCIAL ASPECTS OF NETWORKS

Entrepreneurial networks can often be characterized as a combination of ties that are social (affective) and commercial (instrumental or calculative) (Sjöstrand, 1992). Shared values and mutual sentiments are said to build social ties such as those existing in kinship and friendship. Commercial ties are primarily associated with business exchange, either commercial or professional, that is, the transfer of expertise (Johannisson, 1996). Both kinds of ties are necessary for an entrepreneur.

Processes in small business ventures can never (above all from an understanding research orientation) simply be seen as being totally driven by some form of rational self-interest; they also contain social and cultural elements. The main point of the network perspective is that the interaction between social and commercial dimensions creates extra possibilities in itself (Johannisson, 1996). Social connections make it possible for entrepreneurs to find and to realize new business opportunities.

One may even claim that entrepreneurship, development and similar economic activities are primarily complex social processes and only secondarily physical, technological or psychological ones (Zafirovski, 1999). They cannot be treated as independent and imputed with an intrinsic law of their own, because they are embedded in concrete, ongoing systems of social relationships. We may call this *embeddedness* (Granovetter, 1985). Entrepreneurial embeddedness creates a link between its economic and its social spheres (Jack and Anderson, 2002). Embeddedness is the mechanism by which the entrepreneur becomes part of the local structure, but it is more than that: it includes understanding the nature of the structure, enacting and re-enacting it to forge new ties and maintain both the link and the structure.

Granovetter (1985) shows that every transaction contains a social element. The fact that economic transactions contain social elements will be obvious to many. Market forces are not enough to explain why a customer in a restaurant which he or she has never visited before leaves a tip for a waiter. Granovetter (1985, p. 490) suggests that such a transaction has three simple characteristics:

1. the two actors involved in the transaction are previously unacquainted;
2. they are not likely to transact again;
3. it is unlikely that information about the activities of either will reach other people with whom they might transact in the future.

The conclusion is that some kind of trust must operate in every economic transaction. Southern (2000) offers some relevant points on the embedding process which every small firm goes through:

1. The embedded nature of their business is not simply a property of an economic transaction but of the concrete social relations which are built up between participating actors.
2. A social relationship between the business owner/manager must exist with business contacts before an economic transaction can take place.
3. A moment of lack of trust, opportunism of the worst kind or disorder is always possible in all business transactions.
4. It is difficult to discuss a single business activity in isolation without considering its predecessor and its follower.

There is an important difference between informal, personal relationships (strong ties) and formal relationships such as joint ventures, licences and business relationships with suppliers and customers (weak ties) in a network. A network with strong ties has a small range, but is dense. Weak ties on the other hand form a network with low density but with larger reachability. Mixed results exist as far as the values of strong and weak ties in the entrepreneur's business are concerned. A few conclusions are as follows:

- Successful entrepreneurs seem to have large networks of weak acquaintances, which can offer the right information at the right time, give access to potential customers and introduce them to potential investors. For business success these seem more important than our cherished strong friend- and kinships (Granovetter, 1985).
- A comparative study of successful small and large firm technological innovations found that external inputs for ideas about the best course of the development process mainly consisted of strong ties between the small firms. Supplier contacts among the small firms were more of a weak kind (Conway, 1994).
- In a study by Bruderl and Preisendorfer (1998), strong ties were found to be more critical than weak ties in explaining firm success, but less important for sales growth.

To summarize, we can say that embeddedness is important for entrepreneurs for several reasons:

- discovering social resources,
- gaining social support,
- developing confidence in and knowledge about the way in which businesses are carried on,
- discovering opportunities which 'suit' the local situation's specific needs.

SOCIAL CAPITAL

A concept which is close to social embeddedness and which appeared during the 1990s alongside the then established concepts of financial, real and human capital was *social capital*. It is a common view that social capital is a concept of great relevance for many analyses of small business and entrepreneurship (Westlund and Bolton, 2003). An early definition of social capital was 'the sum of the resources, actual or virtual, that accrue to an individual or a group by virtue of possessing a durable network of

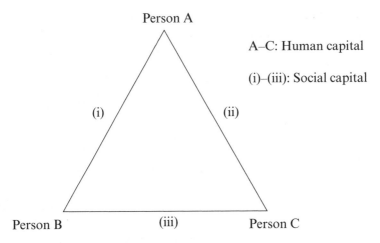

Person A

A–C: Human capital

(i)–(iii): Social capital

(i)   (ii)

Person B   (iii)   Person C

Source: Coleman (1990, p. 305).

Figure 5.4   Social capital

more or less institutionalized relationships of mutual acquaintances and recognition' (Bourdieu and Wacquant, 1992, p. 119).

Coleman's (1990) conceptualization of social capital is not as individual-oriented as Bourdieu and Wacquant's. Figure 5.4 is from Coleman, and illustrates the differences between human capital and social capital.

Human capital relates to individual resources (in the human nodes) while social capital is found in the links (relations) between individuals/actors.

Putnam (1993), in his famous studies of Italy, uses a definition of social capital which is similar to Coleman's and considers social capital to consist in characteristics of social organizations, such as networks, norms and trust, which facilitate coordination and cooperation.

However, social capital can have negative as well as positive consequences for entrepreneurship. It has been described as both the glue that binds to create a network and the lubricant that eases and energizes network interaction (Powell and Smith-Doerr, 1994). Table 5.2 presents some social capital issues related to this.

Social capital can be a restraint on entrepreneurship in a network if the ties are too strong between conservative members (nobody is allowed to differ). It can also facilitate entrepreneurship as it can provide a harbour which 'automatically' legitimizes new business attempts so long as these attempts fit with the content and idea of the social capital.

Table 5.3 offers a summary of similarities and dissimilarities between social capital and other kinds of capital – productivity, vintages, accumulation

Table 5.2   Issues in entrepreneurial social capital

The construction of social capital	Emphasis	Analytical category	Key questions
The nature of social capital	Process	Entrepreneurial networks	What is it? How can we conceptualize it?
As a glue	Bonding (Structure)	Creation of relationships	How is it formed? Ends or means?
As a lubricant	Facilitating (Relational)	Interaction within relationships	How is it maintained? Is it purely exploitative? Are there rules?

Source: Anderson and Jack (2002, p. 199).

and maintenance, rights of possession and complexity and levels of aggregation.

WITHOUT NETWORKING, NO ENTREPRENEURSHIP?

The role of cooperative networks in the entrepreneurial process may seem paradoxical (Schutjens and Stam, 2000). On the one hand, entrepreneurs are presented as independent, self-sufficient persons. On the other, we read that entrepreneurship emerges at the junctions of social and commercial information networks which supply potential entrepreneurs with ideas, opportunities and access to resources. However, this is paradoxical only from the point of view of the explaining-oriented researcher who looks at networks by themselves and entrepreneurs by themselves, even if they are related. The understanding-oriented researcher instead looks at social constructions, including networks, as the basis for comprehending all aspects of society, including entrepreneurship.

No matter what research view one has, an individual's personal network is often seen as the origin of his or her creative idea (we will be back to this in more detail in the next section). One could even conceptualize the entrepreneurial situation as *organizing through personal networking* (Johannisson, 2000).

Management requires structures; entrepreneurship thrives on processes and ambiguity. This leads entrepreneurs to networking as they develop new

Table 5.3   Some similarities and differences between social capital and other kinds of capital

Similarity	Dissimilarity
Productivity	
Social capital is sunk costs that might become obsolete.	
Social capital can be put to good or bad uses (from society's perspective).	Social capital expresses interests of actors, good or bad from society's perspective. It is not neutral with regard to society's interests.
Vintages	
Social capital consists of vintages.	The vintages of social capital are more comparable to a port wine than to other capital forms. The composition of vintages is decisive. There is no simple correlation between age and decreasing productivity.
Accumulation and maintenance	
Social capital is worn out if it is not maintained.	Social capital is a product of both intentional investments and an unintended by-product of other activities.
Social capital is a result of past activities.	Accumulation of social capital does not necessarily need deliberate sacrifices for future benefits.
	Social capital is harder to construct through external interventions.
Rights of possession vs public goods	
Access to social capital is never completely public. Access demands connection to a network and/or certain skills.	Social capital is *social*, that is, it cannot be individually possessed.
Complexity and levels of aggregation	
Diversified social capital means less vulnerability to economic structural changes.	Social capital is the most diversified, least homogeneous form of capital.
	Aggregating social capital belonging to different levels meets great methodological difficulties.

Source: Westlund and Bolton (2003, p. 88).

realities (Johannisson, 2000). There are several reasons why entrepreneurs can prefer informal (personal) relationships to formal relationships of exchange (Johannisson, 1996):

- Personal exchange is more potent, flexible and committing than legal agreements (increased flexibility).
- Casual encounters may appear as opportunities that – by coincidence – initiate and direct the strategic development of the venturing process (elaborate business intelligence).
- Entrepreneurs typically listen to and learn from business partners, such as peers, suppliers and customers, where long-term exchange has created shared understanding and trust.

From the network perspective, the content of a company becomes both wider and undeniably more problematic (Lundgren and Snehota, 1998). The company's horizon should not coincide with a product-based market but with the total base of suppliers and other business partners. The differences from the earlier approach are considerable.

It is now recognized that networks and the activity of networking are important small business assets (Shaw, 2001). One could even say that the intrinsic value of an SME lies in its networks. '[In our new entrepreneurial society] a company's primary focus is shifted from maximizing the value of the firm to maximizing the value of its networks' (Kelly, 1998, p. 91; my translation).

It appears that an intensive use of networks is separating fast-growing companies from slow-growing companies (Hoang and Antoncic, 2003). During the 1990s, companies increasingly began to use networks in which teams with extended formal authority handled not only their internal work processes but also external relationships with upstream and downstream partners. In many networks, it became difficult to determine where one organization ended and another began, as cross-firm teams resolved interface issues, important customers were invited to participate in new product development processes and suppliers were given access to large firms' scheduling and accounting processes through electronic data interchange systems (Miles et al., 2002, p. 283). Networks have been identified as important in the innovation process. They have, for instance, been found to help innovative organizations acquire and understand new technologies and spread the costs of research and development (Shaw, 2000). 'Experimenting, hands-on tests in interaction with others, become building blocks of continuous learning in the business world, no matter whether we look at businesses in established or in young, emerging structures' (Johannisson, 1996, p. 123; my translation). Networks open opportunities for value-creating communication (Figure 5.5).

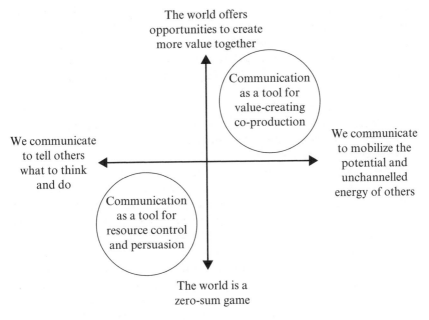

The world offers
opportunities to create
more value together

Communication
as a tool for
value-creating
co-production

We communicate
to tell others
what to think
and do

We communicate
to mobilize the
potential and
unchannelled
energy of others

Communication
as a tool for
resource control
and persuasion

The world is a
zero-sum game

Source: Normann (2001, p. 287).

Figure 5.5 Value-creating communication in networks

Most traditional communication is found in the lower left-hand corner of the figure. Communication leading to growth in knowledge and co-creation is, however, situated in the upper right-hand corner. What is important here is the symmetry between those views which are part of co-creation, such that the view of one participant does not dominate completely. In other words, a genuine dialogue is necessary.

NETWORKS AT DIFFERENT STAGES OF A BUSINESS

Entrepreneurs, at an early stage of enterprise development, rely heavily on an informal network of friends, family members and social contacts from the local neighbourhood to gather relevant data. At a later stage, entrepreneurs rely increasingly on professional bankers, accountants, lawyers, suppliers, government agencies, etc. to gain access to requisite business information. (Birley et al., 1991, p. 59)

Entrepreneurial networking means increasing the operative space for a new business venture (Shaw, 2001). Critical dimensions in the content of the networks are: (1) information, (2) advice, (3) exchange of services and

(4) expressions of friendship and feelings. Personal networks are part of the first stages of a business start-up when innovative and creative thinking are indispensable (McAdam and McGowan, 2003). The particular importance of contacts when building up a business, contacts which exist even before a business starts to be built up, is gaining wide support in research (Hoang and Antoncic, 2003).

At the early stages of new firm creation, information networks represent an important resource that the entrepreneur relies on extensively. Effective information networks enrich the entrepreneur's environment and enhance the other networks and processes in which the entrepreneur engages (McAdam and McGowan, 2003). Social networks are used as a testing ground for new ideas and as a mechanism for gaining access to resources to exploit new opportunities (Aldrich and Zimmer, 1986). Entrepreneurial networking facilitates access to resources which the entrepreneur does not own and enables the entrepreneur to overcome the problem of being a newcomer.

Larson and Starr (1993) posit that the networks constructed and activated for new venture formation follow a three-stage sequence of development. Each stage in the network development process is characterized by distinctive changes in the content of the relationship and the governance mechanisms used to manage the relationship.

In the first stage, the key activities centre on identifying the contacts that will provide the critical resources to begin the venture, particularly the use of ties to family, friends and existing business contacts. During this stage, new contacts are identified and pre-existing contacts are tapped for the venture. Entrepreneurs spend a significant amount of time developing new contacts and maintaining existing contacts.

In the second stage, exchange relationships become more multiplex, with relationships that began for instrumental reasons becoming imbued with social or affective components and ties that were strictly non-instrumental being leveraged for economic purposes. In addition, the governance relationships shift from quid pro quo behaviour as a basis for the exchange to trust and concerns about maintaining one's reputation.

In the third stage, the network content of the relationships gains further complexity and is characterized by more and higher quality information exchange between partners. Partly driven by the resource requirements of the venture, a critical mass of relationships is established and, more significantly, the continued interaction between actors becomes routinized. Ties can be characterized as interorganizational relationships when the direct involvement of the individuals who played a role in their formation is no longer needed for the relationships to be sustained.

Even when companies grow these personal contact networks will still be the building blocks on which strong business relationships are formed

(Dubini and Aldrich, 1991). An established small firm which engages in 'a network of contacts/associates, is able to offer a wide range of services without employing a substantial full-time professional or support staff' (Bryson et al., 1993, p. 267).

A picture of the importance of the personal network at different stages of a new business venture is given in Figure 5.6.

Networks can contribute in all stages of innovation: project stimuli, concept definition, idea-generation regarding features and functionality of innovation, technical problem-solving and field-testing prior to commer‑cialization (Conway, 1997).

PERSONAL, BUSINESS-BASED, VIRTUAL AND IMAGINARY NETWORKS

I see four rather different networks today, even if they can be partly com‑bined: these are personal, business-based, virtual and imaginary networks.

Personal networks consist of friends and relatives, they are built up by strong ties and they are, in some cultures and contexts, indispens‑able for whether an entrepreneur will be able to start a business or not. In other situations, personal networks may play a more generally sup‑portive role.

Business-based networks are necessary in order for a company to develop and to survive. These networks consist of different business partners who exchange products and services on a functional and calculative basis.

Virtual networks can be of two kinds. One is a free-flow organization (Storey, 2002, p. 353). Job responsibilities and responsibilities are here con‑stantly shifting – the notion of being an 'employee' is problematic here as some suppliers and customers spend more time on company premises than do some of the firm's permanently contracted employees. The other kind of virtual network is an organization which is linked up to computers and enclosed within the medium, an increasingly common reality. Latour (1998, p. 303) claims that this is something of a false declaration, a 'game with fiction while it, in fact, is about reality'. The virtual is factual here and should be studied as such.

Imaginary networks have been defined by Hedberg et al. (1994, p. 13) as follows:

> The perspective of the imaginary organization refers to a system in which assets, processes, and actors critical to the 'focal' enterprise exist and function both inside and outside the limits of the enterprise's conventional 'landscape' formed by its legal structure, its accounting, its organigrams, and the language otherwise used to describe the enterprise.

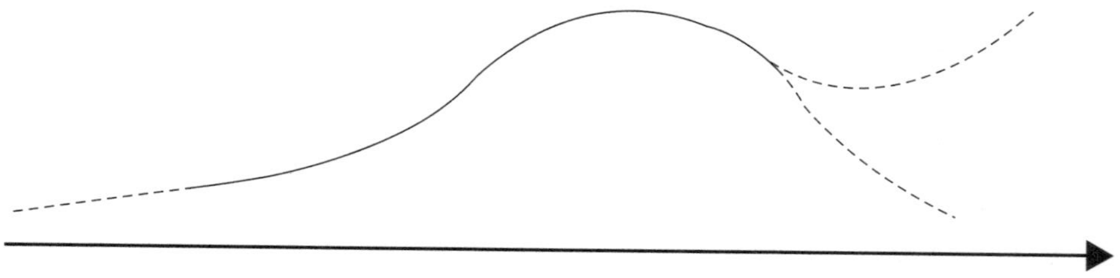

Development stage	Incubation	Take-off	Growth	Maturity	Vitalization/ liquidization	Time
Business leader profile	Innovator	Craftsman	Entrepreneur	Manager	'Renovator'/ 'Liquidator'	
Important actions	Formulate business concept	Mobilize links to market	Organize business partners	Develop control of income and expenditures	Establish strategic alliances/ liquidate	
The main task of network and context	Relate to business concepts and mentors	Establish credibility and market	Offer supplementary skills	Create arena for collegial exchange of experience	Relate to new business concepts/ second-hand market	

Source: Johannisson (1996, p. 33; my translation).

Figure 5.6   Different functions for the personal network and context during the development cycle of a firm

However, to me this is a virtual organization. In my view an imaginary organization is a construct of value to an understanding approach to entrepreneurs, which 'exists' only as a possibility, an image which an entrepreneur has of a network (perhaps only of its possibility) which contains actors and components that it would be necessary to involve in order to realize a business venture. The entrepreneur then sense-makes, language-makes, culture-makes and history-makes this imaginary organization, thereby contributing to the continuous construction of social reality. As the process continues, this imaginary network develops into one of the other three networks above (or a combination).

6. Entrepreneurship and growth

GROWTH IS IMPORTANT FOR AN ECONOMY

An economy cannot, without active steps being taken, maintain its size in the long run. In order to make an economy grow, extra steps are necessary. Growing firms are very important in this process. Harrison and Taylor (1996) claim that in the United States it is estimated that while medium-sized businesses represent just 1 per cent of all businesses, they generate a quarter of all sales and employ a fifth of all private sector labour. In the case of Great Britain, Storey et al. (1987) assert that out of every 100 small firms, the fastest growing four firms create half the jobs in that group over a decade. In other countries, however, it might be difficult to find a small group of companies that dominates the employment growth in the country (Davidsson and Delmar, 2001).

WHAT IS GROWTH?

A company's growth is 'any increase in the level, amount or type of work and outputs in the company'. It involves expanding, enlarging or extending what the company does (Coulter, 2001, p. 283). It is possible to distinguish between growth, expansion and 'gazelles'.

- *Growth.* When a distinction is made between growth and expansion, the growth stage is defined as the first significant increase in sales, in revenue and/or in number of employees after start-up.
- *Expansion.* This is a more controlled increase in market share and business size after the first growth phase.
- *Gazelles.* Birch (1979) has shown that a small proportion of any cohort of new businesses creates a disproportionately large share of jobs. He calls them 'gazelles'. The opposite are referred to by Birch as 'mice' (Bridge et al., 2003, p. 202).

Possible measures of growth are share value, profit, employment, turnover, return on investment, profile/image, number of customers, market share, new products/services and added value. However, the most common measures of

growth are probably employment and turnover. In considerin
among small firms it is important to realize the following facts:

1. Many entrepreneurs are not interested in pursuing growth, at least not
   in terms of number of employees, which is seen more as a means than
   as a goal (Davidsson, 1989; Wiklund, 1998). Growth is sometimes
   associated with less attractive elements of business such as managing
   others, limiting opportunities for personal control, dependence on
   others, sharing responsibility and decisions, perhaps losing some ownership. It may also be seen as an unnecessary risk.
2. Growth orientation can vary at different stages of the business. For a
   newly established business, some growth is likely to be a necessity for
   survival, although after a period of rapid growth, it may be necessary
   to enter a period of consolidation (Smallbone and Wyer, 2000, p. 411).

MODELS DESCRIBING GROWTH

There are many suggestions in the literature as to how to describe a course
of growth for a single business firm. Many of these suggestions consist of
a diagram where different stages are marked. There is one such model in
Figure 6.1.

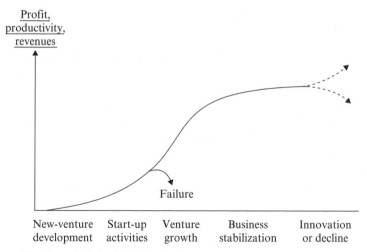

Source: Kuratko and Hodgetts (2004, p. 547).

Figure 6.1   A stage-model for growth (1)

Figure 6.1 distinguishes five stages:

1. *New-venture development.* The first stage is to build the foundation of the entrepreneurial process, which requires creativity as well as assessment. Networking is also very important. The purpose is to formulate the enterprise's general philosophy, mission, scope and direction.
2. *Start-up activities.* These encompass the foundation work needed for creating a formal business plan, possibly searching for capital, carrying out various marketing activities and developing an effective entrepreneurial team if the venture is to consist of more than one person.
3. *Venture growth.* Here, competition as well as other market forces may call for a modification and sometimes even a major reformulation of strategies. These new challenges are to be part of the entrepreneur's efforts to put a more complete set of entrepreneurial skills in place.
4. *Business stabilization.* This is a result of both market conditions and the entrepreneur's efforts. The market becomes mature and the entrepreneur must begin thinking about where the enterprise will go over the next three to five years.
5. *Innovation or decline.* Firms that fail to innovate will die. Financially successful enterprises will often try to acquire other innovative firms to ensure their own growth.

All five stages are important, but they require different actions to be taken and different strategies to be implemented for a business venture to continue to grow.

Some descriptive models for growth are presented as tables. Table 6.1 has, in principle, the same content as Figure 6.1, but begins earlier in the entrepreneurial process.

Figure and table can also be combined (Figure 6.2).

Models describing growth can also be presented as stage-less. Figure 6.3 shows a model for the way in which different external forces can influence the growth of a business venture.

Another variation of growth in which different intrapreneurial efforts in a company lead to growth for the company at large is shown in Figure 6.4.

MODELS EXPLAINING GROWTH

None of the models presented so far provides an explanation. They *describe*, after the fact, a picture of a course of growth of a successful

Table 6.1   A stage-model for growth (2)

Stage	Actions	Priorities	Challenges
1. Idea	Develop ideas for innovation Determine their commercial application	R&D IPR protection	Technical
2. Pre-start	Research the market Acquire skills Decide on the business strategy Prepare the business plan	Feasibility Facilitate partnering The 'business case'	Forecasting
3. Start-up	Raise finance Put the components in place Launch the business	Management Finance Marketing and sales	Development
4. Survival	Run the business Ensure its survival	Early growth Production Distribution	Operational
5. Expansion (and rewards?)	Develop the business Find an exit route	Growth Planning system Procedures Management team	Planning and strategic

Source: Bridge et al. (2003, p. 210).

business. With the terminology presented in Chapter 2 one can say that they present an intrinsic relationship. At some stages or some phases of the development of a business, some grow, some do not. One can also say that it is a logical relationship in that, for instance, a stage called 'Take-off' precedes a stage called 'Maturity'. Causal relationships are of a different kind. They mean coming up with those factors which could cause growth before the fact. These are models *explaining* growth. One could summarize the factors which could be included in such a model as in Figure 6.5.

A more specific model for explaining growth of a single business is presented in Figure 6.6.

Figure 6.6 shows that the entrepreneurial *motivation* for growth is a critical factor in attaining it. This motivation is a result of the fact that the entrepreneur perceives an ability, a need and an opportunity in reality.

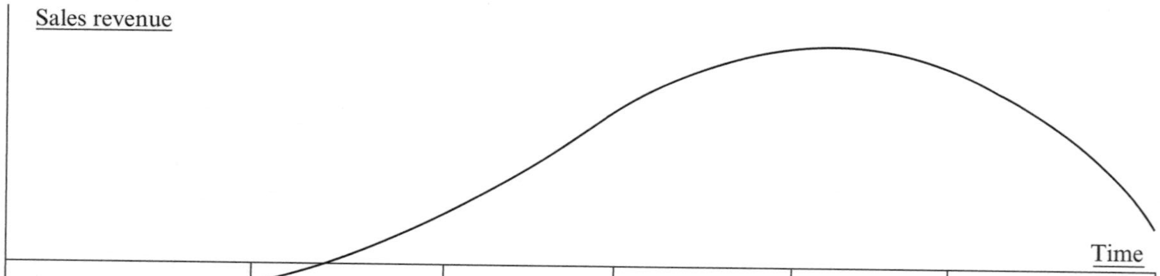

Sales revenue

Time

Business life-cycle	Initiation	Development	Growth	Maturity	Decline
Example					
Changing nature of impacting problems	Need to identify market	Need to consolidate and develop	Need to counter competition	Need to seek alternative markets	Need to develop extension strategies
The need to progressively develop management ability	Informal marketing ability	Formulation of marketing approach	Competition analysis	Broadening of market analysis	Adjustment to existing products and market focus

Source: Smallbone and Wyer (2000, p. 415).

Figure 6.2   A stage-model for growth (3)

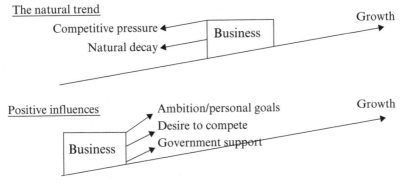

The natural trend

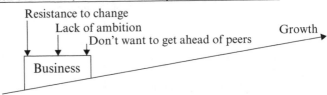

Positive influences

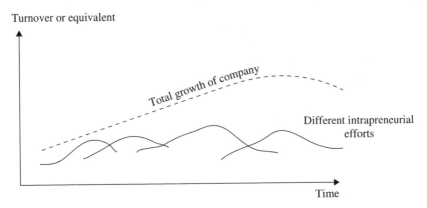

Influences, often overlooked, which tend to keep a business where it is

Source: Bridge et al. (2003, p. 273).

Figure 6.3   A stage-less model for growth

Figure 6.4   Growth through continuous intrapreneurial efforts

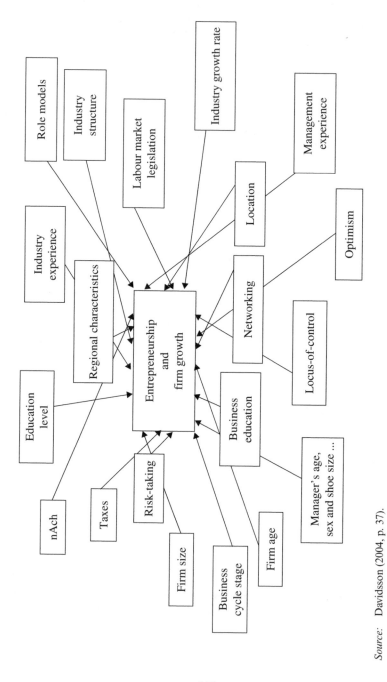

Source: Davidsson (2004, p. 37).

Figure 6.5   Factors that may influence business growth

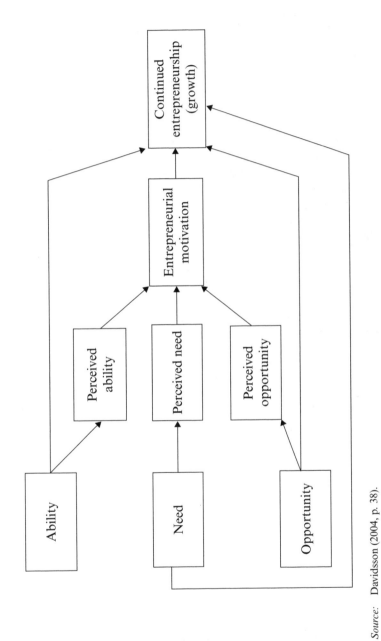

Source: Davidsson (2004, p. 38).

Figure 6.6   A possible model explaining growth

FACTORS FAVOURABLE FOR GROWTH

It is possible to classify factors favourable for growth of a business as in Figure 6.7. These are luck, the entrepreneur, the company, the strategy and the environment. Let us look at these factors one by one in further detail.

Luck

Growth, especially for new business ventures, can never be completely planned in advance in all details. If that were possible, the venture would, almost by definition, not be new! Growth is therefore, at least partly, a result of luck. For example, good timing, an unexpected financial windfall such as an inheritance or a chance meeting with a person who will later become an important customer.

The Entrepreneur

But growth is not only a result of chance. The character of the entrepreneur is also important.

- The entrepreneur should be interested in growth, proactive and have a willingness to expand and a positive belief in the future development of the company.

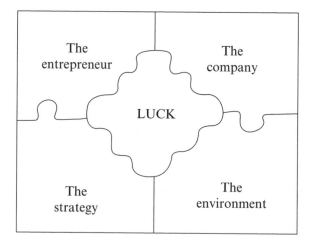

Figure 6.7   The ingredients of successful growth

- The entrepreneur's attitude to risk may influence willingness to use available external financial possibilities for growth.
- The competency of the entrepreneur is crucial. As well as an interest in growth and a favourable attitude to risk, the entrepreneur also needs an ability to adapt to new requirements which appear as the business venture is going on.
- If growth is not possible on the ground on which the company stands, the entrepreneur should have an innovative ability to lead the company into other areas more favourable to growth – if growth is of interest.
- Empirical studies show that one of the most important factors for the growth of a business is the entrepreneur's willingness to delegate (Storey, 1994). This may, for instance, provide more time for the entrepreneur to think about growth and problems related to this. Lack of time is often seen as a major obstacle for growth (see later in this chapter).
- The significance of age is not clear for the explaining-oriented researcher. The chances of belonging to the growth group become smaller when the business leader grows older ('Tillväxt i småföretag', 2003). At the same time greater experience can help in successfully launching another business and making it grow.
- A willingness to share ownership with external individuals or organizations is often seen as a central factor for growth.

The Company

The characteristics of the company which are important for growth include:

- *A growth culture.* The business culture must contain a wish to grow. This is probably more important for growth than the way in which the company is structured.
- *Age.* The younger the company is, the larger the probability is that it belongs to the growth group ('Tillväxt i småföretag', 2003). After a while, the willingness to grow further may decrease (Burns, 1989).
- *Size.* It may sound obvious that it is easier for a small company to double its size, but there are likely to be, in all industries and under various circumstances, limits to growth.
- *Legal form.* A limited company with spread ownership seems to be more likely to grow than a proprietorship or a family firm where ownership is restricted.

The Strategy

Strategies can be important to growth. Storey (1994) notes the following areas:

- *Product development*. A company that wants to grow is rarely relying on only one product.
- *Market*. A company set up to exploit a clearly defined market segment has a higher propensity to grow than a company which is established as a necessity for the founder to be able to support himself financially.
- *Production technology*. Technologies used must be relevant to growth.
- *Financial base*. To use only internally generated means can be a hindrance to growth, a situation which is not uncommon among family firms.
- *Recruitment*. In order to grow, a company should recruit personnel who have the competency and ability to participate and to work for growth, including overcoming existing obstacles to growth.
- *Using advice and assistance from outside*. To abandon what could be seen as an exaggerated need for independence when necessary and to take advice and use assistance from outside the firm when necessary can open opportunities for growth. This may, above all, be the case in high-technology firms.

Harrison and Taylor (1996) identify five winning factors among 179 fast-growing firms:

1. Competing on quality rather than price.
2. Domination of a market niche.
3. Competing in areas of strength.
4. Having tight financial and operating control.
5. Frequent product or service innovation.

The Environment

A company does not, of course, live in a vacuum. There are factors in its environment which may influence its opportunities for growth. These include:

- Regulations.
- Taxes.
- Interest rates.

- The state of the economy.
- Market trends. There may be extraordinary possibilities for growth, but also a higher risk of failure, for instance, in young and volatile areas like IT.
- Competition. Strong competition in a market can hamper growth. At the same time it may stimulate even better performance than before.
- Localization/cluster effects. If a company which exists to fulfil local needs wants to grow, it must be located in the right place. It is the case today that place can be a competitive factor because of cluster effects (see further Chapter 7).
- Access to labour. Access to qualified people, as well as to other production factors, can influence the opportunities for a firm to grow.

Typically fast growing firms seem to be:

- First in a niche market they created and in which they became the leaders.
- Better at what they do than their competitors.
- Leaner in their operations.
- Unique in what they offer (Allen, 2003, p. 393).

Small companies seem to have an advantage over larger companies when it comes to growth (Zimmerer and Scarborough, 2002, p. 502):

- Larger companies' inability to react quickly is a major barrier to their growth. Small companies are naturally quick to respond.
- Rigid internal structures keep big companies from growing rapidly. Small companies typically bypass traditional structures.
- Large companies focus on expanding existing product and service lines, while small businesses concentrate more on creating new ones.
- Large companies are concerned with minimizing risks and defending their market share. Small companies are more willing to take the risks necessary to conquer new markets.
- Large companies are reluctant to eradicate market research and technology that have worked in the past. Entrepreneurial companies have more of a 'clean-slate' approach to research and technology.

GROWTH BARRIERS

There are many growth barriers for small firms. Some of them are presented in Table 6.2.

Table 6.2   Growth barriers for new business ventures

Growth barrier	Cause of barrier	Resources required to overcome
Unestablished or weak competitive position	Competitive deficiencies, small-scale operations	Strategic industry resources, large-scale resources
Lack of organizational legitimacy	Lack of institutional support, non-existent firm reputation	Effective network with key external organizations, longevity
Minimal internal coordination	Lack of organizational development	Efficient administrative structure
Weak exchange relationships	Minimal bargaining power, lack of stable links to clients, suppliers, customers	Limits to appropriation, customer and supplier loyalty

Source: Shelton (2001, p. 14).

Table 6.3   Obstacles to growth according to their origin and character

		The character of growth obstacle	
		Material obstacles	Immaterial obstacles
The origin of growth obstacle	Internal obstacles	Shortage of routines and methods, for instance, control systems for inventory and costs	Unwillingness of the entrepreneur to expand, shortage of competent colleagues, insufficient leadership qualities, etc.
	External obstacles	Shortage of external venture capital, insufficient infrastructure, unfavourable rule system, etc.	Negative opinion about business venturing, tendencies to look for 'safe' jobs, etc.

Source: Barth (2001, p. 236).

One can also distinguish different obstacles to growth according to their origin and character (Table 6.3).

It might be important to identify the origin as well as the character of growth obstacles in order to be able to expand. This, of course, does not exclude the possibility that several different obstacles, in terms of origin as well as of character, may unite to stop growth. This obviously complicates the picture for a growth-hungry entrepreneur.

In a survey carried out in Sweden among small firms ('Tillväxt i småföretag', 2003), a question was asked concerning obstacles to growth. The most common answers were:

- Lack of own time (60 per cent of respondents).
- Tough competition (39 per cent).
- Low profitability (36 per cent).
- Shortage of the right kind of workers (36 per cent).
- Authority rules, approval formalities and the like (35 per cent).
- Weak demand (29 per cent).
- Shortage of external capital for equity (21 per cent).
- Shortage of loans (16 per cent).

Entrepreneurs can, themselves, discourage growth in many different ways. Some of the most common growth traps are (Bjerke, 1989):

- *Trying to attain a false conformity.* It is unproductive for an entrepreneur to impose an artificial conformity on the business objectives, the organization structure, rewards and strategies. This neglects the possibility that an innovative company, to its advantage, can be engaged in several simultaneous approaches to a promising venture; instead, it indicates a false belief, that there are 'typical' approaches to 'typical' problems.
- *Trying to eliminate uncertainty.* In an uncertain world risk cannot be eliminated. To formulate rules of thumb to reduce uncertainty in all situations encourages people to take on the roles of auditors and trouble-shooters rather than as catalysts of change.
- *Trusting traditions.* When confronting fundamental business changes an entrepreneur cannot with certainty trust his or her experience, nor can he or she place significant trust in the assumptions behind the plans intended for implementation.
- *Dominating discussions.* As a company grows in size and variety the entrepreneur must delegate, inevitably losing direct contact with those centres where actions take place, a process which increases over time. Still believing as an entrepreneur that he or she can have the final word on what is most appropriate in all cases can be a serious mistake.
- *Delegating strategy.* It is true that the entrepreneur can leave subordinates to work out and implement different tactical steps, but he or she should still have a reasonably clear overall business strategy and a vision for the organization as a whole.

A summary of growth among small firms in Sweden is summarized in Table 6.4.

STRUCTURES, ORGANIZATIONS AND CULTURES FOR GROWTH

In a classic article, Schollhammer (1982) presents five possible structures (patterns) for organizing intrapreneurship in existing business establishments. These are administrative, opportunistic, imitative, acquisitive and separative.

In the *administrative* structure, growth is seen as a sequential, controllable process. Functional responsibility is divided between scientific or technical personnel on one side and managers or administrators on the other. These two sides are to select viable domains of activity, secure necessary resources, and create and maintain a conducive organizational climate.

Accidental encounters between business interests and technical innovations which become the basis for developing business initiatives are not infrequent. Therefore, for existing companies it may be necessary to have enough contacts to be part of new developments. Conscious scanning and surveillance of internal and external environments for the purpose of detecting and adopting innovative developments can be characterized as the *opportunistic* structure for intrapreneurship.

Imitation may not sound very innovative. To try to copy what others have done already does not seem entrepreneurial. However, to adopt what may seem like a well-tested innovation can, for the imitator, be a step which is as daring as it is for the innovator. Conscious control of what is going on in the environment and, when necessary, taking on the success of others, can be called an *imitative* structure for business development.

By acquiring other establishments, a company can achieve growth, diversification and horizontal or vertical integration in less time and with greater cost efficiency than by internal innovative activities. Acquisition and mergers play a very significant role in the transformation of a single-business company to a multiple-business company. The fact is that acquisition can become a goal in itself. From an entrepreneurial perspective, the *acquisitive* structure for business development can provide technological capabilities that will combine with resources in the acquiring company to provide a basis for accelerated growth, diversification and improved financial performance.

Some multidivisional companies have elected to separate new-product activities from marketing or other functional units within their operative divisions and to put them under the direction of a new-product development

Table 6.4   Growth among small firms in Sweden

At an overall level
- The societal climate in which the firms are to grow has long been unfavourable
- Lately it has become better, but in some respects it is still worse than in many competitive nations
- The external circumstances are important for growth, but
- Business firms in all industries and in all kinds of geographical places can develop and exploit favourable niches for growth
- The companies' own choice and behaviour seem to be of great importance to their development

About fast growing firms
- They are few, and their total ability to create new jobs is not very impressive
- Early growth is organic; later growth is more and more achieved through acquisitions
- This pattern coincides with the pattern for external ownership
- Transition from organic growth to growth based on acquisition is seen when fast growing firms are going international
- There is no general understanding of how to continue in fast growing firms

Concerning venture capital and technology-based firms
- Access to venture capital has exploded in recent years
- External venture capital is of great importance to technology-based firms
- Firms with external venture capital grow more
- The problem mainly concerns seed capital (early venture capital) and the technological competency among venture capitalists
- Spinoffs from other firms grow more than firms started from scratch, and spinoffs from firms grow more than spinoffs from the academic world
- New-technology industries grow more if supplementary industries are already strongly represented in the region

About business strategy
- Companies with an entrepreneurial orientation grow more
- This is also – or perhaps particularly – valid in a turbulent environment; new orientations are important
- Growth firms search for dynamic growth niches

About the entrepreneur
- Many of them do not want to grow
- Non-economic factors influence the willingness to grow; in particular concerns about employees' job satisfaction
- Self-confidence and tolerance of uncertainty are important personal characteristics for growth in hard times

---

Source: Davidsson et al. (2001, pp. 21–3).

department in each division. Others have completely centralized all their new-product activities under a single such department at the corporate level. On both counts a *separative* structure for new products has grown in popularity.

Personally I would like to add a sixth structure, if structure is the right word here. I call it an *incubative* structure (Bjerke, 1989). In this structure all organizational members are of a common opinion that everybody in the company can contribute to developing new business ventures – without necessarily formally feeling that they are part of such an activity. Whether this is possible in practice can be questioned (see, for instance, Forslund, 2002).

Peters (1997) sees a purposeful new innovative organization in our new entrepreneurial society, a post-industrial organization which does not look like its predecessor:

- *At the top.* The top of the pyramid, for instance, the main office, is much smaller, but far more important. It must keep a constantly changing and fluid network organization together at the same time as it is responsible for keeping the vision alive.
- *The old middle.* The old middle as controller, police force and keeper of information is dead.
- *The new middle.* The new middle, even if it is drastically reduced, is more important than ever in its value-adding transformative project role.
- *At the bottom.* This is much more powerful than before. Every person who has an external role should look at his or her task as running a business.
- *From outside.* The outside (for instance, customers) moves in and is given power. This is more important than empowering employees.

It might be wrong to talk about organizational structures in our new entrepreneurial society, because organizing is more important than the organization. An organization must then be organized such that it never stops organizing. One could talk about building a business with the idea of 'unfitness by design'!

There are many proposals as to how to arrive at a business structure which supports development. For example:

- *Keep the lines of communication open.* Employees need to be informed about major issues.
- *Establish trust* by being honest, open and forthright about the challenges and rewards of being a growing organization.

- *Be a good listener.* Find out what employees are thinking and facing.
- *Be willing to delegate duties.* You cannot continue to make every decision.
- *Be flexible.* Although planned growth is desirable, be flexible enough to change your plans.
- *Provide consistent and regular feedback.* Let employees know the outcomes – good and bad.
- *Reinforce the contributions of each person* to the venture's ultimate success. People like to be recognized for their efforts.
- *Continually train employees.* It is important to enhance employees' capabilities and skills.
- *Maintain the focus on the venture's vision and mission.* The organizational vision and mission are the reasons the venture is in business.
- *Establish and reinforce a 'we' spirit.* A successful growing entrepreneurial venture requires the coordinated efforts of all the employees (Coulter, 2001, p. 288).

The basic logic behind the way in which a company manages its businesses (old as well as new) could be called a strategic formula. This includes a number of opinions about where the competency and skills of an organization are situated. This strategic formula is very important (Johnson and Scholes, 1999).

INNOVATION

The modern company must be innovative. One could say that it is more important for a company in our new entrepreneurial society to do the next thing right than do the same thing better (Kelly, 1998, p. 191).

Unfortunately, the course of an innovation is too often presented as a stepwise planned process (Figure 6.8). In this process, the steps are as follows:

1. *Research.* Searching for (own or others') business ideas which could fit with the objective of the company.
2. *Screening.* A quick analysis to decide which ideas are suitable and require further analysis.
3. *Business analysis.* Extension of the idea, through creative analysis, to a tangible business possibility, including product characteristics and a programme for the product. The business opportunity may, in some cases, already be realized in other companies.
4. *Development.* To transform an idea from paper to a product in hand, demonstrable and possible to manufacture.

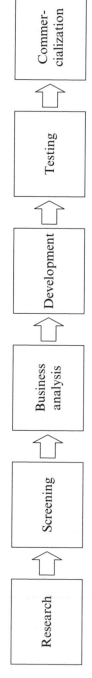

Figure 6.8   A step-wise model of innovation

5. *Testing.* Commercial experiments necessary to verify previous business judgements.
6. *Commercialization.* Launching the product full-scale, in terms of selling as well as in terms of production, and thereby involving the reputation and the resources of the company.

This step-wise model contradicts everything we think we know about innovation. Any 'innovation' produced in this planned, formal and structured way would not, in my opinion, be worthy of the name. New things come from sometimes random collisions between contrary opinions and often only after much anxiety and hesitation. The language picture in Figure 6.9 probably provides a better view of how an innovation can come through (compare Figure 4.2 and Figure 4.3).

FURTHER ON INTRAPRENEURSHIP

Business development is rarely the result only of individual persons' actions, but takes place in groups in the wide sense of the term. Creative groups have certain characteristics in common. They are, for instance, very dependent on a creative leader, what we in this context could call an intrapreneur (Jay, 1970):

1. *The authority of the leader is unquestioned and unchallenged.* In a successful group, the leader is often spoken of with an uncritical admiration which borders on reverence. There is no room here to consider what makes a creative leader, but without such a person the creative group would not exist. He or she is also surrounded by a smaller group which is the central nucleus of the creative group. This is not to say that there cannot be many more trusted and able members of the group, only that the central nucleus must be small.
2. *Within the central nucleus there is a dialogue.* This is a difficult concept to describe to those who have not experienced it, but dialogues (which were discussed in Chapter 2) are important here. They could also be called discussions or debates, but they are usually very informal, open and honest. Attitudes, ideas and critical standards are hammered out until there is a body of shared convictions about methods and products and markets or whatever the group's business is concerned with. And once this is hammered out, it forms a basis for a continuing dialogue, improved understanding and firmer convictions.
3. *Creative groups need results.* They do not work at their best when spirited away to a country house and told to 'have some ideas'. Creative

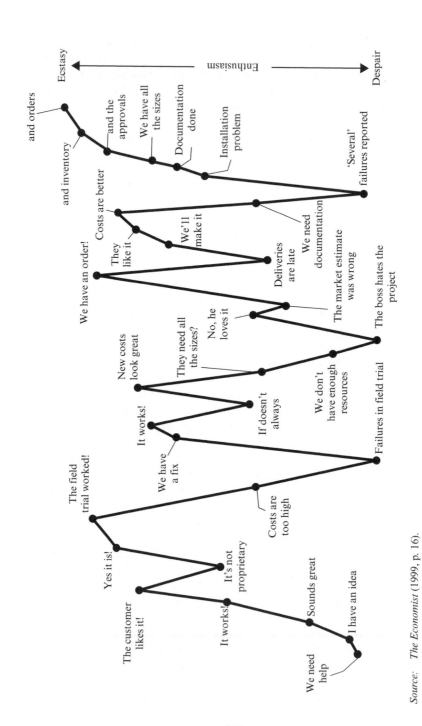

Source: *The Economist* (1999, p. 16).

Figure 6.9   The language way for an innovation

groups belong where the work is being done if they are to come up with ideas that are constructive and practical. Tangible results are also important for morale. Creative groups use up a lot of energy. Often they work hard and long and late, and they cannot be supervised or checked on for punctuality and efficiency as more routine performers can. The third need for tangible results is to provide feedback. If the dialogue is to continue, there must be a continuous supply of new data, a continuous learning process. Only by continuing to produce can improvements be made, new facts revealed, and the body of shared convictions augmented, revised or refined by tangible results.

4. *The leader of a creative group must have as much autonomy as possible.* The leader of a creative group must be able to implement the ideas of the group on his or her own responsibility. If they have to be passed up to somebody else, they will not be put into effect with the same understanding, nor with the same confidence and enthusiasm. And of course the group works more willingly if it knows that the leader is the person who will actually implement the idea.

5. *Creative groups have to grow, or they die.* If they devise and launch a new and successful project, they are unlikely to be satisfied with the running of it once it is established. Indeed the mere fact of being good enough to launch it is proof that they are good enough to run it – at least as a full-time job. They need the constant stimulus of bigger challenges and responsibilities, better resources, larger budget, more staff, as well as sufficient personal promotion and increase of salary to keep their morale high.

6. *If the creative leader is removed from the group, it becomes an extinct volcano.* As with real volcanoes, it takes time to realize that it has become extinct; but it gradually becomes clear that although it is still efficient, the thing is not bubbling any more. Our society has many extinct volcanoes, which were once exciting and important, but which carry on a staid and routine existence after the glory has departed.

7. *Creative groups define their own projects.* This is not to say that they do not need projects given to them – they must have some details of what product is required, how big the budget is, what plant and labour are available, what the time scale is and so on. But the more freedom they are given within these broad limits, the more successful they are likely to be. People tend to devise what they can achieve, and projects devised by creative groups are likely to draw on the skills and expertise and interests which the group possesses. They will not devise a product whose success hinges on metallurgic factors if they have no one with metallurgic qualifications in the group. It therefore follows that there

will be more variety in results, if the members of the group have different backgrounds.

I am well aware that listing some of the shared characteristics of creative groups is not the same as providing a formula for starting them. I am equally aware that some of the most important creative ideas have come, without any particular external stimulus, to people working entirely on their own.

Business development through individual actions and groups within existing companies can be called *intrapreneurship*. In order for intrapreneurship to function in big organizations, the following are needed, according to Allen (2003, p. 23):

- *Senior management commitment.* Without the support of senior management, it will be difficult to move any entrepreneurial ambition forward fast or far enough to be successful.
- *Corporate interoperability.* It is essential to provide an environment that encourages collaboration and gives the intrapreneur access to the knowledge and resources of all the company's functional areas.
- *Clearly defined stages and metrics.* Entrepreneurial ventures inside large organizations need a timeline with stages at which decisions can be made about whether to proceed and if additional or different resources are required. They also need a way to measure progress and success that is not based on the corporation's benchmarks but rather on benchmarks appropriate to start-up ventures with limited resources.
- *A superior team.* Only the best people should be put in corporate venture situations, because by definition they are riskier than projects based on the company's core skills and products. The new venture team also needs a champion among the top management who will assist when the team reaches inevitable roadblocks.
- *Spirit of entrepreneurship.* Entrepreneurship is about opportunity – recognizing it, seizing it and exploiting it – but it is also about failing sometimes. A company that encourages intrapreneurship cannot penalize its intrapreneurs for mistakes, but must support them as they take what they have learnt to a new project.

Pinchot, who coined the term intrapreneurship, talks about ten questions of intrapreneurial freedom (see Table 6.5).

There are many intrapreneurial barriers. Dollinger (2003, p. 341) lists a few:

- corporate bureaucracy
- internal product competition
- competing demands for resources

Table 6.5   The ten intrapreneurial freedom questions

---

1. Does your company encourage the self-appointed intrapreneur?
2. Does you company provide ways for intrapreneurs to stay with their intraprises?
3. Are people in your company permitted to do the job in their own way, or are they constantly stopping to explain their actions and ask for permission?
4. Has your company evolved quick and informal ways to access the resources to try new ideas?
5. Has your company developed ways to manage many small and experimental products and businesses?
6. Is your system set up to encourage risk-taking and to tolerate mistakes?
7. Can your company decide to try something and stick with the experiment long enough to see if it will work, even when that may take years and several false starts?
8. Are people in your company more concerned with new ideas or with defending their turf?
9. How easy is it to form functionally complete, autonomous teams in your corporate environment?
10. Do intrapreneurs in your company face internal monopolies or are they free to use the resources of other divisions and outside vendors if they choose?

Source: Pinchot (1985, pp. 198–9).

- resistance to change
- absence of 'internal venture capitalists' for guidance
- employees' lack of ownership reduces commitment
- corporate environment not as free to creative people as entrepreneurial environment.

A relevant concept here is *learning organizations*. For this concept, there are almost as many conceptualizations as there are for culture. However, some reasonably common ideas are:

- The essence of organizational learning is the organization's ability to use the amazing mental capacity of all its members to create the kind of processes that will improve its learning capacity (Dixon, 1994).
- A learning company is an organization that facilitates the learning of all its members and continually transforms itself (Pedler et al., 1991).
- Organizational learning occurs through shared insights, knowledge and mental models and builds on past knowledge and experience – that is, on memory (Stata, 1989).
- Learning organizations exist where people continually expand their capacity to create the results they truly desire, where new and

expansive patterns of thinking are nurtured, where collective aspirations are free, and where people are continually learning to learn together (Senge, 1990).

- Learning organizations 'unlearn' and forget redundant and unsuccessful past behaviour (Hedberg, 1981). No expert on innovation and learning can exist if there is no expert on breaking down established knowledge (Kelly, 1998, p. 115).

It is interesting in this context to compare how learning takes place in Japanese organizations and how learning takes place in Western organizations (Table 6.6).

Some leaders are better able than others to encourage members of an organization to actively join in learning at work. Such leaders are sometimes called *transformational leaders* (as opposed to *transactional leaders*). Some characteristics of transformative leaders are:

- *They identify themselves as agents of change.* These leaders make a difference and transform the organization for which they have assumed responsibility.

Table 6.6   A comparison between the Japanese and the Western style of learning in organizations

In Japanese organizations learning	In Western organizations learning
is group-based	is individual-based
is oriented to tacit knowledge	is oriented to explicit knowledge
is strong on socialization and internalization	is strong on externalization and combination
emphasizes experience	emphasizes analysis
leads to a danger of 'group think' and an overadaptation to past successes	leads to a danger of 'paralysis by analysis'
leads to ambiguous organizational intention	leads to clear organizational intention
is based on group autonomy	is based on individual autonomy
works with creative chaos through overlapping tasks	works on creative chaos through individual differences
starts from frequent fluctuations from top management	starts from less fluctuations from top management
provides a redundancy of information	provides less variety of information
appreciates requisite variety through cross-functional teams	appreciates requisite variety through individual differences

Source: Nonaka and Takeuchi (1995, p. 199).

- *They are courageous.* They are able to take a stand, able to take risks and able to stand against the status quo in the larger interest of the organization.
- *They believe in people.* They are not dictators. They are powerful yet sensitive to other people, and ultimately work towards the empowerment of others.
- *They are value-driven.* They are able to articulate a set of core values and exhibit behaviour that is congruent with their value positions.
- *They are lifelong learners.* They are able to talk about mistakes they have made. However, they do not view them as failures, but as learning experiences.
- *They have the ability to deal with complexity, ambiguity and uncertainty.* They are able to cope with and frame problems in a complex, changing world.
- *They are visionaries.* They are able to dream and able to translate those dreams and images so that other people can share them (Tichy and Devanna, 1986, pp. 271–80).

Six ingredients which are necessary for change in an organization are (Bjerke, 1989):

1. An awareness of that something is wrong.
2. Support from senior management of the notion that something has to be done.
3. A 'vision' of something new or at least a feeling of a new direction.
4. Agents of change that take it upon themselves to carry changes through.
5. A commitment from all key actors to be there with their brains (to understand what it is all about), their hearts (to feel to be part of something new) and their guts (to dare to be part of a genuine change).
6. Time.

It is possible to identify four different roles in entrepreneurial change within an organization (Bjerke, 1989):

1. *A person with an idea* – somebody who thinks differently.
2. *An entrepreneur* – a person who can bring an idea to application and use.
3. *A supporter* – a person in a senior position who supports the project (one could call such a person a 'godfather' or a 'godmother').
4. *A 'gate keeper'* – a person who (often informally) knows all the technical details necessary to make it all work.

BUSINESS VOCABULARY AND MANAGING LANGUAGE

To explain how organizations create growth, for instance through new products and new organizational structures, is important. But more important is to understand how organizations create the new knowledge that makes such growth possible.

An important part of a company's ability to renew itself is its *vocabulary*. An organization that wishes to handle a changing environment in a dynamic fashion needs to be able to *create* new information and knowledge, not only to treat existing information more effectively.

> [M]any of the most important artefacts are purely symbolic, with no *a priori* physical manifestations. *Concepts* are incredibly important artefacts. They are memes often resulting from a long 'cultural' process, or they may be expressions of deliberate rhetorical innovation. When Enron describes itself as a risk management company in (and recently also outside) the energy business, when Xerox goes from the copying machine company to 'The Document Company', or when Mercedes-Benz or Ford talk about selling 'mobility' instead of cars, these notions are highly significant as artefacts. When Observer (a very successful Stockholm headquartered company) launches concepts such as 'communication audit' and 'value-creating communications' they create mental analysts for reframing the company's business, which started as press clippings where they were the world's leader. The power of concepts is further proven by how extremely conserving they can be. (Normann, 2001, p. 255)

What is not always obvious is that because language is never neutral and because of the natural process of self-referentiality in language, people in groups are constantly in the process of creating new language and new meanings, even if they share the same mother tongue (Roos and von Krogh, 2002, p. 257). We have more options to create memes than genes. Language-making ability is a strategic advantage. We can call this *languaging* capability (Normann, 2001, p. 253).

This capability is probably even more important in entrepreneurial situations. As we saw in Chapter 4, we can look at an entrepreneur as a language-maker. The more the world becomes blurred (as in 'our new entrepreneurial society'), the more a sense of identity must come from reflection – from language activities.

As mentioned in chapters 2 and 4, language activities and action orientation are two sides of the same coin (Figure 6.10).

There are particular phrases floating around in companies that can easily kill something as sensitive as a new idea. Some of these 'killer phrases' are listed in Table 6.7.

Languaging means considering every moment as a symbolic moment, which is both good and bad news for entrepreneurs and other business

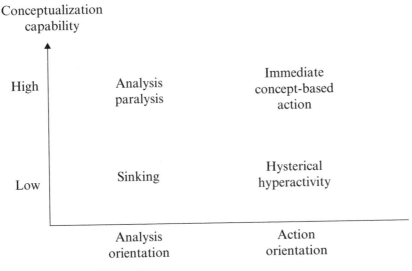

Source: Normann (2001, p. 274).

Figure 6.10   Conceptualization and action go together

people. Good news, because it does not involve any investment costs. Bad news, because *every moment* is a symbolic opportunity. It is an opportunity that you consciously – or unconsciously – choose to grasp or squander:

> It all adds up to this: *Every* system, *every* seating arrangement, *every* visit is symbolic behavior. Questioning routines: What's the first question the boss invariably asks? Market-oriented people ask about marketing. Financially oriented people ask about finance. Want to change your strategic emphasis? Determined shifts in time-honored questioning habits can be a big part of it. Seating arrangements. Who gets invited to what kinds of meeting? In 'Staff-oriented' organizations, a disproportionate share of staff gets invited to meetings. Want to take the emphasis off staff? Quit inviting staff people to meetings! Visits: Who gets visited, in what order? What functions first? Junior or senior people first? How much time is spent with what level people in which functions? The word gets around – at approximately the speed of light (some argue faster). (Peters and Austin, 1985, p. 273)

A genuine dialogue should exist in a company which aims at constructive change:

> The creative dialogue will not be more open than our thoughts permit. When confronting new questions and thoughts something old must always be abandoned! In a learning and creative organization love flows to these quantum leaps of thoughts, where we for brief moments have only the wings of our inner courage to trust. An indicating important criterion that we are really participating in a

Table 6.7   Killer phrases

'You are on the wrong track'	'It is too risky'
'It does not give enough return'	'We have already too much to worry about'
'Let's put the idea aside for a while'	'You are too young to know anything about this'
'Who shall do it?'	'Who are you? Some kind of snob?'
'I don't understand what you hope to achieve'	'Somebody must have done it'
'Is this your business?'	'Be sensible'
'Something else that is new?'	'I thought about it last year; we didn't use it then'
'The boss will laugh'	'You must be joking'
'We tried this two years ago'	'Who needs this?'
'Competitors are ahead of us'	'It is against our common logic'
'It sounds good – but . . .'	'For what purpose?'
'Who asked you?'	'Why not start today?'
'We are too big for this'	'Who cannot be without *that*?'
'The public is not ready for it yet'	'You will never get an approval'
'It does not suit our orientation'	'We tried this 25 years ago'
'Sixth floor will not like it'	'We have enough problems already'
'It will not work'	'Why?'
'It is not a new concept'	'One day there will be somebody who needs it'
'It is probably illegal'	'The public will laugh at us'
'Why now? Let us check it later'	

creative dialogue is that the wing-strokes of our own inner courage bring us forward. (Arbnor, 2004, p. 372; my translation)

Languaging concerns the future.

> The management of conversation needs to be a central concern of every manager who wishes to succeed in a knowledge-intensive age. The process through which we both create new meaning and share meaning and frames of reference in language is at the heart of knowledge development in organizations. It is a powerful concept within the domain of corporate epistemology. It is about the future of management. (Roos and von Krogh, 2002, p. 263)

We live in the world we know. We also live in the world we created ourselves. And I do not refer to the physical world here, but to the social world, which is by and large built up by our language and which, above all, can only be understood through language and be changed by language.

Language and thought are related. The language that we acquire in the culture of our workplace can be almost as binding as the first language we acquired as children. This binding is usually as unnoticed as the movements we make when we are out walking.

New actions and new thoughts require a new language. The language of our new entrepreneurial society should be a language in and of change: not only a language that can handle change, but a changing language. It should be able to interpret a culture (say, in a company), perceived primarily as consisting in language acts between people, and also, as far as is humanly possible, when necessary to develop our conventional language. In such language exercises there are, according to Ehn and Löfgren (1982) several things to keep in mind.

- To see everyday life as a problem of interpreting culture can undermine people's needs for safety and predictability. To concern oneself with interpreting culture can, therefore, be experienced as a threat and must be pursued with tact and care.
- Everyday reality is maintained, most of the time, without people actually being able to verbalize the basic ruling principles. Most of what is governing socially constructed reality cannot even be verbalized in retrospect. We cannot therefore, expect people to have any clear understanding of their cultural behaviour.
- Cultural interpretation is not a scientific process in the sense that every thought and step is ruled by logic, rationality and empirical safety. The analysis is often fragmented and uncertain. Such a situation has to be worked through, the process intensified, and new platforms for analysis built in order to see other patterns, for instance, reading a meeting as a soccer game between two teams.
- You should shift between different levels of thought, from the concrete to the abstract and back. As a member of a culture you are inevitably an insider, but you should as far as possible play the role of an outsider.
- It is useful to think in terms of analogies. Break out of habitual thinking by calling well-known things by other names. An imaginative language filled with images can revitalize an analysis. The key word is *as*. Envisage a company as a make of car ('Volvo' or 'Toyota') or a department as a season ('spring' or 'autumn').
- To look for synonyms means to look beneath the tip of the iceberg at the mass of connotations and associations which flourish in an often implicit way. By exchanging habitual words (such as 'manager', 'system' and 'strategy') thinking can move on to new tracks and provide a better understanding for that reality built on words.
- Everything should be seen as symbolic. Things, acts and concepts all represent something other than themselves. To see the symbolism in

what is taken for granted – how a room is furnished, how people dress, how coffee is served or how the order of a meeting is effected – will reveal the unthinking acceptance of so much of everyday life.

- Compare your working place with completely different places – a marathon race, a petrol station, a department store or a lecture theatre – and discuss similarities and differences. This can generate unexpected feelings of freedom and, thereby, new thinking.

Arbnor et al. (1980) offer four interesting principles as guidance in order to rid ourselves of our language dependence:

1. *Language cleaning.* The idea is to promote curiosity and reflection over what is taken for granted in language. It can be liberating to unmask hidden connotations in different terms, for instance:
   - We used to say 'unemployed' when somebody was out of work. Today we sometimes see the term 'released manpower'. Why?
   - When I buy commodities I am called a buyer. When I buy labour I am not called a 'labour buyer', but a 'work provider' or something else. Why?
   - Should not some data collection rather be called data construction?
   - Why are systems for managing insecurity called security systems?
2. *Language polarization.* By playing with opposites in parts of words, we realize how we have used them traditionally. Some examples ('in' is opposite to 'out', 'pro' is opposite to 'con'):

insight	outsight
outcome	income
protest	contest
conflict	proflict.

3. *Language shift.* All languages have a tendency to fix and justify their own existence with their own words. To get away from this means to try to see something *as* something else. We have talked about this several times.
4. *Language subjectification.* Our language – our present language – is hiding something. In our eagerness to be part of something, we have taken over this language, but it is taking us ever further from the acting subject. The consequence in many business settings is a scientific language ideal and a blind faith in an objective and neutral attitude which dissociates itself from all subjective acts and emotions. 'I' has become 'one', 'action' has become 'planning', 'understanding' has become 'analysis', 'agents of change' have become 'moments of uncertainty'. We can never step *outside* our own culture, but we can see it as something *between* us people. For the first time we should be able to create new business ventures as part of our everyday life!

SOME *GROWTH PICTURES*

This section presents some pictures of growth which were introduced in Bjerke and Hultman (2002) and summarized in Bjerke and Hultman (2003). First a few general concepts:

- I look at a *manager* as, basically, a person who practises a profession. Managers need technical skills in a wide sense, the skills to be able to run a business or part of it. They relate to their firm and its environment. Whether they do a good job or not is judged by the firm (and its owners).
- I look at a *leader* as a person who plays a role – which is to live up to expectations. Leaders need social skills in order to encourage other people to work. They relate to these other people – the followers – and it is the followers' judgement that determines whether they should be called a leader. We may need types of leaders in our new entrepreneurial society, but they are still role-based.
- I look at *entrepreneurship* as a mental disposition (a form of life) ('a meaningful lifestyle for many'; Thornton, 1999, p. 19). Entrepreneurs need mental skills. They relate to themselves, but they are judged by the users of the result of their efforts.

Why make this distinction between management, leadership and entrepreneurship? As I see it, as an understanding-oriented researcher, there are at least two reasons. First, Carson et al. (1995) have shown that entrepreneurship is, traditionally, intimately connected with 'good management'. Sexton and Bowman-Upton (1991), for instance, refer to an entrepreneur as 'a special kind of manager' and Peter Drucker believes in what he calls 'entrepreneurial management' (1985a). This may have been useful and relevant in the past, but in our new entrepreneurial society it is important to be aware that the extent of management, leadership and entrepreneurship needed in a company depends on the context.

Second, following from the first point, a company which is growing needs a different mix of management, leadership and entrepreneurship over time and depending on variable circumstances.

Three components or attitudes are necessary to an entrepreneurial disposition:

1. Everything is not perfect (if that would be the case, why do anything?).
2. There are many exciting opportunities to improve the condition of things.
3. *I* want to be part of implementing at least one of these opportunities.

To foster these three attitudes (not convey technicalities, nor train in roles) I see it as necessary when building up an entrepreneurship programme at a school to encourage entrepreneurship and foster it, not teach it or train it (I will come back to this in Chapter 8).

But to return to my growth pictures, I see two alternative courses of growth (these were discussed in the context of entrepreneurs as language makers in Chapter 4). They are illustrated in Figure 6.11. Cells 1–3, I call *managerial growth*. Only cell 4 is genuine *entrepreneurial growth*.

Let us further discuss the differences between managerial and entrepreneurial growth. First of all, we can consider two different sets of terms which are adequate in the two cases (Table 6.8; compare Table 4.3).

In *managerial growth*, it is important to plan united, structured systems, which are guided by business concepts. It is important to be efficient, utilize economies of scale, apply different standards, be financially successful and have educated managers in senior positions. In *entrepreneurial growth*, it is, on the other hand, important to learn from variations and act in processes which are guided by visions. It is important to change, to be committed in small ongoing units where surprises are welcome. Entrepreneurs act in these situations as leaders and support a purposeful business culture.

In relation to these two kinds of growth it is also possible to talk

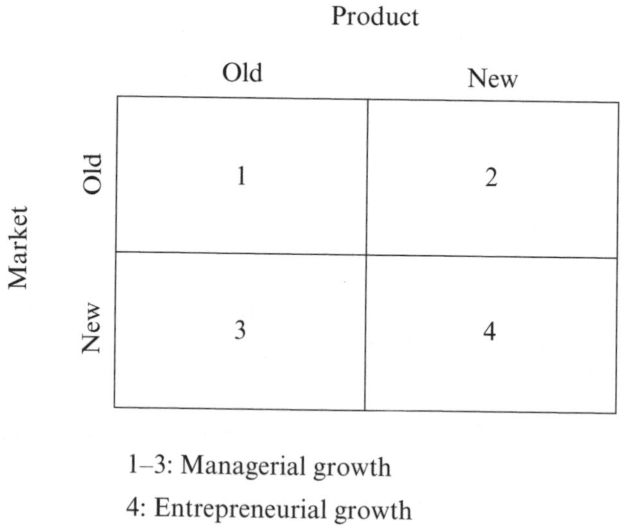

Product

	Old	New
Old	1	2
New	3	4

Market

1–3: Managerial growth

4: Entrepreneurial growth

Figure 6.11   Two alternative courses of growth

Table 6.8   Terminological pairs in two kinds of growth

Managerial growth	Entrepreneurial growth
Planning	Learning
Unity	Variety
Systems	Actors
Structures	Processes
Business concepts	Visions
Efficiency	Commitment
Economies of big scale	Economies of small scale
Standardizations	Surprises
Financial capital	Entrepreneurs
Education	Culture
Management	Leadership

Source: Bjerke and Hultman (2002, p. 150).

about two kinds of marketing, transactional marketing and relationship marketing:

1. *Transactional marketing* means planning and executing the conception of ideas, goods and services to create exchanges that satisfy individual and organizational objectives.
2. *Relationship marketing* means identifying and establishing, maintaining and deepening, and if necessary, ending relationships with customers (and other parties) in order to accomplish the economic and other goals of all parties. This is achieved through mutual exchange and by carrying out promises given.

And, again, two kinds of organizations, focal organizations and imaginary organizations:

1. *Focal organizations* (often called formal organizations) are clearly built up and consist of connections, often in hierarchies, between people and departments in specific firms and/or legal units.
2. *Imaginary organizations* (often called networks) consist of loosely related, constantly changing connections between members in different focal organizations as well as stand-alone individuals – connections, which in principle exist only as potentialities and can be realized only by those who feel that they are part thereof and who are strong enough to use them.

And two kinds of learning, exploitative learning and explorative learning:

1. *Exploitative learning* aims to create reliability in experience: to refine, routinize, come up with and apply knowledge (to learn more and understand more about what you already know). It usually leads to improvements, but is blind to important new directions.
2. *Explorative learning* aims to create variety in experience: to research, find something new, vary and innovate (to learn genuinely new things). It often leads to failure, but sometimes to important new directions and discoveries.

And two kinds of value-adding, value chains and value stars:

1. *Value chains* follow existing value-adding courses, adapting to existing connections between existing and incoming participants in market arenas.
2. *Value stars* build new value constellations and construct (or find) at least partly new connections between existing and incoming partici-pants in market arenas.

Figure 6.12 illustrates the connections between these five pairs of concepts.

Entrepreneurial growth and managerial growth can be seen as two stages in the growth of a single business venture. Let us simply call them *entre-preneurship* and *small business economics*. This is shown in Figure 6.13.

This can give us different growth patterns. Six such patterns are presented in Figure 6.14.

I call Pattern A in Figure 6.14 'The fledgling that didn't fly'. This means that even if the firm tried to achieve growth, it never happened. Perhaps the firm concentrated too much on transactional marketing and too little on relationship marketing, or tried to learn the wrong things at the wrong time. Perhaps it never understood its proper role in its value-adding constellation or perhaps, most importantly, it never really offered something new enough to the market.

Pattern B is called 'Icarus'. In Greek mythology Icarus and his father, Daedalus, escaped from imprisonment on an island using wings which Daedalus had made, holding the feathers together with wax. Ignoring his father's warning, Icarus flew too near to the sun. The wax on his wings melted and he fell into the sea and died. This could represent an entrepre-neur who never could become a manager (or enter a partnership with such a person). The entrepreneur was entrepreneurial for too long, applied too much relationship marketing for too long, and was never able to generate enough transactions to survive.

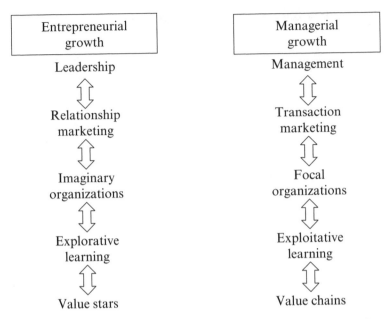

Figure 6.12   Different connections in entrepreneurial and managerial growth

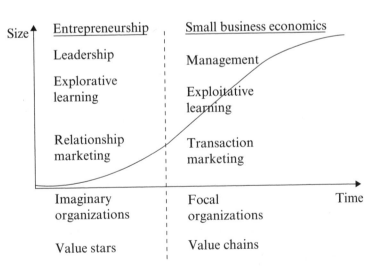

Figure 6.13   Entrepreneurship and small business economics – two stages in growth of a single business venture

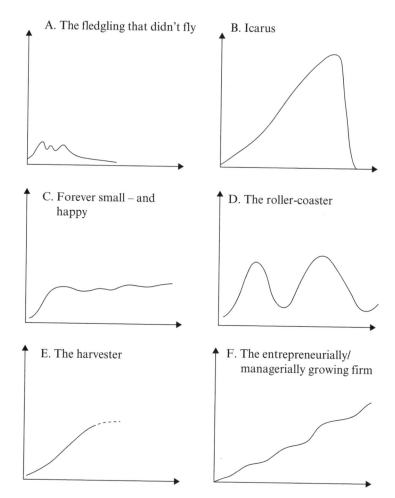

Figure 6.14   Six possible growth patterns

Most small firms resemble Pattern C, that is, 'Forever small – and happy'. They start their business by finding a market niche of their own. However, they lack the ambition to grow over a certain size, and concentrate on exploitative learning, their own focal firm, management and transactional marketing, occasionally applying a bit of explorative learning, networking, entrepreneurship and relationship marketing in order to survive.

'The roller-coaster' (Pattern D) is no good at timing various actions, applying each of the two sides of learning, focal and imaginary life, management and entrepreneurship, and each of the two kinds of marketing

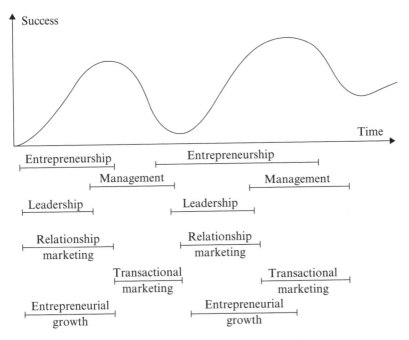

Figure 6.15   The roller-coaster

for too long, thereby running a very volatile and unstable firm. If there are any employees in the firm, labour turnover is probably very high.

Pattern E, that is, 'The harvester' is a bit like Pattern B ('Icarus') with a happier ending. The business was founded on a good idea, but the entrepreneur sold it to another, possibly bigger company, cashing in before things turned bad. What happened to the business after the firm was sold is not part of this pattern.

Pattern F, 'The entrepreneurially/managerially growing firm', is an excellent example of what can be done in our new entrepreneurial society, applying a well-balanced and timely mix of various types of learning, growth and marketing. It is about concentrating on explorative learning when necessary, on exploitative learning when necessary, on the imaginary organization when necessary, on the focal organization, when necessary, and so on.

Let us look at two of these patterns in further detail, that is, 'The roller-coaster' and 'The entrepreneurially/managerially growing firm'. Figure 6.15 shows the roller-coaster growth pattern together with some of our conceptual pairs. The horizontal bars in the figure are supposed to indicate periods when different activities, such as 'management' and 'relationship marketing', are focused on. Figure 6.15 shows that the firm is entrepreneurial for too

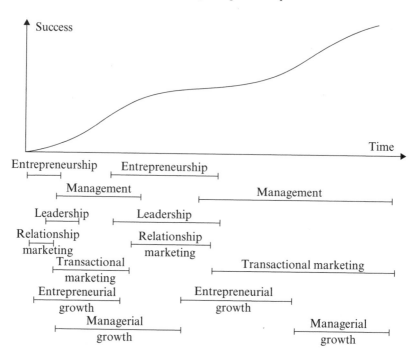

Figure 6.16   The entrepreneurially/managerially growing firm

long, management comes in too late, leadership should have come earlier the second time. Focusing on relationship marketing for too long and transactional marketing for not long enough leads to entrepreneurial growth only (when there is growth). Similarly, 'The entrepreneurially/managerially growing firm' is pictured in Figure 6.16. The figure shows good timing. Entrepreneurship is taken over by management, and relationship marketing by transactional marketing, before it is too late; entrepreneurship starts a second time even when the firm seems to be growing well, leadership coincides with entrepreneurship and there are consecutive periods of entrepreneurial and managerial growth.

7.   Entrepreneurship and regional development

THE INTEREST IN REGIONAL DEVELOPMENT TODAY

There exists today considerable interest in clusters, regions, regional development and so on, and in the role of entrepreneurship in such contexts. There are several reasons for this:

- During the 1970s, the conditions for economic development in industrialized countries changed dramatically. Previously it had been taken for granted that mass production gave winning advantages. Now this growth model ran into trouble (see, for instance, Nyström, 2002). The industrialized countries could no longer compete with low-cost countries when manufacturing standard products. Companies in the Western world instead had to compete through innovation, flexibility and productivity, which did not turn out to be easy for large companies. Small and medium-sized firms proved to be better at handling this situation in decentralized systems in geographically limited areas.
- In a globalized production and finance economy, countries' central governments have lost control of the flow of investments and labour. At the same time a more knowledge-intensive economy has developed. Regions supporting processes of learning and innovation have been identified as a key source of competitive advantage (MacKinnon et al., 2002).
- Localization has become a competitive factor. Thinking about competition and competitive strategy has previously been dominated by what goes on inside companies. Yet the prominence of clusters suggests that much of competitive advantage lies outside companies, residing in the locations at which their business units are based (Porter, 1998). Companies may actually benefit from having more local companies in the same business field as themselves, in spite of the tendency to believe that this will create more local competition, drive up input costs and make it more difficult to retain employees.

- Geographic concentration occurs because proximity serves to amplify productivity and innovation (Porter, 1998). Transaction costs are reduced, the creation and flow of information is improved and local institutions turn out to be more responsive to the specialized needs of companies, when there are more of them and peer pressure and competitive pressure are more keenly felt.

> Paradoxically, then, the enduring competitive advantages in a global economy are often heavily local, arising from concentrations of highly specialized skills and knowledge, institutions, rivals, and sophisticated customers in a particular nation or region. Proximity in geographic, cultural, and institutional terms allows special access, special relationships, better information, powerful incentives, and other opportunities for advantages in productivity and productivity growth that are difficult to tap from a distance. (Porter, 1998, p. 11)

- Knowledge is a non-rivalrous production factor which, when used more, will not lead to decreasing returns but can be used by a large number of actors at the same time. Several studies point out that knowledge-intensive production tends to organize itself in clusters (Braunerhjelm et al., 1998).

A BRIEF DESCRIPTION OF THE HISTORY OF RELEVANT THEORIES

Since the earliest days of industrialization similar types of operation have tended to locate in specific places. Groups of firms are established near each other and specific industries are concentrated in certain cities and regions. This was not particularly surprising given the need for proximity to different raw materials, energy sources in the form of coal, timber and water, and transportation. What is new today is that companies locate close to each other because it is valuable in itself. We can call this *localization as a means of competition*.

Alfred Marshall was the first specifically to recognize the mutual advantages that firms could obtain from proximity to each other, especially if they are small and medium-sized enterprises (Hansen, 2001). The idea was that a concentration of firms in close geographical proximity would allow all to benefit from large-scale industrial production and technical and organizational innovation which are beyond the scope of any individual firm. He described these concentrations as *industrial districts*.

Marshall (1898) focused on factors which determined the localization of industries; factors which are external to individual firms, but advantageous to those firms which are part of the district. Two such factors in his discussion were *agglomerations* and *externalizations* (another expression for this is '*spillover effects*').

Both these factors depend on decisions made by other firms in the same district. Effects of agglomerations originally discussed by Marshall include (Jonsson and Olander, 2000):

- the creation of a labour pool facilitating the recruitment of personnel;
- improvement in the coordination of different steps in the production process;
- stocks can be reduced as firms have quick access to suppliers;
- communication channels between business actors become more effective and less costly.

Later research has added some advantages from industrial districts, for instance, the dissemination of communication and access to ideas are improved, and the geographic concentration of a diverse knowledge base stimulates innovative activities.

As far as knowledge externalities in industrial districts goes there is a much-quoted passage by Marshall:

> When an industry has thus chosen a locality for itself, it is likely to stay there long; so great are the advantages which people following the skilled trade gets from near neighbourhood to one another. The mysteries of the trade become no mysteries; but are as if it were in the air. Good work is rightly appreciated, inventions and improvements in machinery, in processes and the general organization of the business have their merits promptly discussed; if one man starts a new idea, it is taken up by others and combined with suggestions of their own; and thus it becomes the source of further ideas. (Marshall, 1898, p. 271)

It has been pointed out that Marshall's industrial districts do not describe all types of dynamic regional economies, but it seems to be a general opinion that their basic ideas are suitable to many regions in both Europe and the United States (Håkanson, 2003).

Renewed interest in the significance of localized economies in industrial districts came about in the 1980s, largely due to the work of Piore and Sabel (1984) on the 'third Italy', which was a name they used to distinguish their topic from the old industrial area in northwest Italy and from the less developed area south of Rome. Instead of, as Marshall did, focusing on agglomeration models based on transaction costs, however, Piore and Sabel stressed flexible production backed up by wider social and institutional support. Similarly, Granovetter (1985) stressed the fact that a social structure and culture only comes about through proximity, through his concept of embeddedness (which we saw in Chapter 5), and which, as mentioned, points out the importance of collective and institutional grounds for successful coordination.

At about the same time there was another important contribution to the explanation of regional economic growth. Paul Romer (1986) presented a new growth theory and found that the divergence in growth rates may be the result of *increasing returns to knowledge*.

Michael Porter (1990), in his study on the competitiveness of nations, argues that many successful industries locate within a single town or region to such an extent that it is questionable whether the nation is a relevant unit of economic analysis. Instead it is more meaningful to look at regional units, where industries are connected in *clusters* in vertical and horizontal relationships. Porter suggests that successful regions operate in so-called 'diamonds', which has become a much quoted model. Any equitable history of theories of regional development must include this model (Figure 7.1). At the points of Porter's diamond are:

- *Factor conditions.* The situation of the region when it comes to production factors such as skilled labour or advanced infrastructure which are necessary to compete successfully.
- *Demand conditions.* The nature of home demand for the industry's product or service.
- *Related and supporting industries.* The presence or absence in the region of supplier industries and related industries which are internationally competitive.

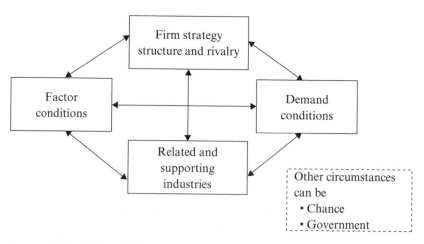

Source: Porter (1990, p. 127).

Figure 7.1   Regional success pattern

- *Firm strategy, structure and rivalry*. The conditions in the region governing how companies are created, organized and managed, and the nature of the domestic competition.

Examples of *chances* that can play a role in regional development according to Porter are:

- pure inventions
- breakthroughs in basic technologies (such as biotechnology, microelectronics)
- discontinuities in input costs, such as the oil crises
- significant shifts in the world's financial markets or exchange rates
- major shifts in market demand globally or regionally
- political decisions in foreign governments
- war.

Porter claims that *governments* can influence (and be influenced by) each of the four determinants in the diamond, either positively or negatively. However, he asserts that their influence can only be indirect.

Paul Krugman (1991) has a more active approach. He claims that even if regions have an advantage due to historical circumstances, they can keep their leadership only if they can use agglomeration and spillover effects together with consideration of the importance of transport costs and the size of different markets available.

Rosenberg et al. (1992) emphasize the importance of high technology for the wealth of nations. High technology is the result of research at tertiary institutes of technology and universities which is transferred to companies through higher education or has been developed by the companies themselves. The authors also emphasize the 'path dependency' in a region's development of a technology, that is, the tendency to continue on the technological path once an industry has invested in it to achieve its competence.

Maryann Feldman (1994) introduced the concept of 'regional technological infrastructure', which, in her opinion, contains four classes of factors which are required to complete a commercialization process: agglomeration effects and networks of firms in related industries, concentration of university R&D, concentrations of industrial R&D and networks of business service firms in close contacts with the market.

The available part of our total stock of knowledge in society seems to be correctly classified if it is assumed to have two portions (Acs, 2002): one perfectly accessible part consisting of already established knowledge elements (obtainable via scientific publications, patent applications and so on) and a novel, *tacit* element, accessible only by interactions between actors in an innovation system. The importance of the latter was pointed out in the 1960s by Michael Polanyi (Polanyi, 1966), but interest in the phenomenon grew with the discussions of regional development and the like in the 1990s. For example:

> The propensity for innovative activity to cluster spatially will be the greatest in industries where tacit knowledge plays an important role . . . it is tacit knowledge, as opposed to information, which can only be transmitted informally, and typically demands direct and repeated contact. (Audretsch, 1998, p. 23)

Implicit knowledge is unarticulated, highly contextual and can only be transmitted in face-to-face interaction or through individuals' physical movements. Access to tacit knowledge is obtained through embeddedness in local networks (Håkanson, 2003). That knowledge which is not tacit is called *codified*.

Innovation is seen here as a social process (Henton et al., 2002):

- it is interactive; it does not occur in a straight line;
- it is built on tacit knowledge through interaction and personal experiences;
- it takes place in networks based on trust, where key business agents participate;
- it works only when it tears down walls;
- it combines cooperation and competition;
- it is place-based.

In 1994, Saxenian presented her famous study on a comparison between Silicon Valley (a successful region in the United States) and Route 128 (a less successful region in the United States). She maintains (Saxenian, 1994) that Silicon Valley has been much more resilient and adaptable than Route 128. Despite similar origins and technologies, the two regions have evolved two different forms of industrial arrangements. Silicon Valley has an industrial system based on regional networks that promote entrepreneurship, collective learning, flexible adjustment and experimentation. Route 128, on the other hand, is dominated by a small number of relatively vertically-integrated corporations that by and large keep to themselves. A summary of Saxenian's results is seen in Table 7.1.

Bo Carlsson launched the concept of 'technological systems' in 1997 (Carlsson, 1997). He studied the interactions between the actors in a system of competence networks in markets and non-markets. He claims that the approach to public policy based on the theory of market failures is insufficient, since failures in networks, institutions and systems exist as well.

Table 7.1   A comparison between Silicon Valley and Route 128

Silicon Valley	Route 128
A technical culture which crosses over firms and functions	An industrial order which is based on individual firms
Less formal social relationships and cooperative traditions which support experimentations	Relationships between individuals and firms, where secrecy and territorialism rules
	Traditional hierarchies within firms
Firms organized as loosely coupled engineering teams	Distant – even antagonistic – relationships with local institutions
A flexible industrial structure which is organized around the region and its professional and technical networks rather than around individual firms	A number of independent firms, which lack social and commercial relationships with each other

Source: Saxenian (1994).

FOUR TYPES OF EXPLANATORY MODELS

Four types of explanatory models are discussed in relation to regional development:

1.   Agglomeration theories.
2.   Transaction cost theories.
3.   Neoinstitutional theories.
4.   Resource dependency theories.

Agglomeration theories show that cost reductions may result from shared infrastructure, such as communication and transportation facilities, and access to specialized labour and machinery and the like. In addition, consumer search costs may be reduced and spillover effects may occur as companies learn more quickly about new technologies and market opportunities. Increased returns and positive feedback may also arise as more companies join the region.

Transaction cost theories show that under conditions of uncertainty it may be most efficient to locate near your business partners. Spatial proximity facilitates firms' learning and increase the likelihood that they will react faster to suppliers and customers.

Neoinstitutional theories emphasize cognitive, regulatory and normative frameworks within which firms are located. Geographic closeness fosters a strong local culture which legitimizes homogeneous behaviour in interactions between people and firms:

- similarity through pressure exerted on organizations by other organizations
- similarity in order to reduce uncertainty
- similarity because members in the networks have the same education and backgrounds.

Resource dependency theories provide an alternative to neoinstitutional theories. They make it possible to explain 'deviant' competitive behaviour in those firms in a region that are able to influence their environment.

Neoinstitutional theories and resource dependency theories can be combined in a number of different business strategies (Figure 7.2).

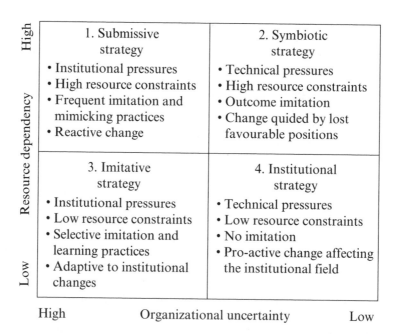

Source: Alberti (2002, p. 12).

Figure 7.2 Different strategies for firms in a region explained by neoinstitutional theories and resource dependency theories

CLUSTERS

The concept of the *cluster*, which has been mentioned already, has become very prominent during the past decade or so. It is possible to trace four, more or less overlapping, perspectives and uses of the cluster concept (Assmo, 2003):

- A model for explaining why a region is competitive within a certain industry in comparison to other regions.
- A perspective from which to describe and structure complex production systems in which actors in different ways form and support a manifold interconnected production structure, often within a more or less geographically concentrated area.
- A tool for regional planning.
- A model for social networks, which are thriving through social capital.

But we have many names for the things we love. Instead of clusters, we may talk about industrial districts, local/regional industrial environments, local business venturing for global use, competence blocks, learning regions or districts of excellence. Further:

Clusters are defined as production of similar products and services in a geographically well-defined area. Unlike branch and industry definitions, clusters are usually composed by firms from several branches and are characterized by a differentiated supply of products as well as services. (Braunerhjelm et al., 1998, p. 420; my translation)

Cluster is partially replacing the old concepts of sector (for instance, service sector) and branch (for instance, graphic industry). Sector is today too broad and branch classifications are too narrow. A cluster is branch-transgressing. The purpose of thinking and acting in clusters is to start a dynamic interaction between firms in a common strategic knowledge area and interaction between these firms and other actors concerned (educators, research, regional and local community institutions). If we turn to international experiences and research, we can say that cluster is a holistic approach to work with growth, development of regional innovation and profiling, where different actors are working with different parts. ('Regionala vinnarkluster', 2001, p. 14; my translation)

A cluster is a critical mass of companies in a particular field in a particular location, whether it is a country, a state or region, or even a city. Clusters take varying forms depending on their depth and sophistication, but most include a group of companies, suppliers of specialized inputs, components, machinery, and services, and firms in related industries. Clusters also often include firms in downstream (e.g., channel, customer) industries, producers of complementary products, specialized infrastructure providers and other institutions that provide specialized

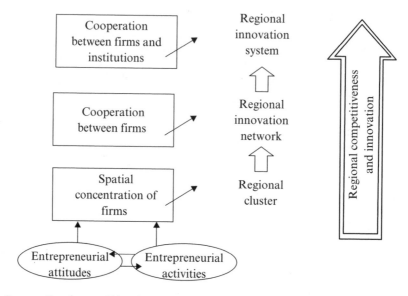

Source: Sternberg and Litzenberger (2003, p. 2).

Figure 7.3   Three hierarchical cluster levels

training, education, information, research, and technical support, such as universities, think tanks, vocational training providers, and standard-setting agencies. Finally, many clusters include associations and other collective bodies covering cluster members. (Porter, 1998, p. 10)

It is possible to separate three hierarchical cluster levels (Figure 7.3).

The idea behind clusters may also be structured in a theoretical taxonomy (Table 7.2).

A few comments are worth making in this context:

- Which type of region is relevant when studying the regional anchorage of entrepreneurship depends on which factors are influencing the existence of entrepreneurship in the region. Is it natural conditions, the history of the region or the local culture that are playing the crucial roles (Nilsson, 2002, p. 202)?
- Cluster is not purely a high-technology phenomenon. Clusters occur for many types of industry, such as textiles in Georgia, fashion goods in Milan, diamond cutting in Belgium and scientific pens and pencils in Nuremberg (Cooper and Folta, 2000, p. 348).
- Even if localization in a cluster may be important for all firms, it appears to have particular implications for start-ups and small firms.

Table 7.2   Cluster roles – a theoretical taxonomy

	Spatial logic	
	Territorial approach	Network approach
Cognitive logic		
Functional approach	Cluster	Interconnection
	Diversification and specialization of activities	Cluster as a node in multiple and interactive technological, communication and economic networks
	Concentration of externalities	
	Density of proximity contacts	
	Concentration of tacit knowledge	Cluster as interconnection between place and node
	Reduction of transaction costs	
Symbolic approach	Milieu	Symbol
	Substrate of collective learning	Cluster as a 'landmark' for an innovative region
	Uncertainty-reducing operator through:	Cluster as a status symbol for local or regional promotion agencies and politicians
	• information transcoding	
	• ex-ante co-ordination of private decisions (collective action)	Cluster as a producer of symbols and codes for 'change towards a brighter future' and as 'change agent'
Normative approach	Learning region	International competitiveness
	Promotion of regional innovation and production systems (RIPS)	Ranking of international technological centres of excellence
	Support of higher educational system (HES) to foster human capital	Support of incubator centres, start-up or spin-off firms
	Information and mobilizing platform for local and regional actors of small size clusters	International promotion platforms of locations and cluster competencies

Source: Dümmler and Thierstein (2003, p. 426).

These are unlikely to have all the resources that they need in-house and often lack credibility as well as experience. These may be easier to acquire by locating in a cluster (Cooper and Folta, 2000, p. 349).

Clusters rarely appear out of nowhere. A local pioneer usually provides the spark that sets off the process (*Metro*, 2001)

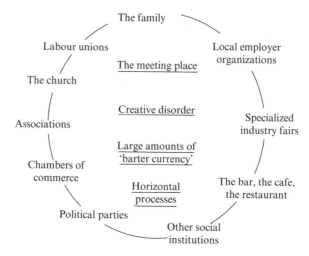

Source: Normann (2001, p. 302).

Figure 7.4 The Italian small business clusters

1. *The pioneer stage.* A single individual gets a successful business idea.
2. *Spinoffs by imitation.* The success of the first company simulates others to start similar companies and employees leave to start on their own.
3. *Creating local business networks.* The companies start to exchange products and services. Information and knowledge are spread between them.
4. *Creating a local culture.* When the companies become numerous enough they start to make an impact on the region. Education and infrastructure are adapted to the companies.
5. *The region becomes a brand.* Sometimes the cluster may become so big that the region itself becomes part of the brand of the companies – for instance, Hollywood.

An example of the intimacy that may exist between different actors in a cluster can be seen in the Italian small business clusters as shown in Figure 7.4.

SILICON VALLEY – AN IDEAL MODEL?

Many commentators are of the opinion that Silicon Valley is one of the best examples of a successful region. Here are ten of its 'secrets for success':

1. *Failure is tolerated.* Having been bankrupt is almost seen as a merit; as a necessary step towards credibility. This attitude may be the region's major strength.

2. *Unfaithfulness is tolerated.* Silicon Valley is not known for traditional loyalty. To jump from one company to another and to exchange secrets is one of the recipes for success.

3. *Risk-seeking.* A venture capitalist in Silicon Valley calculates 20 investments the following way: four will go bankrupt, six will lose money, six will go OK, three will go well . . . and one will win the jackpot.

4. *Reinvest.* The enormous cash flow that is generated in Silicon Valley is, by and large, reinvested.

5. *Enthusiasm for change.* 'Only the paranoid survive' is a traditional slogan (which is associated with Intel's legendary chairman Andy Grove). Cannibalism is the key.

6. *Support merit.* There are wide opportunities for women and immigrants in Silicon Valley, they say. An understatement! If women and immigrants did not come there, they may as well close the place down. Generally things are moving so fast that politics is of hardly any practical importance. No small thing in itself!

7. *Fixation with the product.* In Silicon Valley, they always think of the latest, the coolest. The innovators love their product.

8. *Cooperation.* Generations last for months. Sometimes for weeks. The answer: mix the latest with the tried and tested borrowed from all and sundry.

9. *Variation.* There are lots of things going on all the time – most are gone rather quickly.

10. *Anybody can play.* The old American dream has come alive again in Silicon Valley. Everybody who lives in the Valley thinks he or she can be rich. Maybe it is an exaggeration. But not too much of one.

It is not simply the concentration of skilled labor, suppliers and information that distinguish the region. A variety of regional institutions – including Stanford University, several trade associations and local business organizations, and a myriad of specialized consulting, market research, public relations, and venture capital firms – provide technical, financial, and networking services which the region's enterprises often cannot afford individually. These networks defy sectoral barriers: individuals move easily from semiconductor to disk drive firms and from computer to network makers. They move from established firms to start-ups (or vice versa) and even to market research or consulting firms, and from consulting firms back into start-ups. And they continue to meet at trade shows, industry conferences, and the scores of seminars, talks, and social activities organized by local business organizations and trade associations. In these forums, relationships are easily formed and maintained, technical and market information is exchanged, business contacts are established, and new enterprises are conceived ... This decentralized and fluid environment also promotes the diffusion of technological capabilities and understandings. (Saxenian, 1994, pp. 96–7)

A successful region in Sweden is Gnosjö. According to Johansson (2001) some central concepts for the Gnosjö spirit are:

- It is concentrated into three clusters – metal, plastics and machinery – which together account for more than 40 per cent of employment there.
- There is cooperation as well as competition.
- Many companies are suppliers to large industries in the country, such as car manufacturers and engineering, which sometimes means that the companies compete for the same order.
- Cooperation means buying from, borrowing from or using each other as sub-suppliers.
- Everybody is positive towards the development of business networks, which are created by business connections and personal relationships.
- It is based on well-developed social capital with a very positive attitude towards business venturing.

If we compare Silicon Valley and Gnosjö, we can state the following (Johannisson, 2002, pp. 139–43):

1. *Role in the global economy.* The technological innovations of Silicon Valley have strongly contributed to changing global society, above all within information technology. Gnosjö has proven its role as a successful centre for industrial development, but not at the global level.
2. *Key resources.* In Silicon Valley the key resource is knowledge capital at a high level. The educational level in Gnosjö is, on average, lower, but it is compensated with a kind of confidence capital (social capital) for creating and spreading knowledge.
3. *Organization of competence.* In Silicon Valley as in Gnosjö, the competence has been organized locally and regionally. In Silicon Valley you can get access to this competence, if you have an idea to test. In Gnosjö the local knowledge bank is opened if you can demonstrate your solidarity.
4. *Focus of learning processes.* What you can learn in Silicon Valley is high technology, above all information technology. In Gnosjö the technical development is not that high, but equally fast. There, learning is dominated by what could be described as ingenuity and shrewdness.

5. *Geographic mobility, industrial dynamism and social variation.* Silicon Valley is characterized by high mobility between firms and across the borders of the region. In Gnosjö the opposite is the case. In Gnosjö, however, social mobility relates to a way of life, between being employed and becoming your own boss.

6. *Attractiveness.* Silicon Valley offers nature, climate and a spirit of creativity and freedom. Gnosjö has long been admired for its vital small business venturing and its, by and large, total lack of unemployment.

7. *Infrastructure of networks.* In Silicon Valley and in Gnosjö networking between firms and other actors plays a decisive role in the development of the region. In Silicon Valley this is run by what we could call individual calculative ambitions. In Gnosjö networking mirrors a more collective capital.

8. *Dominant institutions.* As far as formal structures are concerned, economic institutions dominate in Silicon Valley, while the social networks in Gnosjö have been generated by and continue to generate formal institutions such as free churches, sports organizations and business associations. The basic systems of the informal institutions also differ.

9. *Entrepreneurship.* Dense, regional environments generally generate different forms of partnership. Team entrepreneurship is common in Silicon Valley. Gnosjö can be characterized as a kind of collective entrepreneurship, that is, business venturing in a wide sense, which is less tied to individual firms.

10. *Identity.* Silicon Valley rests on 'the American dream' and its entrepreneurial values. In Gnosjö they want to show that they can 'do what is impossible in other parts of the country'.

11. *Variation.* Variation is big in both Silicon Valley and Gnosjö, although the information and communication industries dominate in Silicon Valley and plastics and engineering industries dominate in Gnosjö.

Many commentators claim that the business climate is generally more progressive in the US than in Sweden. Still on the subject of regions, Braunerhjelm et al. (1998) saw the following advantages in the American clusters, when comparing biochemical and polymer clusters in Sweden and Ohio:

- established links between researchers, industry and potential financiers exist;
- applied research has priority (important basic research is bought);
- supply of venture capital is much broader and more competent in the sense that money is followed by available management and marketing competence;

- there is access to a great number of so-called 'business angels', that is, private persons who want to become venture financiers;
- mechanisms for introducing new products and/or services on the market are more developed;
- a clear reward structure exists for successful entrepreneurs.

SUCCESSFUL REGIONS

The driving forces underpinning successful regions are considered by Mascanzoni and Novotny (2000), *Entreprenör* (2003), *Metro* (2001), Berggren and Brulin (1985) and Johannisson (2002). Among their proposals are:

- *Access to labour*. The more companies there are in the same industry in one place, the greater are the chances of recruiting competent labour.
- *Locomotive companies*. Something like 'hidden champions', these are centres which coordinate the production of a large number of companies in the region and work at the front of the value-added chain. It is important to keep them!
- *Coordination*. When companies in the same industry are agglomerating, they start to buy from and sell to each other, develop new ideas and increase the competence in the cluster at large.
- *Rivalry*. If the toughest competitor is located across the street, it seems to stimulate more rivalry than if it is invisible.
- *Variations*. Including other activities of a social and cultural kind in dense local networks.
- *A demanding home market* which hones the companies' ability.
- *Societal service*. Schools, development centres and the like.

According to Normann (2001) the crucial question is: How to become a good home for value creation activities? He presents a list of desiderata for successful regions (pp. 313–14):

- they should be nerve centres to some locomotive companies,
- there should be clusters of different kinds and sizes around these internationally competitive locomotive companies,
- they should be the home of some highly competitive knowledge-intensive service companies, since these now lead the development of an economy,

- physical and informational infrastructures should be of a high standard,
- there should be a high quality of life for 'global knowledge entrepreneurs', including in areas such as health care, culture, ecology and nature,
- there should probably be a high proportion of people from unconventional business circles, such as entrepreneurial immigrants and women, involved with business innovation and new start-ups,
- there should be several meeting-places for exchanging tacit knowledge, both within industry clusters and across various areas of society including between industry, culture and politics,
- people move from one context to another at the same time as they change the way they organize themselves,
- there should be a high degree of reconfigurability,
- there should be a high level of quality of the 'strategic conversation' and probably an informal but effective 'strategic management coalition' between actors from all areas of society,
- there should be experiments going on to break taboos and boundaries with regard to traditionally structured areas such as welfare services,
- there should be a high degree of externalization of support functions for city services in infrastructure, education, health care and so on, as well as a certain level of 'outsourcing' of such services to international players,
- the area should be recognized as one in which aesthetic and cultural issues are particularly high priorities and there should be a range of people from around the world visiting for this reason.

Some 'buts' added to common proposals as to content in successful regions:

- They should be guided by a vision, *but* this should not be pronounced as *one* vision and it should be shared by the people who live and work in the region.
- Key actors should be involved in the development, *but* they should be there with their brain (understanding), heart (wishing) as well as their stomach (daring).
- There should be lots of networks, *but* they should overlap and intersect with each other, not consist only of friends and camaraderies.
- There should be locomotive companies, *but* they should be admired and talked about with pride.

- There should be lots of entrepreneurship, *but* within all sectors of society, not only among business firms.
- There are many proposals for what should be contained in a successful region, *but* timing is very important. The situation should rather be compared with baking a soufflé than baking a sponge cake (Nilsson, 2002, p. 204).

TECHNOLOGY AND SCIENCE PARKS

There are many technology and science parks, that is, formal arrangements for cooperation between industry and higher educational institutions, being built in countries like Sweden today. This could be because such countries are over-dependent on their large corporations. In some places in Sweden, for instance, employment is totally dependent on one Swedish (and increasingly foreign-owned) branch of a multinational corporation. It is striking to note that where these employers dominate there are conspicuously few spinoffs, no positive attitudes to entrepreneurship and no stable ownership, which could secure employment (Jonsson et al., 1996).

To compensate for this, to avoid a drain of knowledge to other parts of a country and to ensure that the potential for regional growth will benefit the local communities, regions in many advanced societies (above all where universities and tertiary institutes are situated) have established (and continue to establish) such technology and science parks. The main aim is to stimulate the regional economy by attracting investment from outside and to encourage more start-ups of small firms (Lindelöf, 2002). Some functions attributed to technology and science parks are:

- To facilitate industrial cooperation and technology transfer between trade and industry and universities/tertiary institutes;
- To facilitate the creation of new firms;
- To provide a good locality for academicians who want to commercialize their scientific results;
- To support synergy between firms;
- To support economic development for localized firms.

A name sometimes given to a functioning cooperation between trade and industry, knowledge centres such as universities, educational and research institutes, and society as local, regional, national and/or supranational resource for knowledge-based innovation is a *triple-helix-constellation* (Ylinenpää, 2002).

LEARNING REGIONS AND ENTREPRENEURIAL CITIES

One concept which is relevant to this chapter is that of *learning regions*. There are differences of opinion about the meaning of the term, but the following provides a reasonable summary (Maillat and Kebir, 2001):

- Non-material resources are basic in our modern entrepreneurial economy. More emphasis is placed on constructed resources (skills, know-how, qualifications, but also methods of doing and acting) than on natural resources.
- These constructed resources cannot, however, be learnt once and for all. Different actors (firms, organizations, regions) must constantly keep them up to date, reproduce them and process them.
- Maintaining competitive advantage follows from the creation of non-material resources which are constructed through learning processes.
- The concept of 'learning economy' (for instance in a region) provides the theoretical basis for understanding a context in which change takes priority over the allocation of resources and in which knowledge and learning processes occupy a central position. The learning economy is a dynamic concept which highlights the ability to learn and to expand the knowledge base.
- The concept of learning economy refers not only to the importance of the science and technology systems, universities, research organizations, R&D departments, and so on, but also to the learning implications of the economic structure, organizational forms and institutional set-up.
- It is the ability of firms as well as regions and countries to learn, change and adapt rather than their allocative efficiency which determines their long-run performance.
- In a learning economy, the competitive advantages of firms and regions are based on their ability to innovate.
- In a globalized context and one of competition between regional systems, it is accepted that innovation has become a permanent necessity and that therefore the actors cannot act alone. They must cooperate in order to benefit from their complementary competencies.
- In a learning region, the economic model is no longer focused on the allocation of resources and exchanges; it is a system which integrates learning and change. One could even say that externalities linked to a region no longer suffice to explain the significance of proximity. They

are the result of involuntary actions. What counts is the partners' deliberate will to cooperate, to achieve projects together.

- The concept of learning regions makes sense where companies are interested in and willing to develop their ability to learn and intend to use this ability.
- Four processes are important in a learning region: (1) interactive learning (learning to cooperate), (2) organizational learning (learning one's own role in the region), (3) institutional learning (the ability of institutions to question themselves, to adapt their structures and objectives and to regenerate themselves in line with the changes in the environment), and (4) to learn the ability to learn.

Another current concept of relevance here is that of the *entrepreneurial city* (Hubbard and Hall, 1998; Czarniawska and Solli, 2001):

1. The idea that the modern city is organized and managed differently is heard more and more. One talks increasingly about a 'new urban politics'.
2. The new urban politics is distinguished from the old by virtue of the ways in which the policies pursued by local governments are being steered away from the traditional activities associated with cities and urban districts. A reorientation takes place through a shift from the local provision of welfare and services to more outward-orientated policies designed to foster and encourage local growth and economic development.
3. These policies are supported and financed by a large number of urban districts and local offices and institutions, which try as best they can to encourage growth on its own terms.
4. The concept of the entrepreneurial city is here to stay.

SOME FINAL QUESTIONS

I would like to pose five critical questions at the end of this chapter:

1. What is an industrial region?
2. How important is entrepreneurship to an industrial region?
3. Is it possible to successfully build an industrial region top-down?
4. Is it possible to successfully pick the geese that will lay the golden eggs to be part of the industrial region?
5. How to humanize visions, networks, ideals and systems in an industrial region?

1. What is an industrial region?

- There are many who claim that what is happening when specific senior actors get together is that industrial regions are constructed rationally using plans, decisions and coordinated action. An alternative (and in my opinion more fruitful) view is the social constructionistic one (compare Alberti, 2003). An industrial region gradually comes into existence through repeated discussion and materializes as names and labels come to be given to events and activities that take place and by endorsing supportive organizations with the name of the region (Berg, 2001).
- One is 'invoking' (Berg, 2001) and one 'makes sense of' (Weick, 1995) the region in such a way.
- An industrial region then becomes a sense of belonging (Alberti, 2003), a way of thinking, a discourse and an epistemic community (Håkanson, 2003) more than anything else.

2. How important is entrepreneurship to an industrial region?

- As I see it, entrepreneurship is crucial for the success of the industrial region. Nothing happens if nobody acts. Entrepreneurship is, after all, about coming up with things that the environment can use.
- However, one should look at entrepreneurship in all varieties that exist in the modern society. It appears (or should appear) in all sectors of society, that is, in the public, private and voluntary sectors.

3. Is it possible to successfully build an industrial region top-down?

- Industrial districts have almost exclusively been studied and treated as objective phenomena, on the assumption that it is possible to identify the crucial parameters that are necessary to succeed and then work (hard) to apply them (Acs, 2002).
- Human abilities such as will-power, passion and empathy have hardly been considered at all. Social capital is assumed to be produced by formal institutions, which generate trust and absorb uncertainty (Hjorth and Johannisson, 2002).
- A more realistic alternative is to discover the unique, organic conditions existing in an industrial region and then to support and participate in dialogues in creative and constructive networks, where key actors move forward together.
- The enabling role of authorities then becomes more important than the task of providing service (Karlsson et al., 2001).

- Industrial regions (and clusters) are extremely difficult (or impossible) to create from the outside or top-down. Existing regions have a history and have taken time to develop, from within and bottom-up.

4.   Is it possible to successfully pick the geese that will lay the golden eggs to be part of the industrial region?

- Too many power-holders in incubators, industrial villages and local community institutions believe they can decide beforehand which types of industries ('they shall belong to the future') and business firms ('they shall have a growth potential') should be included in their region, and also that they can pick out those that will be most successful.
- This conflicts with everything we think we know about how innovation works. Innovative processes cannot be planned, they behave in a random, almost arbitrary way and they are practically unpredictable.
- The task is rather to do one's best in an industrial region to create even more turbulence, even more variety, to 'let a thousand flowers bloom'. Participating actors then have the best conditions in which gradually to build something which is meaningful and sustainable.

5.   How to humanize visions, networks, ideals and systems in an industrial region?

- People interpret their belonging (or lack of belonging) in an industrial region in different ways, which may seem coherent and meaningful only to themselves (people are 'embedded' in their social context). There are, however, several problems associated with the dominant, super-rational view on how to develop successful industrial regions (Hjorth and Johannisson, 2002):
    - There is a need for a gradualist approach and social constructionism.
    - One should listen to local 'storytellers'.
    - One needs a local 'worldview'.
    - One should study local history.
    - One should invoke and make sense of a collective identity.

8. Can entrepreneurship be taught?

IT HAS ALL EXPLODED RECENTLY

Although entrepreneurship education has existed at university level for more than fifty years, it is, as a wider practice, a relatively young and emerging discipline. And the past 20 years have witnessed an enormous growth in the number of small business management and entrepreneurship courses at different educational institutions around the world.

According to Alberti et al. (2005), entrepreneurship education was pioneered by Shigeru Fijii, who started teaching in this field in 1938 at Kobe University in Japan. In the United States, the first entrepreneurship course was introduced by Myles Mace at Harvard Business School in 1947 (Katz, 2003). Half a century later this phenomenon gained a more universal recognition (Dana, 1992).

The total number of universities offering courses in entrepreneurship seems to be more than 1600 worldwide (Katz, 2003), of which more than half are in the United States alone (Fiet, 2001). However, European governments are also recognizing entrepreneurship as a resource to be cultivated. This is true also in post-communist Eastern Europe (Dana, 2005). Business schools in Asia have launched programmes in entrepreneurship as well as new journals and scientific publications addressing entrepreneurship issues (Dana, 2001). However, in spite of the fact that China and India have proven themselves as entrepreneurs in practice, entrepreneurship is still a relatively new field in education in these countries (Li et al., 2003).

There are, no doubt, pressures for greater individual and collective entrepreneurial behaviour, and thereby education, at all levels in our new entrepreneurial society (Gibb, 2005). Examples of pressures at the global level are:

- constant political realignments,
- the reduction of trade barriers,
- the growth of information and communication technologies opening up the world to the individual,
- growing lifestyle choices,
- the impact of massive international capital flows.

Examples of pressures at the societal level are:

- public spending reductions,
- privatization of public services,
- deregulation,
- increasing business involvement in partnership with governments,
- new forms of governance involving non-governmental organizations (NGOs).

Examples of pressures at the organizational level are:

- decentralization,
- re-engineering,
- more partnerships and strategic alliances,
- increasing importance of the human knowledge base of a firm.

Examples of pressures at the individual level are:

- a work environment with greater career and occupational mobility and job uncertainty,
- greater probability of part-time and contract employment,
- more pressure for geographic mobility,
- stronger prospects for self-employment.

HOW MUCH TO TEACH AND TO WHOM?

The title of this chapter is 'Can entrepreneurship be taught?' The debate about this question has been going on for years. There are those who state clearly that the answer is 'Yes!' Peter Drucker said (Drucker, 1985b) that entrepreneurship 'is not magic', 'it is a discipline' and can be learned like any discipline. Not surprisingly, most entrepreneurship scholars seem to agree that entrepreneurship can be learned – and taught. The argument might be that entrepreneurship education would generate more and better entrepreneurs than there have been in the past (Ronstadt, 1985) or that education would increase the chances of obtaining entrepreneurial success (Kirby, 2002).

Nevertheless, there has been very little empirical proof of the positive impact of education on entrepreneurship and entrepreneurial success (Storey, 1994) and very few studies have shown proof of the positive impact of entrepreneurship education on the development of entrepreneurial skills and values (McMullan et al., 2001).

Perhaps one could say that it is possible successfully to learn as well as to teach entrepreneurship but it is necessary to clarify under what circumstances this education takes place and what we mean by success. Questions to ask when considering good or bad teaching of entrepreneurship include:

- What are the educational objectives?
- Who are the students?
- How much of the entrepreneurship/small business management range should be included?
- To what extent should we ask the students actually to start a venture during or after joining an educational programme?
- What are the teaching techniques and pedagogy used?
- What dimensions should be included when we assess the effect of the educational programme?

All these will have a bearing on the entrepreneurship teaching programme. Let us explore them as we move on in this chapter.

According to Alberti et al. (2005), the most commonly cited objectives of entrepreneurship education are (Curran and Stanworth, 1989; Block and Stumpf, 1992; Garavan and O'Cinneide, 1994):

- *To acquire knowledge germane to entrepreneurship.* To gain knowledge, concepts and techniques about some specific area or discipline related to entrepreneurship.
- *To acquire skills in the use of techniques, in the analysis of business situations and in the synthesis of action plans.* To promote the skills of analysis and synthesis of entrepreneurship in a holistic way.
- *To identify and stimulate entrepreneurial drive, talent and skill.* To increase individuals' awareness of new venture career possibilities and support them in developing such possibilities.
- *To undo the risk-averse bias of many analytical techniques.* To counter this bias and to find progressive solutions.
- *To develop empathy and support for the unique aspects of entrepreneurship.* To help individuals understand and learn concepts related to entrepreneurship.
- *To revise attitudes towards change.* To educate people on how to encourage their subordinates to innovate.
- *To encourage new start-ups and other entrepreneurial ventures.* To stimulate in fostering new ventures, self-employment and entrepreneurial oriented careers.
- *To stimulate the 'affective socialization element'.* To inculcate attitudes, values, psychological mindsets and strategies necessary for taking on the entrepreneurial role.

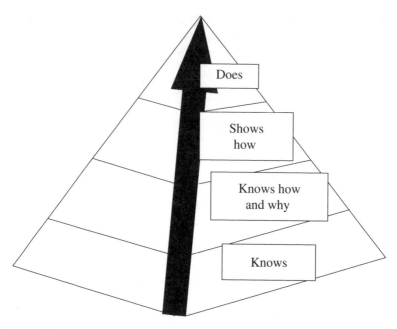

Source: Adapted from Miller (1990).

Figure 8.1   What should participants in an entrepreneurial programme learn?

In more general terms, any competence-based learning should enable an individual to climb one or several stages of a pyramid (Figure 8.1). Thus, a programme for teaching entrepreneurship can stop at trying to transfer knowledge of what entrepreneurship is or go all the way to trying to teach how to do something entrepreneurially (or to any stage in between).

Another aspect related to the objectives of an entrepreneurial programme is whether it should focus on only the set-up stage or include techniques for surviving (the small business management stage) as well (Figure 8.2; compare Figure 6.13). Which objectives to adopt will influence the design and implementation of the entrepreneurial programme. So will the students. They could be (Alberti et al., 2005):

- entrepreneurs
- managers
- entrepreneurial sympathizers
- scholars
- people willing to develop their entrepreneurial spirit.

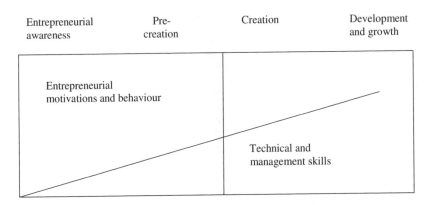

Source: Duchéneaut (2001, p. 137).

Figure 8.2   Progression of motivations and behaviour/technical skills through phases surrounding company creation

Table 8.1   Two learning systems

The classroom learning system
1. Receiving information through a symbolic medium such as a book or lecture.
2. Assimilating and organizing information so that the general principle is understood.
3. Being able to infer a particular application from the general principle.
4. Moving from the cognitive and symbol-processing sphere to the sphere of action.

The experiential learning system
1. Carrying out an action in a particular instance and seeing the effects of the action.
2. Understanding the effects in a particular instance.
3. Understanding the general principle under which the particular instance falls.
4. Applying the concept through action in a new circumstance within the range of generalization.

Source: Coleman (1979).

It is not difficult to understand that there is a tremendous variation in the way entrepreneurial programmes are designed and implemented. Bill Bygrave, the Director of Entrepreneurial Studies at Babson College, said in 1993 (according to Fiet, 2001, p. 83), that there are two ways to spoil an entrepreneurship course. One is to have it to consist entirely of the practical application and analysis of cases. The other is to have it to be entirely

Table 8.2   *Teaching methods: characteristics of 'didactic' and*
'entrepreneurial' models

Didactic model	Enterprising model
Learning from teacher alone	Learning from each other
Passive role as listener	Learning by doing
Learning from written texts	Learning from personal exchange and debate
Learning from 'expert' frameworks of teacher	Learning from discovering (under guidance)
Learning from feedback from one key person (the teacher)	Learning from reaction of many people
Learning in well organized, timetabled environment	Learning in flexible, informal environment
Learning without pressure of immediate goals	Learning under pressure to achieve goals
Copying from others discouraged	Learning by borrowing from others
Mistakes feared	Mistakes learned from
Learning by notes	Learning by problem solving

Source: Gibb (1992, p. 24).

theory. I agree. Most likely a mix of two learning systems are required for a good entrepreneurship education (Table 8.1).

On the pedagogical side, however, it is likely that most entrepreneurship education programmes tend towards the right-hand column in Table 8.2.

This whole discussion also hinges, of course, on what we mean by success in an entrepreneurial programme. In general, there are different viewpoints from which to evaluate the performance of an entrepreneurship programme (McMullan and Gillin, 2001):

- *For the economy*
  The likelihood of graduates starting a business
  Early indications of business outcome in terms of employment, sales and perhaps even choice of industry
- *For the individual*
  Earnings
  Capital gains
  Non-tangible aspects such as enhanced job satisfaction
- *For the programme*
  Is the entrepreneurship programme growing in terms of number of graduates, international recognition and financial success?

Is new knowledge being generated?
Has there been any diffusion of the programme elsewhere?

Still, evaluation of any entrepreneurship educational programme will remain heterogeneous due to a number of factors characterizing entrepreneurship education (Alberti et al., 2005). These include:

- Target groups.
- University/school vs entrepreneurship education/training focus.
- Objectives of entrepreneurship education.
- Levels of analysis.
- Time dimension.

SOME EXAMPLES OF ENTREPRENEURSHIP EDUCATION PROGRAMMES

Let us look at some examples of entrepreneurship education programmes in order to illustrate variety and perspectives.

A Graduate Degree Programme in Entrepreneurship Offered at Swinburne University of Technology in Australia

Here the focus is on a very specific, clearly-defined and well-motivated group of participants; if you have a group of people clearly on their way to becoming entrepreneurs, you can help them; which is proven by the fact that the authors of the chapter from which I have used the Swinburne programme here – McMullan and Gillin, 2001 – claim that 87 per cent of the participants in the programme have started a business of their own. Some aspects of this programme follow:

- It is a three-year programme:
- *Year one*
  Semester 1: entrepreneurial organization opportunity, evaluation techniques.
  Semester 2: new venture marketing and commercializing innovation.
- *Year two*
  Semester 3: innovation, creativity and leadership, managing the growing business.
  Semester 4: new venture financial planning, the business plan.
- *Year three*
  Semester 5: growth venture evaluation, advanced business plan, entrepreneurial research project 1.

Semester 6: strategic intent and corporations, advanced business plan 2, entrepreneurial research project 2.

- From year two, courses are taught by teams typically consisting of one academic practitioner and one practitioner academic.
- Students are selected, by interview, for their entrepreneurial potential; qualities looked for are:
  level of responsibility attained in their career to date
  their apparent commitment to entrepreneurship
  evidence of creative and/or lateral thinking.
- Experiential learning is achieved through active participation of students in 'live' and relevant growth ventures in conjunction with appropriate reading.
- Students are directed to begin searching for opportunities early in their first term.

A German View on the Theory and Practice of Entrepreneurship Education

This employs a Schumpeterian economic approach using interdisciplinary instruments of analysis for management of new and small enterprises.

In Germany, the first professorship in entrepreneurship was only founded in 1998 and the country is making intensive efforts to catch up; 17 active institutions already include the subject. Seeing universities as a 'reservoir of competency', politicians hope to draw on generator, incubator and accelerator effects regarding innovation and technology-oriented new enterprises (Koch, 2003). The content of the programmes extends beyond opportunity recognition and relevant thinking for nascent entrepreneurs to include issues such as creating an institutional framework for fostering entrepreneurship. Entrepreneurship education stands in opposition to established, mainly business economics-oriented education concepts in which the image of managers employed in large companies dominates; the demand is for an integrated, action-oriented education which focuses on the genesis and management of new and smaller enterprises and the accompanying problems.

One programme up and running is that at the University of Wuppertal. It offers a two-semester programme for economists and a three-semester programme for non-economists. The former contains courses such as:

- Case studies in entrepreneurship.
- Entrepreneurial management.
- Advanced entrepreneurial management.
- Soft skills for entrepreneurs, and
- New venture map exercises.

The three-semester programme contains courses such as:

- Business and social scientific aspects of founding and developing new enterprises.
- Legal aspects of founding and developing new enterprises, and
- National economic aspects of founding and developing new enterprises.

Then the two groups of students join together for one term on a business plan seminar.

An Entrepreneurship Master Programme at Dauphine University in France

This programme is designed to provide French students with an entrepreneurial spirit in order to prepare them for international careers in small, innovative and high-potential companies, to integrate large companies, to create new companies or to take over existing ones (Léger-Jarniou, 2006).

The French government is encouraging strong growth in entrepreneurship education. Proposals have been developed to target three levels of intervention: to raise awareness of all students irrespective of the subject studied; to support students who are promoters of projects to set up a business; and to provide specialization for motivated students to allow them to obtain specific managerial skills (Klapper, 2005). Very few French students look at entrepreneurship as their first career choice.

The entrepreneurship education programme at Dauphine University in Paris has the following features:

- It is a two-year programme.
- *Compulsory courses are*
  Fundamentals.
  Project management.
  Entrepreneurial behaviour.
  Entrepreneurial marketing.
  Entrepreneurial finance.
  Negotiation and communication.
- *Optional courses are*
  International entrepreneurship.
  Law and taxation.
- Students are to write a dissertation (on participation in a 'Business Plan Workshop').
- Students also go through a training period of six months in France or abroad, under the supervision of a tutor, based on an entrepreneurial theme.

- *Knowledge control takes place through*
  Participation.
  Reports from different classes.
  Final exam.
  Dissertation and oral presentation.
  Training period report.

The NES (New Entrepreneurship Scholarship) Programme at Manchester Metropolitan University Business School (MMUBS)

Some entrepreneurship education programmes are set up to help new entre-preneurs to survive and the programme at Manchester Metropolitan University Business School is one such. A few of its characteristics are (Boles, 2005):

- A six-month, part-time, business development programme for new entrepreneurs.
- The ambition is to develop a sustainable enterprise culture.
- A balance of knowledge about business methods and a process of personal development.
- Based on the idea of action learning, the participants work in small groups, which over time offer individuals a safe but challenging environment in which to focus on a particular problem.
- Faculty members act as mentors, or as sounding boards for the entre-preneurs' aspirations and concerns, rather than as experts in a particular field.

Intrapreneurship as Part of the Masters of Technology Management (MTM) at Stevens Institute of Technology in the US

This programme is designed to teach corporate entrepreneurship to students from large companies) (Koen, 2001).

A course for training intrapreneurs is given at Stevens Institute of Technology in the United States. It is divided into four parts and is taught weekly for two half hours over a fourteen-week period. The four parts are:

1. Key factors for corporate venture success.
2. Evaluation of organizational and cultural factors.
3. Guidance in how to write a business plan.
4. Development of an actual business venture in student's company.

Key criteria, determined from the executive champions working with the venture teams, for obtaining start-up funds are corporate strategic fit, the teams' understanding of the business, the market and the product and their ability to develop a comprehensive business plan.

A MASTER'S PROGRAMME IN ENTREPRENEURSHIP

My aim in the rest of this chapter is to present a one-year master's programme in entrepreneurship that I started myself and which has been running at Stockholm University since autumn 2000 and at Malmö University College since autumn 2003 and which is based on ideas presented in this book. Let me simply call this the Master's Programme. As will become clear, I do not think entrepreneurship can be 'taught' in the traditional sense of the term.

The Basic Assumptions behind the Master's Programme

The basic assumptions behind the Master's Programme will be familiar to those who have read earlier sections of this book:

- I am of the opinion that even if entrepreneurship has obvious economic consequences (such as development and employment), it should not only (maybe not even primarily) be understood economically, but also, say, historically, politically, sociologically and psychologically. Furthermore, entrepreneurship exists in all social strata and classes. The Master's Programme is, consequently, not an education in business but a stand-alone education, common to the whole of Stockholm University and Malmö University College, respectively. You can have a bachelor's degree in any subject when starting the programme (more of this shortly).
- There is no single or generally best way to become an entrepreneur. There is also no specific set of traits characterizing a successful entrepreneur. I see management as a profession, leadership as a role, but entrepreneurship as a mental disposition. You can, therefore, teach management, you can train leadership, but you cannot in general (except in very specific situations with very similar individuals) teach or train entrepreneurship, in the traditional sense of these two terms. How can you teach or train a mental disposition, a way of life, a life form? At most, you can foster it or inspire it!
- I make a definite distinction between entrepreneurship and small business economics (or between an entrepreneur and a small business manager). Both are necessary for a business to survive and, eventually,

grow, but entrepreneurship is about starting a business venture, management about helping it survive. This point is related to the previous one.

The Foundation of the Master's Programme

If you look at entrepreneurship as a mental disposition, the primary task is not to teach techniques, such as how to write a business plan or how to build effective accounting and control systems in new business firms. I do not deny that planning and control can be necessary for a business firm (or any other organized activity) to survive, but these functions concern its small business economics stage, which comes later. I am firmly convinced that most entrepreneurial activities start without any formal plan; if an entrepreneur thinks in terms of control too early, the result could be a disaster. Entrepreneurship is not about planning or controlling to any major degree. To try to do so would, in my opinion, go against the very entrepreneurial idea.

The ambition of the Master's Programme is to inspire, encourage and demonstrate possibilities, in short, to foster the entrepreneurial mental disposition. As mentioned earlier, I see the entrepreneurial disposition as consisting of three attitudes, all of which are necessary for an individual to have an entrepreneurial potential:

1. The world is full of problems and we all look at them differently, at least partly so!
2. There are many exciting possibilities and solutions in our (socially constructed) reality (or they can be created)!
3. *I* want to be part of exploiting and implementing at least one of these possibilities and solutions!

Attitudes 1 and 2 are developed by letting the participants in the Master's Programme work with genuinely different people (remember that all kinds of people with all kinds of backgrounds will join this programme). If you put, say, six economists together in a project group, not much will happen – they are too similar and they will use much of the project work to confirm the social reality that they were already part of. On the other hand, if you put together, say, a doctor, a philosopher, a historian, an archaeologist and an engineer in a project group, exciting things start to happen. The participants will start to demonstrate new aspects of and possibilities in reality. A genuinely new creation of socially constructed reality will take place; reality will not just be confirmed as in the first example.

Attitude 3 will develop by having the participants make a large number of visits to real entrepreneurial settings and by having entrepreneurs and other people involved in entrepreneurial efforts to visit the class as guest lecturers. The idea is that the interest of the participants in the entrepreneurial direction will be inspired by all these visits and guest lecturers; sooner or later most (or at least many) of the participants will meet somebody, of whom they can say afterwards: 'If he (or she) can do it, so can I!'

The Master's Programme is undoubtedly Sweden's most multi-disciplinary education. Anybody can apply, no matter what their educational background. The only requirement is a three-year bachelor's degree (or equivalent).

Let me show the variety of students in the programme during the first three years at Stockholm University:

Year 2000–01

- 20 students.
- 11 men and 9 women.
- Average age 31 years (range: 24–44).

Study orientation	Number
Business	6
Medicine	3
Sociology	2
Computer	2
Theatre	1
Philosophy	1
Law	1
Biology	1
Health	1
Political science	1
Meteorology	1

It is interesting to note the even distribution of the two sexes. There are no typically male or female subject areas favoured, as anybody can apply (and join). Furthermore, there is a huge variation in age among the participants. I see it as an advantage if the students can work in heterogeneous groups over the course of the Master's Programme, not only in terms of background, but also in terms of sex and age. Such a variation is also shown in later years.

Year 2001–02

- 24 students.
- 12 men and 12 women.
- Average age 32 years (range: 22–56).

Study orientation	Number
Business	8
Technology	3
Film, theatre, photography	3
Computer, information design	2
Literature, language	2
Sociology	2
Media	1
Sports/health	1
History	1
Tourism	1

Year 2002–03

- 20 students.
- 11 men and 9 women.
- Average age 31 years (range: 23–60).

Study orientation	Number
Business	7
Political science	2
Fine arts	2
Computer	2
Technology	2
Tourism	1
Health care	1
Hotel management	1
Language	1
Law	1

Examples of professions which are not normally associated with entrepreneurship, but which have been represented in the Master's Programme at Stockholm University are:

- study counsellor
- secondary school teacher
- midwife
- dietician
- historian
- philosopher
- actor
- doctor (of medicine)

- officer
- meteorologist.

The Objective and Design of the Master's Programme

In line with my conceptualization that entrepreneurship is about coming up with new solutions which other people can use, the objective of the Master's Programme has been formulated as 'to learn to understand how to create, implement and maintain new user-friendly change processes'. A somewhat more informal formulation is 'to learn how to realize one's ideas'. The participants do not, however, need to have any entrepreneurial idea when they start the Master's Programme.

A few ideas behind the design of the Master's Programme are:

- to use the whole potential that exists in those students that participate in the programme.
- to let, in all situations, theory support practice – and the other way round.
- to maintain a holistic view.
- to develop a mental disposition rather than professional knowledge or a role.

The Master's Programme consists of four courses, each five weeks long:

- Entrepreneurship software.
- Entrepreneurship hardware.
- Entrepreneurship variations.
- Entrepreneurship applications.

There are also two projects, each ten weeks long, in the programme:

- Entrepreneurial pictures from life.
- Entrepreneurial project.

It is important to understand that the combined four courses should not be seen as comprising some kind of general or complete knowledge of what the characteristics or behaviour of a successful entrepreneur should be. Such general knowledge does not exist, according to my basic assumptions. Each of the four courses rather constitutes a holistic view in the sense that they all look at the subject 'as a whole', but from different angles: software, hardware, variations and applications. The courses are meant to be some

kind of 'smorgasbord' from which individual participants can pick whatever they find suitable according to their backgrounds and special needs
which I do not know when we start. The courses can, therefore, be given in
any order.

As far as the projects are concerned they are arranged such that
'Entrepreneurial pictures from life' is completed during the first term and
'Entrepreneurial project' during the second.

The content of the courses and the projects are presented in more detail
in Tables 8.3–8.8 below.

Table 8.3   The Master's Programme: course 'Entrepreneurship Software'

Entrepreneurship software
This course looks at the subject of entrepreneurship from a process point of
view. It stresses the more human aspects of entrepreneurship and those processes
of which these aspects are an expression. Items discussed are, for instance,
differences and similarities between creativity, innovation and entrepreneurship,
team work/group dynamism, favourable entrepreneurial environments,
networking in practice and what else is part of a successful project.

Another name for this course could be 'Projecting'

Table 8.4   The Master's Programme: course 'Entrepreneurship Hardware'

Entrepreneurship hardware
This course is functionally oriented and stresses the more technical aspects of
entrepreneurship. The course discusses entrepreneurship from a structural point
of view and contains items such as marketing and entrepreneurship, business law,
entrepreneurship financing and entrepreneurial growth.

Another name for this course could be 'Doing business'

Table 8.5   The Master's Programme: course 'Entrepreneurship Variations'

Entrepreneurship variations
This course thematizes different parts of the theory of entrepreneurship, for
instance, male and female entrepreneurship, history of entrepreneurship theory,
entrepreneurship and business venturing, entrepreneurship and culture and the
core of entrepreneurship.

Another name for this course could be 'Entrepreneurship theory'

Table 8.6   The Master's Programme: course 'Entrepreneurship Applications'

Entrepreneurship applications
This course means that the participants will take part in real, ongoing, sharp practical cases concerning entrepreneurship and business development. Students are to actively participate in discussions about how to run these further successfully. A variety of activities and elements of entrepreneurship in application will be touched upon. The idea of the course is partly to illustrate how different these activities and parts may look in practice, partly to show that they play different roles in different stages of a business development process.

Another name for this course could be 'Entrepreneurship practice'

Table 8.7   The Master's Programme: project 'Entrepreneurial Pictures from Life'

Entrepreneurial pictures from life
This project involves individual presentations of what the participants think they have understood of the subject of entrepreneurship half-way into the programme. The basis for the project is:
- reading recommended literature
- reading other literature that the participants choose themselves
- listening to stories from visiting entrepreneurs and business developers
- participating in various study visits as the programme goes on
- taking material from daily press, business journals, the Internet and so on

---

Note: The presentation can take any form, preferably as entrepreneurial as possible. Besides 'traditional' essays, I have seen presentations as a stage drama, a video, a children's tale read as role play, an artistic installation and a game ('Monopoly' rewritten), to give a few examples.

Table 8.8   The Master's Programme: project 'Entrepreneurial Project'

Entrepreneurial project
This project involves writing a master's thesis, with those academic rules which normally govern an essay at such an academic level.

The experience for the final project (the master's thesis) is gained in three alternative ways:

1. To be placed with a project host and to work in a real business development project.
2. To work on a personal entrepreneurial idea.
3. To write an essay on a chosen entrepreneurial topic.

In practice, half of the participants tend to choose the first alternative, and the other half tend to choose the second. Writing an essay on an entrepreneurial topic (without any contact with an ongoing real entrepreneurial project) is rarely done.

Examples of essay subjects resulting from being placed with a host are:

- Building up an internal consulting company in a major multinational corporation.
- Developing a new business connected with a cultural museum.
- Devising a telecommunications solution for a transport company.
- Evaluating a site for e-commerce hosted by a larger corporation.
- Making winter sports villages more attractive.
- Building up a system for collecting (with compensation) old sewing machines from people's homes.
- Solving an intrapreneurial logistical problem.

Examples of essay subjects based on participants' own ideas are:

- Starting a place for producing fruit wine.
- Starting a company for teaching the art of presenting oneself.
- Starting an idea laboratory.
- Developing businesses between Sweden and China.
- Launching a programme for interpreting text.
- Building up a manpower company.
- Commercialization of one's own inventions.
- Distribution of dairy products through the Internet.
- Start an event café.

Two examples of essays in a chosen topic are:

- Studying, with entrepreneurial eyes, the care of the elderly in some Stockholm local government institutions.
- Study the climate for Kurds to start a business in Sweden.

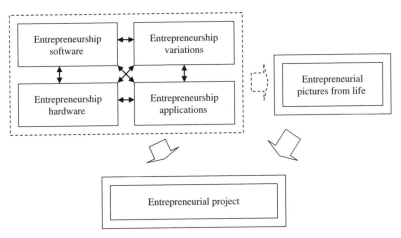

Figure 8.3   The Master's Programme (of Entrepreneurship)

The courses and the projects are related as in Figure 8.3.

The four courses are, to the extent that they are finished, part of the background to the project 'Entrepreneurial pictures from life' (consequently a dotted line). All courses and the project 'Entrepreneurial pictures from life' are part of the background to 'Entrepreneurial project'.

How to Apply

Selection of participants is based on three factors:

1. The participants' CVs.
2. A letter in which the applicants explain why they want to join the programme.
3. Interviews with all qualified applicants.

The content of the CV is worth as much as the letter and the interview together.

A Few Results

Of those approximately one hundred students who have gone through the programme so far, about half run their own businesses today (to be fair, many of them already had a business when they joined the programme) and approximately one-third are employed in the business sector, in another organization or with an authority whose mission is to encourage entrepreneurship in society.

References

Achrol, R.S. and P. Kotler (1999), 'Marketing in the network economy', *Journal of Marketing* (Special Issue), **63**, 146–63.

Ackerman, P.L. and L.G. Humpreys (1990), 'Individual differences theory in industrial and organizational psychology', in M.D. Dunnette and L.M. Hough (eds), *Handbook of Industrial and Organizational Psychology*, Vol. 1, 2nd edition, Palo Alto, CA: Consulting Psychology Press, pp. 223–82.

Acs, Z.J. (2002), *Innovation and the Growth of Cities*, Cheltenham, UK and Northampton, MA, USA: Edward Elgar.

Ajzen, I. (1991), 'The theory of planned behaviour', *Organizational Behaviour and Human Decision Processes*, **50**, 179–211.

Alberti, F. (2002), 'The embeddedness of competitive behaviour in industrial districts', paper presented at 12th Nordic Conference on Small Business Research, Kuopio, Finland, June 16–19.

Alberti, F. (2003), 'What makes it an industrial district? A cognitive perspective', paper presented at Uddevalla Symposium 2003, June 12–14.

Alberti, F., S. Sciascia and A. Poli (2005), 'The domain of entrepreneurship education: key issues', *International Journal of Entrepreneurship Education*, **2**(4), 453–82.

Aldrich, H. and C. Zimmer (1986), 'Entrepreneurship through social networks', in D.L. Sexton and R.W. Smilor (eds), *The Art and Science of Entrepreneurship*, Cambridge, MA: Ballinger, pp. 2–23.

Allen, K.R. (2003), *Launching New Ventures. An Entrepreneurial Approach*, 3rd edition, Boston, MA: Houghton Mifflin Company.

Alvesson, M. (1993), *Cultural Perspectives on Organizations*, Cambridge: Cambridge University Press.

Alvesson, M. and K. Sköldberg (2000), *Reflexive Methodology. New Vistas for Qualitative Research*, London: Sage.

Anderson, A.R. and S.L. Jack (2002), 'The articulation of social capital in entrepreneurial networks: a glue or a lubricant?', *Entrepreneurship and Regional Development*, **14**, 193–210.

Andersson, S. (1979), *Positivism kontra hermenutik* [Positivism versus hermeneutics], Göteborg: Bokförlaget Korpen.

Apel, K.-O. (1984), *Understanding and Explanation*, Cambridge, MA: The MIT Press.

Arbnor, A. (2004), *Vägen från Klockrike. Om liv och ledarskap* [The road from the industrial kingdom. About life and leadership], Stockholm: SNS Förlag.

Arbnor, I. and L. Andersson (1977), *Att förstå sociala system* [To understand social systems], Lund: Studentlitteratur.

Arbnor, I. and B. Bjerke (1997), *Methodology for Creating Business Knowledge*, Thousand Oaks, CA: Sage Publications.

Arbnor, I., S.-E. Borglund and T. Liljedahl (1980), *Osynligt ockuperad* [Invisibly occupied], Malmö: Liber.

Assmo, P. (2003), 'Creative clusters. Ideas and realities for cluster growth', paper, University of Trollhättan/Uddevalla.

Audretsch, D.B. (1995), *Innovation and Industry Evolution*, Cambridge, MA: MIT Press.

Audretsch, D.B. (1998), 'Agglomeration and the location of innovative activity', *Oxford Review of Economic Policy*, **14**, 18–29.

Austin, J.L. (1965), *Philosophical Papers*, Oxford: Clarendon Press.

Baldwin, J.R. and J. Johnson (1999), 'Entry, innovation and firm growth', in Z.J. Acs (ed.), *Are Small Firms Important? Their Role and Impact*, Dordrecht: Kluwer, pp. 51–78.

Bandura, A. (1995), 'Perceived self-efficacy', in A.S.R. Manstead and M. Hewstone (eds), *The Blackwell Encyclopedia of Social Psychology*, Oxford: Blackwell Publishers Ltd, pp. 434–6.

Barabási, A.-L. (2002), *Linked. The New Science of Networks*, New York: Perseus Publishing.

Baron, R.A. (1998), 'Cognitive mechanisms in entrepreneurship: why and when entrepreneurs think differently than other people', *Journal of Business Venturing*, **12**, 275–94.

Baron, R.A. and S.A. Shane (2005), *Entrepreneurship. A Process Perspective*, Mason, OH: Thomson Corporation.

Barth, H. (2001), 'Tillväxthinder i mindre företag' [Obstacles for growth in smaller firms], in P. Davidsson, F. Delmar and J. Wiklund (eds), *Tillväxtföretagen i Sverige* [Growth companies in Sweden], Stockholm: SNS Förlag, pp. 234–49.

Bartunek, J.M. (1984), 'Changing interpretive schemes and organizational restructuring: the example of a religious order', *Administrative Science Quarterly*, **29**, 355–72.

Bauman, Z. (1978), *Hermeneutics and Social Science. Approaches to Understanding*, London: Hutchinson and Sons.

Baumol, W.E. (1993), *Entrepreneurship, Management, and the Structure of Payoffs*, Cambridge, MA: MIT Press.

Benner, M. (2002), 'Time and the new economy', in I. Holmberg, M. Salzer-Mörling and L. Strannegård (eds), *Stuck in the Future?*

Tracing the 'New Economy', Stockholm: Bookhouse Publishing, pp. 135–57.

Berg, P.O. (2001), 'The summoning of the Øresund region', in B. Czarniawska and R. Solli (eds), *Organizing Metropolitan Space and Discourse*, Solna: Liber, pp. 175–91.

Berger, P.L. and T. Luckmann (1981), *The Social Construction of Reality*, Harmondsworth: Penguin.

Berggren, C. and G. Brulin (1985), *Från myt till människa* [From myth to man], Stockholm: FA-rådet.

Birch, D. (1979), *The Job Generation Process*, Cambridge, MA: MIT Program on Neighborhood and Regional Change.

Birley, S., S. Cromie and A. Myers (1991), 'Entrepreneurial networks: their emergence in Ireland and overseas', *International Small Business Journal*, **9**(4), 56–74.

Bjerke, B. (1989), *Att skapa nya affärer* [Creating new business ventures], Lund: Studentlitteratur.

Bjerke, B. (1996), 'Understanding or explaining entrepreneurship', paper presented at UIC/AMA Research Symposia on Marketing and Entrepreneurship, Stockholm, June 14–15.

Bjerke, B. (1998), 'Some aspects of inadequacies of Western entrepreneurship and SME models in understanding Southeast Asia business', paper presented at 43rd ICSB World Conference, Singapore, June 8–10.

Bjerke, B. (1999) *Business Leadership and Culture*, Cheltenham, UK and Northampton, MA, USA: Edward Elgar.

Bjerke, B. (2000a), 'A typified, culture-based, interpretation of management of SMEs in Southeast Asia', *Asia Pacific Journal of Management*, **17**(1), 103–32.

Bjerke, B. (2000b), 'Understanding entrepreneurship – a new direction in research', paper presented at ICSB World Conference 2000, Brisbane, June 7–10.

Bjerke, B. (2005), 'Public entrepreneurship – marginal made central', paper presented at Enterprise and Innovation Conference, University of Waikato, New Zeeland, June 7–10.

Bjerke, B. (forthcoming), 'Face-to-face research: interviews, conversations and dialogues', in B. Gustavsson (ed.), *The Principles of Knowledge Creation: Research Methods in the Social Sciences*, Cheltenham, UK and Northampton, MA, USA: Edward Elgar.

Bjerke, B. and A.R. Al-Meer (1994), 'A behavioural consciousness view of corporate culture', paper presented at the Association of Management 12th Annual International Conference, Dallas, Texas: Proceedings of the Organizational Studies Group, **12**(1), pp. 174–9.

Bjerke, B. and C.-J. Asplund (2005), 'Social entrepreneurs – a new breed?', paper presented at European Summer University in Entrepreneurship Research and Education, University of Dauphine, Paris, September 23–30.

Bjerke, B. and C. Hultman (2002), *Entrepreneurial Marketing. The Growth of Small Firms in the New Economic Era*, Cheltenham, UK and Northampton, MA, USA: Edward Elgar.

Bjerke, B. and C. Hultman (2003), 'A dynamic perspective on entrepreneurship, leadership and management as a proper mix for growth', *International Journal of Innovation and Learning*, 1(1), 72–83.

Block, Z. and I.C. MacMillan (1985), 'Milestones for successful venture planning', *Harvard Business Review on Entrepreneurship*, Boston, MA: Harvard Business School Press, pp. 117–33.

Block, Z. and S.A. Stumpf (1992), 'Entrepreneurship education research: experience and challenge', in D.L. Sexton and J.D. Kasarda (eds), *The State of the Art of Entrepreneurship*, Boston, MA: PWS-Kent Publishing Company, pp. 123–141.

Boland, R.J. (1987), 'The in-formation of information systems', in R. Boland and R. Hirchheim (eds), *Critical Issues in Information Systems Research*, Chichester: John Wiley & Sons, pp. 363–79.

Boles, K. (2005), 'The Manchester Metropolitan University Business School model for enterprise start-up: an action learning approach', in P. Kyrö and C. Carrier (eds), *The Dynamics of Learning Entrepreneurship in a Cross-Cultural University Context*, Entrepreneurship Education Series 2/2005, Hämeenlinna: University of Tampere, Research Centre for Vocational and Professional Education, pp. 260–83.

Bornstein, D. (1998), 'Changing the world on a shoestring', *Atlantic Monthly*, 281(1), 34–9.

Boschee, J. (1998), 'What does it take to be a social entrepreneur?', http://www.socialentrepreneurs.org/whatdoes.html.

Bottomore, T. and R. Nisbet (eds) (1979), *A History of Sociological Analysis*, London: Heinemann.

Bourdieu, P. (1990), *The Logic of Practice*, Cambridge: Polity Press.

Bourdieu, P. and L. Wacquant (1992), *An Invitation to Reflexive Sociology*, Chicago, IL: University of Chicago Press.

Boyd, N. and G.S. Vozikis (1994), 'The influence of self-efficacy on the development of entrepreneurial intentions and actions', *Entrepreneurship Theory and Practice*, Summer, 63–77.

Braunerhjelm, P., B. Carlsson and D. Johansson (1998), 'Industriella kluster, tillväxt och ekonomisk politik' [Industrial clusters, growth and economic policy], *Ekonomisk Debatt*, 26(4), 419–30.

Bridge, S., K. O'Neill and S. Cromie (2003), *Understanding Enterprise, Entrepreneurship and Small Business*, 2nd edition, New York: Palgrave Macmillan.

Bruderl, J. and P. Preisendorfer (1998), 'Network support and the success of newly founded businesses', *Small Business Economics*, **10**, 213–25.

Bryson, J., P. Woods and D. Keeble (1993), 'Business networks, small firm flexibility and regional development in UK business services', *Entrepreneurship and Regional Development*, **5**, 265–77.

Buber, M. (1954), *Det mellanmänskliga* [What goes on between human beings], Ludvika: Dualis.

Burns, P. (1989), 'Strategies for success and routes to failure', in P. Burns and J. Dewhurst (eds), *Small Business and Entrepreneurship*, London: Macmillan, 32–67.

Burns, P. (2001), *Entrepreneurship and Small Business*, New York: Palgrave.

Butler, J.E. and G.S. Hansen (1991), 'Network evolution, entrepreneurial success, and regional development', *Entrepreneurship and Regional Development*, **3**, 1–16.

Byars, L.L. (1987), *Strategic Management*, 2nd edition, New York: Harper & Row.

Cannon, C. (2000), 'Charity for profit: how the new social entrepreneurs are creating good by sharing wealth', *National Journal*, June 16, 1898–904.

Cantillon, R. (1955/1755), *Essai sur la nature du commerce en general*, London: Fletcher Gyles.

Carlsson, B. (1997), *Technological Systems and Industrial Dynamics*, Norwell, MA: Kluwer Academic Publishers.

Carlsson, B. (1999), 'Small business entrepreneurship and industrial dynamics', in Z.J. Acs (ed.), *Are Small Firms Important? Their Role and Impact*, Dordrecht: Kluwer, pp. 99–110.

Carree, M. and A.R. Thurik (1999), 'Industrial structure and economic growth', in D.B. Audretsch and A.R. Thurik (eds), *Innovation, Industry Evolution and Employment*, Cambridge: Cambridge University Press, pp. 86–110.

Carson, D., S. Cromie, P. McGowan and J. Hill (1995), *Marketing and Entrepreneurship in SMEs*, Hemel Hempstead: Prentice-Hall International (UK) Ltd.

Carter, S. (2000), 'Gender and enterprise', in S. Carter and D. Jones-Evans (eds), *Enterprise and Small Business. Principles, Practice and Policy*, Upper Saddle River, NJ: Prentice Hall, pp. 166–81.

Castells, M. (1998), *Nätverkssamhällets framväxt* [The rise of the network society], Göteborg: Daidalos.

Catford, J. (1998), 'Social entrepreneurs are vital for health promotion – but they need a supportive environment too', Editorial, *Health Promotion International*, **13**, 95–8.

Chell, E. (2001), *Entrepreneurship: Globalization, Innovation and Development*, Stamford, CT: Thomson Learning.

Chia, R. (1995), 'The problem of reflexivity in organizational research. Towards a postmodern science of organization', *Organization*, **3**(1), 31–59.

Churchill, N. (1991), 'The components of entrepreneurship', in J. Roure and S. Bradley (eds), *Growth Capital and Entrepreneurship*, Barcelona: EFER/ICSE, pp. 27–32.

Coase, R.H. (1937), 'The nature of the firm', *Economica*, **4**(4), 386–405.

Coffield, F. (1990), 'From the decade of enterprise culture to the decade of the TECs', *British Journal of Education and Work*, **4**(1), 59–78.

Coleman, J.S. (1979), 'Experiential learning and information assimilation: toward an appropriate mix', *Journal of Experiential Education*, **4**(1), 6–9.

Coleman, J.S. (1990), *Foundations of Social Theory*, Cambridge, MA: Harvard University Press.

Conway, S. (1994), 'Informal boundary-spanning links and networks in successful technological innovation', PhD Thesis, Aston Business School.

Conway, S. (1997), 'Informal networks of relationships in successful small firm innovation', in D. Jones-Evans and M. Klofsten (eds), *Technology, Innovation and Enterprise: the European Experience*, Basingstoke: Macmillan, pp. 236–73.

Cooper, A. and T. Folta (2000), 'Entrepreneurship and high-technology clusters', in D.L. Sexton and H. Landström (eds), *Handbook of Entrepreneurship*, Oxford: Blackwell Publishers Ltd, pp. 348–67.

Coulter, M. (2001), *Entrepreneurship in Action*, Upper Saddle River, NJ: Prentice Hall.

Cunningham, J.B. and J. Lischeron (1991), 'Defining entrepreneurship', *Journal of Small Business Management*, **29**(1), 43–51.

Curran, J. and R.A. Blackburn (1991), *Paths of Enterprise*, London: Routledge.

Curran, J. and J. Stanworth (1989), 'Education and training for enterprise: some problems of classification, evaluation, policy and research', *International Small Business Journal*, **7**(2), 11–22.

Czarniawska, B. (1998), *A Narrative Approach to Organization Studies*, Thousand Oaks, CA: Sage.

Czarniawska, B. and R. Solli (2001), 'Big city as a societal laboratory', in B. Czarniawska and R. Solli (eds), *Organizing Metropolitan Space and Discourse*, Solna: Liber, pp. 7–12.

Czinkota, M.R., P. Rivoli and I.A. Ronkainen (1994), *International Business*, 3rd edition, Orlando, FL: Harcourt Brace.

Dana, L.P. (1992), 'Entrepreneurial education in Europe', *Journal of Education for Business*, **68**(2), 74–9.

Dana, L.P. (2001), 'The education and training of entrepreneurs in Asia', *Education and Training*, **43**(8/9), 405–15.

Dana, L.P. (2005), 'Entrepreneurship training in post-communist Europe', in J.R. McIntyre and I. Alon (eds), *Business and Management Education in Transitioning and Developing Countries: A Handbook*, Armonk, NY: M.E. Sharpe, Inc., pp. 75–94.

Davidsson, P. (1989), *Continued Entrepreneurship and Small Firm Growth*, doctoral thesis, Stockholm: Stockholm School of Economics.

Davidsson, P. (2003), 'The domain of entrepreneurship research: some suggestions', in J. Katz and D. Shepherd (eds), *Cognitive Approaches to Entrepreneurship*, Vol. 6, Cambridge, MA: Elsevier Science, pp. 315–72.

Davidsson, P. (2004), *Researching Entrepreneurship*, New York: Springer.

Davidsson, P. and F. Delmar (2001), 'Tillväxtföretag i Sverige: förekomst och utvecklingsmönster' [Growth companies in Sweden: existence and growth pattern], in P. Davidsson, F. Delmar and J. Wiklund (eds), *Tillväxtföretagen i Sverige* [Growth companies in Sweden], Stockholm: SNS Förlag, pp. 83–115.

Davidsson, P., F. Delmar and J. Wiklund (2001), 'Hur förväntningar påverkar småföretagens tillväxtvilja' [How expectations are influencing the willingness of small firms to grow], in P. Davidsson, F. Delmar and J. Wiklund (eds), *Tillväxtföretagen i Sverige* [Growth companies in Sweden], Stockholm: SNS Förlag, pp. 146–67.

Davis, S.J. and M. Henrekson (1997), 'Industrial policy, employer size and economic performance in Sweden', in R.B. Freeman, B. Swedenborg and R. Topel (eds), *The Welfare State in Transition*, Chicago: University of Chicago Press, pp. 353–98.

Davis, S.J., J. Haltiwanger and S. Schuh (1996), *Job Creation and Destruction*, Cambridge, MA: The MIT Press.

Deakins, D. and G. Whittam (2000), 'Business start-up: theory, practice and policy', in S. Carter and D. Jones-Evans (eds), *Enterprise and Small Business. Principles, Practice and Policy*, Upper Saddle River, NJ: Prentice-Hall, pp. 115–31.

Deal, T. and A. Kennedy (1988), *Corporate Cultures*, Harmondsworth: Penguin Books.

de Bruin, A. and A. Dupuis (eds) (2003), *Entrepreneurship: New Perspectives in a Global Age*, Aldershot: Ashgate Publishing Limited.

Dees, J.G., J. Emerson and P. Economy (2001), *Enterprising Nonprofits. A Toolkit for Social Entrepreneurs*, New York: John Wiley & Sons, Inc.

Deetz, S. (1986), 'Metaphors and the discursive production of organization', in I.L. Thayer (ed.), *Communication – Organization*, Norwood, NJ: Ablex, pp. 112–36.

Delmar, F. (2000), 'The psychology of the entrepreneur', in S. Carter and D. Jones-Evans (eds), *Enterprise and Small Business. Principles, Practice and Policy*, Upper Saddle River, NJ: Prentice-Hall, pp. 132–54.

Delmar, F. and P. Davidsson (2000), 'Where do they come from? Prevalence and characteristics of nascent entrepreneurs', *Entrepreneurship and Regional Development*, **12**, 1–23.

Dennis, C. (2000), 'Networking for marketing advantage', *Management Decision*, **38**(4), 287–92.

Derrida, J. (1998), *Rösten och fenomenet* [The voice and the phenomenon], Stockholm: Thales.

'Det nya näringslivet' [The new economy] (2001), a publication from The Swedish Confederation of Employers.

Devins, D. and J. Gold (2002), 'Social constructionism: a theoretical framework to underpin support for the development of managers in SMEs?', *Journal of Small Business and Enterprise Development*, **9**(2), 111–19.

Dixon, N. (1994), *The Organizational Learning Cycle*, New York: McGraw-Hill.

Dollinger, M.C. (2003), *Entrepreneurship. Strategies and Resources*, 3rd edition, Upper Saddle River: NJ: Prentice Hall.

Dredge, C.P. (1985), 'Corporate culture: the challenge to expatriate managers and multinational corporations', in H.V. Wortzel and L.H. Wortzel (eds), *Strategic Management and Multinational Corporations: The Essentials*, New York: John Wiley & Sons, pp. 410–24.

Droysen, J.G. (1858), *Grundrisse der Historik*, published (1897) as *Outline of the Principles of History* (trans. E.B. Andrews), Boston, MA: Ginn & Co.

Drucker, P. (1969), *The Age of Discontinuity: Guidelines to our Changing Society*, London: Heinemann.

Drucker, P. (1985a), *Innovation and Entrepreneurship*, New York: Harper and Row.

Drucker, P. (1985b), *The Changing World of the Executive*, New York: Times Books.

Dubini, P. and H. Aldrich (1991), 'Personal and extended networks are central to the entrepreneurial process', *Journal of Business Venturing*, **6**, 305–13.

Duchéneaut, B. (2001), 'Entrepreneurship and higher education from real-life context to pedagogical challenge', in R.H. Brockhaus, G.E. Hills, H. Klandt and H.P. Welsch (eds), *Entrepreneurship Education*, Aldershot: Ashgate, pp. 128–46.

Dümmler, P. and A. Thierstein (2003), 'Identifying and managing clusters – evidence from Switzerland', paper presented at Uddevalla Symposium 2003, June 12–14.

The Economist (1998), 'Entrepreneurs in order', 14 March, 63–5.

The Economist (1999), 'Innovation in industry', 20 February.

The Economist (2000), 'The new economy. Untangling e-conomics', 23 September.

The Economist (2001), 'The next society. A survey of the near future', 3 November.

Ehn, B. and O. Löfgren (1982), *Kulturanalys. Ett etnologiskt perspektiv* [Cultural analysis. An ethnological perspective], Malmö: LiberFörlag.

Entreprenör (2003), 'Kluster – vår tids företagsmagneter' [Clusters – the business magnets of our time], 1–2, 30–34.

Eriksson, K. and M. Ådahl (2000), 'Finns det en ny ekonomi och kommer den till Europa?' [Is there a new economy and will it come to Europe?], *Penning och valutapolitik*, 1, Stockholm: Bank of Sweden.

Fay, B. (1996), *Contemporary Philosophy of Social Science*, Oxford: Blackwell Publishers.

Feldman, M. (1994), *The Geography of Innovation*, Norwell, MA: Kluwer Academic Publishers.

Ferguson, M. (1980), *The Aquarian Conspiracy*, Los Angeles: Jeremy P. Tarcher.

Fiet, J.O. (2001), 'Education for entrepreneurial competency: a theory-based activity approach', in R.H. Brockhaus, G.E. Hills, H. Klandt and H.P. Welsch (eds), *Entrepreneurship Education*, Aldershot: Ashgate, pp. 78–93.

Forslund, M. (2002), *Det omöjliggjorda entreprenörskapet* [Entrepreneurship made impossible], Doctoral thesis, Växjö: Växjö University Press.

Foucault, M. (1972), *The Archeology of Knowledge*, London: Routledge.

Garavan, T.N. and B. O'Cinneide (1994), 'Entrepreneurship education and training programmes: a review and evaluation – part I', *Journal of European Industrial Training*, **18**(8), 3–12.

Garfinkel, H. (1967), *Studies in Ethnomethodology*, Englewood Cliffs, NJ: Prentice Hall.

Gartner, W.B. (1988), 'Who is an entrepreneur? is the wrong question', *American Journal of Small Business*, **12**(4), 11–32.

Gartner, W.B. and S.A. Shane (1995), 'Measuring entrepreneurship over time', *Journal of Business Venturing*, **10**, 283–301.

Gartner, W.B., B.J. Bird and J.A. Starr (1992), 'Acting as if: differentiating entrepreneurial from organizational behavior', *Entrepreneurship Theory and Practice*, **16**, Spring, 13–30.

Gavron, R., M. Cowling, G. Holtman and A. Westall (1997), 'The entrepreneurial society', Institute for Public Policy Research, London.

Geertz, C. (1973), *The Interpretation of Cultures*, London: Fontana Press.

Gendron, G. (1997), 'Flashes of genius: interview with Peter Drucker', *Inc.*, 16 May, **18**(7), 30–37.

Gephart, R.P.J. (1993), 'The textual approach: risk and blame in disaster sensemaking', *Academy of Management Journal*, **36**(6), 74–81.

Gergen, K.J. (1999), *An Invitation to Social Construction*, Thousand Oaks, CA: Sage Publications.

Gibb, A. (1992), 'The enterprise culture and education', *International Small Business Journal*, **11**(3), 20–33.

Gibb, A. (1993), 'The enterprise culture and education. Understanding enterprise education and its links with small business, entrepreneurship and wider educational goals', *International Small Business Journal*, **11**(3), 11–34.

Gibb, A. (1998), 'Entrepreneurial core capacities, competitiveness and management development in the 21st century', research paper, Durham University Business School.

Gibb, A. (2005), 'The future of entrepreneurship education – determining the basis for coherent policy and practice?', in P. Kyrö and C. Carrier (eds), *The Dynamics of Learning Entrepreneurship in a Cross-Cultural University Context*, Entrepreneurship Education Series 2/2005, Hämeenlinna: University of Tampere, Research Centre for Vocational and Professional Education, pp. 44–67.

Giddens, A. (1984), *The Construction of Society. Outline of the Theory of Structuration*, Cambridge: Polity Press.

Gioia, D.A. (1986), 'Symbols, scripts and sensemaking: creating meaning in organizational experience', in H.P. Sims and D.A. Gioia (eds), *The Thinking Organization*, San Francisco: Jossey-Bass Publishers.

Gioia, D.A. and J.B. Thomas (1996), 'Identity, image and issue interpretation: sensemaking during strategic change in academia', *Administrative Science Quarterly*, **41**, 370–403.

Global Entrepreneurship Monitor, 2002 Executive Report, Ewing Marion Kauffman Foundation.

Granovetter, M. (1985), 'Economic action and social structure: the problem of embeddedness', *American Journal of Sociology*, **91**, 481–510.

Hacking, I. (1999), *Social konstruktion av vad?* [Social construction of what?], Stockholm: Thales.

Håkanson, L. (2003), 'Epistemic communities and cluster dynamics: on the role of knowledge in industrial districts', paper, Copenhagen Business School.

Håkansson, H. and J. Johanson (2001), 'Business network learning', in H. Håkansson and J. Johanson (eds), *Business Network Learning*, Amsterdam and Oxford: Elsevier Science Ltd, pp. 1–16.

Hansen, N. (2001), 'Knowledge workers, communication, and spatial diffusion', in B. Johansson, C. Karlsson and R.R. Stough (eds), *Theories of Endogenous Regional Growth*, New York: Springer-Verlag, pp. 315–29.

Harding, S. (1986), *The Science Question in Feminism*, London: Cornell University Press.

Harrison, J. and B. Taylor (1996), *Supergrowth Companies: Entrepreneurs in Action*, Oxford: Butterworth-Heinemann.

Hedberg, B. (1981), *How Organizations Learn and Unlearn*, London: Oxford University Press.

Hedberg, B. and S.-E. Sjöstrand (eds) (1979), *Från företagskriser till industripolitik* [From corporate crises to industrial policy], Malmö: LiberLäromedel.

Hedberg, B., G. Dahlgren, J. Hansson and N.-G. Olve (1994), *Virtual Organizations and Beyond*, New York: John Wiley & Sons.

Henrekson, M. (2001a), 'The entrepreneur and the Swedish model', in M. Henrekson, M. Larsson and H. Sjögren (eds), *Entrepreneurship in Business and Research. Essays in Honour of Håkan Lindgren*, Institute for Research in Economic History, Stockholm School of Economics, pp. 139–64.

Henrekson, M. (2001b), 'Institutionella förutsättningar för entreprenörskap och företagstillväxt' [Institutional conditions for entrepreneurship and company growth], in P. Davidsson, F. Delmar and J. Wiklund (eds), *Tillväxtföretagen i Sverige* [Growth companies in Sweden], Stockholm: SNS Förlag, pp. 38–82.

Henton, D., J. Melville and K. Walesh (2002), 'Collaboration and innovation: the state of American regions', *Industry and Higher Education*, **16**(1), February, 9–17.

Herskovits, M.J. (1955), *Cultural Anthropology*, New York: Knopf.

Hisrich, R. and C.G. Brush (1986), *The Woman Entrepreneur: Starting, Financing and Managing a Successful New Business*, Lexington, MA: Lexington Books.

Hjorth, D. and B. Bjerke (2006), 'Public entrepreneurship – from social/consumer to public/citizen', in C. Steyeart and D. Hjorth (eds), *Entrepreneurship as Social Change*, Cheltenham, UK and Northampton, MA, USA: Edward Elgar, pp. 97–120.

Hjorth, D. and B. Johannisson (1998), 'Entreprenörskap som skapelse och ideologi' [Entrepreneurship as creation and ideology], in B. Czarniawska (ed.), *Organisationsteori på svenska* [Organizational theory in Swedish], Solna: Liber Ekonomi, pp. 86–104.

Hjorth, D. and B. Johannisson (2000), 'Training for entrepreneurship: playing and language games – an inquiry into the Swedish Education System', SIRE, Växjö University.

Hjorth, D. and B. Johannisson (2002), 'Conceptualising the opening phase of regional development as the enactment of a "collective identity"', paper presented at 2nd Conference of the International Entrepreneurship Forum 'Entrepreneurship & Regional Development', Beijing, September 5–7.

Hjorth, D., B. Johannisson and C. Steyaert (2003), 'Entrepreneurship as discourse and life style', in B. Czarniawska and G. Sevón (eds), *The Northern Lights – Organization Theory in Scandinavia*, Solna: Liber AB, pp. 91–110.

Hoang, H. and B. Antoncic (2003), 'Network-based research in entrepreneurship. A critical review', *Journal of Business Venturing*, **18**, 165–87.

Holmberg, I., M. Salzer-Mörling and L. Strannegård (eds) (2002a), *Stuck in the Future? Tracing the 'New Economy'*, Stockholm: Bookhouse Publishing.

Holmberg, I., M. Salzer-Mörling and L. Strannegård (2002b), 'Epilogue: stuck in the future?', in I. Holmberg, M. Salzer-Mörling and L. Strannegård (eds), *Stuck in the Future? Tracing the 'New Economy'*, Stockholm: Bookhouse Publishing, pp. 268–72.

Holmquist, C. and E. Sundin (2002), 'Kvinnors företagande – siffror och synliggörande' [Women entrepreneurship – numbers and publicity-making], in C. Holmquist and E. Sundin (eds), *Företagerskan. Om kvinnor och entreprenörskap* [The entrepreneuse. About women and entrepreneurship], Stockholm: SNS Förlag, pp. 11–26.

Holt, D.H. (1992), *Entrepreneurship – New Venture Creation*, Englewood Cliffs, NJ: Prentice Hall.

Hubbard, P. and T. Hall (1998), 'The entrepreneurial city and the "New Urban Politics"', in T. Hall and P. Hubbard (eds), *The Entrepreneurial City. Geographies of Politics, Regime and Representation*, New York: John Wiley & Sons, pp. 1–23.

Huizinga, J. (1971), *Homo Ludens*, Boston, MA: Beacon Press.

Ifvarsson, C. (2000), 'Sensemaking and management', licentiate dissertation, Department of Business Administration and Social Sciences, Luleå University of Technology.

Jack, S.L. and A.R. Anderson (2002), 'The effects of embeddedness on the entrepreneurial process', *Journal of Business Venturing*, **17**, 467–87.

Jay, A. (1970), *Management and Machiavelli*, Harmondsworth: Penguin Books.

Johannisson, B. (1994), 'Entrepreneurial networks – some conceptual and methodological notes', paper presented at 8th Nordic Conference on Small Business Research, Högskolan i Halmstad, June 13–15.

Johannisson, B. (1996), 'Personliga nätverk som kraftkälla i företagandet' [Personal networks as a source of power in business venturing], in

254 References

B. Johannisson and L. Lindmark (eds), *Företag, företagare, företagsamhet* [Ventures, venturers, venturing], Lund: Studentlitteratur, pp. 122–50.

Johannisson, B. (2000), 'Networking and entrepreneurial growth', in D.L. Sexton and H. Landström (eds), *The Blackwell Handbook of Entrepreneurship*, Oxford: Blackwell Publishers Ltd, pp. 368–86.

Johannisson, B. (2002), 'Entreprenörskapets regional organisering – bortom storskalighet och teknologi' [The regional organizing of entrepreneurship – beyond economy scale and technology], in P. Aronsson and B. Johannisson (eds), *Entreprenörskapets dynamic och regionala förankring* [The dynamics and regional connection of entrepreneurship], Växjö: Växjö University Press, pp. 127–57.

Johannisson, B., M. Ramirez-Pasillas and G. Karlsson (2002), 'Theoretical and methodological challenges bridging firm strategies and contextual networking', *Entrepreneurship and Innovation*, August, 165–74.

Johansson, I. (2001), 'Nätverk och Gnosjöanda' [Network and the spirit of Gnosjö], in M.-L. von Bergmann-Winberg and W. Skoglund (eds), *Lokalt utvecklingsarbete och entreprenörskap i Gnosjö, Åseda och Bispgården* [Local development work and entrepreneurship in Gnosjö, Åseda and Bispgården], Seminarium in Bispgården, 22 November, pp. 18–25.

Johnson, G. and K. Scholes (1999), *Exploring Corporate Strategy*, 5th edition, Upper Saddle River, NJ: Prentice Hall.

Johnson, S. (2000), 'Literature review on social entrepreneurship', Canadian Centre for Social Entrepreneurship, Alberta.

Johnson, S. (2003), 'Young social entrepreneurs in Canada', Canadian Centre for Social Entrepreneurship, Alberta.

Jones-Evans, D. (2000), 'Intrapreneurship', in S. Carter and D. Jones-Evans (eds), *Enterprise and Small Business. Principles, Practice and Policy*, Upper Saddle River, NJ: Prentice Hall, pp. 242–58.

Jonsson, O. and L.-O. Olander (2000), 'Production and innovation networks – a regional matter', paper presented at Uddevalla Symposium 2000, June 15–17.

Jonsson, O., A. Malmberg and L.-O. Olander (1996), *Geografisk närhet och konkurrenskraft: om industrins beroende av lokala och regionala produktionsmiljön* [Geographic closeness and competitive power: on industry's dependence on the local and regional production environment], Närings- och handelsdepartmentet: Fritzes.

Jonung, L. (2000), 'Den nya ekonomin i ett historiskt perspektiv utifrån debatten och litteraturen' [The new economy in a historical perspective in the public debate and in the literature], *Ekonomisk Debatt*, **28**(6), 561–6.

Kanter, R.M. (1983), *The Change Masters*, New York: Simon & Schuster.

Karlsson, C., B. Johansson and R.R. Stough (2001), 'Introduction: endogenous regional growth and politics', in B. Johansson, C. Karlsson and

R.R. Stough (eds), *Theories of Endogenous Regional Growth*, Berlin, Heidelberg and New York: Springer-Verlag, pp. 3–13.

Katz, J. (2003), 'The chronology and intellectual trajectory of American entrepreneurship education – 1876–1999', *Journal of Business Venturing*, **18**, 283–300.

Keller, E.F. (1985), *Reflections on Gender and Science*, New Haven: Yale University Press.

Kelly, K. (1998), *Den nya ekonomin. 10 strategier för en uppkopplad värld* [New rules for the new economy], Stockholm: Timbro.

Kirby, D.A. (2002), 'Entrepreneurship education: can business schools meet the challenge?', paper presented at ICSB World Conference, San Juan, Puerto Rico, June 16–19.

Kirzner, I.M. (1973), *Competition and Entrepreneurship*, Chicago: University of Chicago Press.

Klapper, R. (2005), 'The projet entreprendre – an evaluation of an entrepreneurial project at a grande ecole in France', in P. Kyrö and C. Carrier (eds), *The Dynamics of Learning Entrepreneurship in a Cross-Cultural University Context*, Entrepreneurship Education Series 2/2005, Hämeenlinna: University of Tampere, Research Centre for Vocational and Professional Education, pp. 188–212.

Kluckhohn, C. and W.H. Kelly (1945), 'The concept of culture', in R. Linton (ed.), *The Science of Man in the World Crisis*, New York: Columbia University Press, pp. 78–106.

Koch, L.T. (2003), 'Theory and practice of entrepreneurship education: a German view', *International Journal of Entrepreneurship Education*, **1**(4), 633–60.

Koen, P.A. (2001), 'Becoming a successful corporate entrepreneur', in R.H. Brockhaus, G.E. Hills, H. Klandt and H.P. Welsch (eds), *Entrepreneurship Education*, Aldershot: Ashgate, pp. 214–31.

Koestler, A. (1964), *The Act of Creation*, London: Hutchinson.

Krackhardt, D. and J. Hanson (1993), 'Informal networks: the companies behind the chart', *Harvard Business Review*, July–August, 104–11.

Kroll, L. (1998), 'Entrepreneur moms', *Forbes*, 18 May, 84–91.

Krugman, P. (1991), 'Increasing returns and economic geography', *Journal of Political Economy*, **99**, 14–31.

Kuhn, T. (1962), *The Structure of Scientific Revolutions*, Chicago: University of Chicago Press.

Kuratko, D.F. and R.M. Hodgetts (2004), *Entrepreneurship. Theory, Process, Practice*, 6th edition, Stanford, CT: Thomson South-Western.

Landström, H. (2005), *Entreprenörskapets rötter* [The roots of entrepreneurship], 3rd edition, Lund: Studentlitteratur.

Lans, H., H. Lööf and S. Hilstad (1997), *Uppfinn framtiden* [Invent the future], Stockholm: ISF, Ingenjörsssamfundet.

Larson, A. and J.A. Starr (1993), 'A network model of organization formation', *Entrepreneurship: Theory and Practice*, **17**(2), 5–15.

Latour, B. (1998), *Artefaktens återkomst* [The return of the artefact], Stockholm: Nerenius and Santérus Förlag.

Léger-Jarniou, C. (2006) (Director of the program), Global Management Master Entrepreneurship Program.

Levander, A. and I. Raccuia (2001), 'Entrepreneurial profiling – stimuli, reaction, action. A cognitive approach to entrepreneurship', essay, Stockholm School of Economics.

Li, J., Y. Zhang and H. Matlay (2003), 'Entrepreneurship education in China', *Education and Training*, **45**(8/9), 495–505.

Liang, S. (1974), *The Basics of Chinese Culture*, Hong Kong: Zhicheng Books.

Liedman, S.-E. (2002), *Ett oändligt äventyr* [An infinite adventure], Stockholm: Albert Bonniers Förlag.

Lindelöf, P. (2002), *Teknik- och forskningsparker som entreprenöriell miljö* [Technology and science parks as an entrepreneurial environment], Borås: Multitryck.

Locke, E.A. (1991), 'The motivation sequence, the motivation hub and motivation core', *Organizational Behaviour and Human Decision Processes*, **50**, 288–99.

Lucas, R.E., Jr (1978), 'On the size distribution of business firms', *Bell Journal of Economics*, **9**(3), 508–23.

Lundgren, A. and I. Snehota (1998), 'Ekonomisk organisation som nätverk' [Economic organization as network], in B. Czarniawska (ed.), *Organisationsteori på svenska* [Organization theory in Swedish], Malmö: Liber ekonomi, pp. 9–21.

MacKinnon, D., A. Cumbers and K. Chapman (2002), 'Learning, innovation and regional development: a critical appraisal of recent debates', *Progress in Human Geography*, **26**(3), 293–311.

Maillat, D. and L. Kebir (2001), 'The learning region and territorial production systems', in B. Johansson, C. Karlsson and R.R. Stough (eds), *Theories of Endogenous Regional Growth*, New York: Springer-Verlag, pp. 255–77.

Marshall, A. (1898), *Principles of Economics*, London: Macmillan.

Mascanzoni, D. and M. Novotny (2000), *Lokomotivföretagen i Italien* [The locomotive companies in Italy], Rådet för arbetslivsforskning, rapport no. 12.

McAdam, M. and P. McGowan (2003), 'An investigation into the role of entrepreneurial networks within a high technology cluster: a comparative study', paper, University of Ulster.

McClelland, D. (1961), *The Achieving Society*, Princeton, NJ: D. Van Nostrand.

McMullan, W.E. and L.M. Gillin (2001), 'Entrepreneurship education in the nineties: Revisited', in R.H. Brockhaus, G.E. Hills, H. Klandt and H.P. Welsch (eds), *Entrepreneurship Education*, Aldershot: Ashgate, pp. 57–77.

McMullan, W.E., J.J. Chrisman and K.H. Vesper (2001), 'Some problems in using subjective measures of effectiveness to evaluate entrepreneurial assistance programs', *Entrepreneurship Theory and Practice*, **26**(1), 37–54.

Mead, G.H. (1934), *Mind, Self and Society from the Standpoint of a Social Behaviorist*, Chicago: Chicago University Press.

Metro (2001), 'Trängsel ger framgång' [Crowdedness brings success], 29 May, 14.

Miles, R.E., C.C. Snow, J.A. Mathews, G. Miles and H.J. Coleman, Jr (2002), 'Organizing in the knowledge age: anticipating the cellular form', in S. Little, P. Quintas and T. Ray (eds), *Managing Knowledge. An Essential Reader*, Thousand Oaks, CA: Sage Publications, pp. 280–98.

Miller, G. (1990), 'The assessment of clinical skills, competence/performance', *Academic Medicine*, **9**, 565–9.

Molander, B. (1996), *Kunskap i handling* [Knowledge in action], Göteborg: Daidalos.

Morgan, G. (1986), *Images of Organizations*, Beverly Hills, CA: Sage Publications.

Naisbitt, J., N. Naisbitt and D. Philips (2001), *High Tech High Touch: Our Accelerated Search for Meaning*, London: Nicholas Brealey Publishing.

Nationalencyclopedin (2005), www.ne.se.

Neergaard, H. and J.P. Ulhøi (forthcoming), 'Preface: methodological variety in entrepreneurship research', in H. Neergaard and J.P. Ulhøi (eds), *Handbook of Qualitative Methods in Entrepreneurship*, Cheltenham, UK and Northampton, MA, USA: Edward Elgar.

Nilsson, J.-E. (2002), 'Entreprenörskapets dynamic och regionala förankring – generella drag' [The dynamics and regional connection of entrepreneurship – general characteristics], in P. Aronsson and B. Johannisson (eds), *Entreprenörskapets dynamik och regionala förankring* [The dynamics and regional connection of entrepreneurship], Vaxjö: Växjö University Press, pp. 199–206.

Nonaka, I. and H. Takeuchi (1995), *The Knowledge-Creating Company: How Japanese Companies Create the Dynamics of Innovation*, New York: Oxford University Press.

Norén, L. (1995), *Tolkande företagsekonomisk forskning* [Interpretive business research], Lund: Studentlitteratur.

Normann, R. (1975), *Skapande företagsledning* [Creative business leadership], Stockholm: Aldus.

258 References

Normann, R. (2001), *Reframing Business. When the Map Changes the Landscape*, New York: John Wiley & Sons.

Nyström, L. (2002), 'Det tredje Sverige' [The third Sweden], in P. Aronsson and B. Johannisson (eds), *Entreprenörskapets dynamik och regionala förankring* [The dynamics and regional connection of entrepreneurship], Växjö: Växjö University Press, pp. 21–30.

OECD (1989), 'Towards an enterprising culture', *Educational Monographs*, **4**, 37–8.

Parker, I. (ed.) (1998), *Social Constructionism, Discource and Realism*, Thousand Oaks, CA: Sage Publications.

Pedler, M., J. Burgoyne and T. Boydell (1991), *The Learning Company: A Strategy for Sustainable Development*, New York: McGraw-Hill.

Peters, T. (1997), *The Circle of Innovation*, New York: Alfred A. Knopf.

Peters, T. and N. Austin (1985), *A Passion for Excellence*, London: William Collins Sons.

Pinchot III, G. (1985), *Intrapreneuring*, New York: Harper & Row.

Piore, M. and C. Sabel (1984), *The Second Industrial Divide*, New York: Basic Books.

Pitkin, H.F. (1972), *Wittgenstein and Justice*, Los Angeles: University of California Press.

Polanyi, M. (1966), *The Tacit Dimension*, London: Routledge & Kegan Paul.

Porter, M. (1990), *The Competitive Advantage of Nations*, New York: The Free Press.

Porter, M. (1998), 'The Adam Smith address: location, clusters, and the "New" microeconomics of competition', *Business Economics*, January, 7–13.

Potter, J. and M. Whetherell (1987), *Discourse and Social Psychology: Beyond Attitudes and Behaviour*, London: Sage.

Powell, W.W. and L. Smith-Doerr (1994), 'Networks and economic life', in N. Smelser and R. Swedberg (eds), *Handbook of Economic Sociology*, Princeton, NJ: Princeton University Press, pp. 93–112.

Prabhu, G.N. (1999), 'Social entrepreneurship leadership', *Career Development International*, **4**(3), 140–45.

Putnam, R.D. (1993), *Making Democracy Work. Civic Traditions in Modern Italy*, Princeton, NJ: Princeton University Press.

Quanyu, H., J. Leonard and C. Tong (1997), *Business Decision Making in China*, Binghamton, NY: The Haworth Press.

Quinn, J.B. (1980), *Strategies for Change: Logical Incrementalism*, New York: Irwin.

Rajan, A., P. van Eupen and A. Jaspers (1997), 'Britain's flexible labour market', report, Create (UK).

Ranson, S., B. Hinings and R. Greenwood (1980), 'The structuring of organizational structures', *Administrative Science Quarterly*, **25**, March, 1–17.

'Regionala vinnarkluster' [Regional winning clusters], booklet published by NUTEK.

Ricoeur, P. (1971), 'The model of the text: meaningful action considered as a text', *Social Research*, **38**, 529–62.

Romer, P. (1986), 'Increasing returns and long-run growth', *Journal of Political Economy*, **94**, 23–33.

Ronstadt, R. (1985), 'The educated entrepreneurs: a new era of entrepreneurial education is beginning', *American Journal of Small Business*, **10**(1), 7–23.

Roos, J. and G. von Krogh (2002), 'The new language lab – parts 1 and 2', in S. Little, P. Quintas and T. Ray (eds), *Managing Knowledge. An Essential Reader*, Thousand Oaks, CA: Sage Publications, pp. 255–63.

Rosenburg, N., R. Landau and D. Mowery (1992), *Technology and the Wealth of Nations*, Palo Alto, CA: Stanford University Press.

Russell, B. (1948), *Human Knowledge*, London: Allen & Unwin.

Sandberg, J. (1999), 'Konstruktioner av social konstruktion' [Constructions of social construction], in S.-E. Sjöstrand, J. Sandberg and M. Tyrstrup (eds), *Osynlig företagsledning* [Invisible leadership], Lund: Studentlitteratur.

Sanner, L. (1997), 'Trust between entrepreneurs and external actors. Sensemaking in organizing new business ventures', doctoral thesis, Department of Business Administration, Uppsala University.

Saxenian, A. (1994), *Regional Advantage. Culture and Competition in Silicon Valley and Route 128*, Cambridge, MA and London: Harvard University Press.

Say, J.B. (1855), *A Treatise on Political Economy*, 4th edition, Philadelphia: Lippincott, Grambo & Co.

Scase, R. (2000), 'The enterprise culture: the socio-economic context of small firms', in S. Carter and D. Jones-Evans (eds), *Enterprise and Small Business. Principles, Practice and Policy*, Upper Saddle River, NJ: Prentice Hall, pp. 32–47.

Schollhammer, H. (1982), 'Internal corporate entrepreneurship', in C.A. Kent, D.L. Sexton and K.H. Vesper (eds), *Encyclopedia of Entrepreneurship*, Englewood Cliffs, NJ: Prentice Hall, pp. 209–23.

Schon, D.A. (1983), *The Reflective Practitioner: How Professionals Think in Action*, New York: Basic Books.

Schulyer, G. (1998), 'Social entrepreneurship: profit as a means, not an end', Kauffman Center for Entrepreneurial Leadership Clearing-house on Entrepreneurial Education (CELCEE), www.celcee.edu/products/digest/Dig 98-7html.

Schumpeter, J.A. (1934), *The Theory of Economic Development*, Cambridge, MA: Harvard University Press.

Schutjens, V. and E. Stam (2000), 'The evolution and nature of young firm networks: a longitudinal perspective', paper presented at Uddevalla Symposium 2000, June 15–17.

Schutz, A. (1962), *Collected Papers I. The Problem of Social Reality*, Leiden: Martinus Nijhoff Publishers.

Schutz, A. (1964), *Collected Papers II. Studies in Social Theory*, Leiden: Martinus Nijhoff Publishers.

Schutz, A. (1967), *The Phenomenology of the Social World*, Evanston: Northwestern University Press.

Schwartz, H. and S.M. Davis (1981), 'Matching corporate culture and business strategy', *Organizational Dynamics*, Summer, 30–48.

Searle, J.R. (1995), *The Construction of Social Reality*, New York: Free Press.

Senge, P. (1990), *The Fifth Discipline: The Art and Practice of the Learning Organization*, London: Doubleday.

Sexton, D.L. and N.B. Bowman-Upton (1991), *Entrepreneurship: Creativity and Growth*, New York: Macmillan.

Shane, S. and S. Venkataraman (2000), 'The promise of entrepreneurship as a field of research', *Academy of Management Review*, **25**(1), 217–26.

Shapero, A. and L. Sokol ((1982), 'The social dimension of entrepreneurship', in C.A. Kent, D.L. Sexton and K.H. Vesper (eds), *Encyclopedia of Entrepreneurship*, Englewood Cliffs, NJ: Prentice Hall, pp. 72–90.

Shaw, E. (2000), 'Social networks: their impact on the innovative behaviour of small service firms', paper, University of Strathclyde.

Shaw, E. (2001), 'What is the point in networking? An insight into the motivating factors for small business networking', paper, University of Strathclyde.

Shaw, E. and S. Conway (2000), 'Networking and the small firm', in S. Carter and D. Jones-Evans (eds), *Enterprise and Small Business. Principles, Practice and Policy*, Upper Saddle River, NJ: Prentice Hall, pp. 367–83.

Shelton, L.M. (2001), 'Expansion barriers and the organizational life cycle: another look at new venture development phases', paper presented at 15th Annual Symposium on Marketing and Entrepreneurship, August 8–10.

Sjöstrand, S.-E. (1992), 'The socioeconomic institutions of organizing: origin, emergence, and reproduction', *Journal of Socio-Economics*, **22**, 323–51.

Smallbone, D. and P. Wyer (2000), 'Growth and development in the small firm', in S. Carter and D. Jones-Evans (eds), *Enterprise and Small Business. Principles, Practice and Policy*, Upper Saddle River, NJ: Prentice Hall, pp. 409–33.

'SMEs in Europe. Competitiveness, innovation and the knowledge-driven society' (2002), publication from European Commission.

Smircich, L. (1983), 'Concepts of culture and organizational analysis', *Administrative Science Quarterly*, **28**(3), 339–58.

Smircich, L. and C. Stubbart (1985), 'Strategic management in an enacted world', *Academy of Management Review*, **10**(4), 724–36.

Snyder, M. and N. Cantor (1998), 'Understanding personality and social behaviour: a functionalist strategy', in D.T. Gilbert, T. Fiske and G. Lindsey (eds), *The Handbook of Social Psychology*, Vol. 1, 4th edition, Boston, MA: The McGraw-Hill Companies, pp. 635–79.

Southern, A. (2000), 'The social and cultural world of enterprise', in S. Carter and D. Jones-Evans (eds), *Enterprise and Small Business. Principles, Practice and Policy*, Upper Saddle River, NJ: Prentice Hall, pp. 78–94.

Spinosa, C., F. Flores and H.L. Dreyfus (1997), *Disclosing New Worlds. Entrepreneurship, Democratic Action, and the Cultivation of Solidarity*, Cambridge, MA: The MIT Press.

Stacey, R.D. (1996), *Complexity and Creativity in Organizations*, San Francisco, CA: Berret-Koehler.

Stata, R. (1989), 'Organizational learning: the key to management innovation', *Sloan Management Review*, Spring, 63–73.

Statistiska centralbyrån (2005), http://www.scb.se/templates/Standard_34546.asp.

Sternberg, R. and T. Litzenberger (2003), 'Industrial clusters and entrepreneurial activities – empirical evidence from German regions', paper presented at Symposium on Entrepreneurship, Spatial Clusters and Inter-Firm Networks, University of Trollhättan/Uddevalla, June 12–14.

Stevenson, H.H. (1983), 'A new paradigm for entrepreneurial management', in J.J. Kao and H.H. Stevenson (eds), *Entrepreneurship – What It Is and How We Teach It*, Cambridge, MA: Harvard Business School.

Stevenson, H.H. (1995), 'We create entrepreneurs', *Success*, September, 50–4.

Storey, D. (1980), *Job Generation and Small Firms Policy in Britain*, Centre for Environmental Studies.

Storey, D. (1994), *Understanding the Small Business Sector*, London: Routledge.

Storey, D., K. Keasey, R. Watson and P. Wynarczyk (1987), 'Fast growth small business: case studies of 40 small firms in Northern Ireland', Department of Employment, Research Paper no. 67.

Storey, J. (2002), 'HR and Organizational Structures', in S. Little, P. Quintas and T. Ray (eds), *Managing Knowledge. An Essential Reader*, Thousand Oaks, CA: Sage Publications, pp. 349–55.

Suchman, M.C., D.J. Steward and C.A. Westfall (2001), 'The legal environment of entrepreneurship', in C.B. Schoonhoven and E. Romanelli (eds), *The Entrepreneurship Dynamic*, Palo Alto, CA: Stanford University Press, pp. 349–82.

Thalbuder, J. (1998), 'How nonprofit and for-profit differ', http://www.socialentrepreneurs.org/entredef.html.

Thompson, J. (2002), 'The world of the social entrepreneur', *International Journal of Public Sector Management*, **15**(5), 412–31.

Thompson, J., G. Alvy and A. Lees (2000), 'Social entrepreneurship – a new look at the people and the potential', *Management Decision*, **38**(5), 328–38.

Thornton, P.H. (1999), 'The sociology of entrepreneurship', *Annual Review of Sociology*, **25**, 19–46.

Tichy, N.M. and M.A. Devanna (1986), *The Transformational Leader*, New York: John Wiley & Sons.

'Tillväxt i småföretag' [Growth among small firms] (2003), paper published by NUTEK.

Timmons, J.A. (1999), *New Venture Creation. Entrepreneurship For the 21st Century*, 5th edition, New York: IrwinMcGraw-Hill.

Toffler, A. (1984), *The Third Wave*, New York: Bantam Books.

Trigg, R. (1985), *Understanding Social Science*, Oxford: Basil Blackwell Publishers Ltd.

US Department of Labor (2005), http://www.osha.gov/dcsp/smallbusiness/sb_facts.html.

Ushido, Y. (1995), 'Small and medium enterprises and government policy', paper presented at APEC Symposium on Human Resources Development for SMEs, Taipei, November 8–10.

Varadarajan, P.R. and M. Cunningham (1995), 'Strategic alliances: a synthesis of conceptual foundations', *Journal of the Academy of Marketing Science*, **23**(4), 282–96.

Watts, A.G. and R. Hawthorn (1991), 'Careers education and enterprise in higher education', An Interim Report, National Institute for Careers Education and Counselling, Cambridge, pp. i–iv.

Weick, K.E. (1988), 'Enacted sensemaking in crisis situations', *Journal of Management Studies*, **25**(4), 305–17.

Weick, K.E. (1995), *Sensemaking in Organizations*, Thousand Oaks, CA: Sage.

Wenneberg, S.B. (2001), *Socialkonstruktivism – positioner, problem och perspektiv* [Social constructivism – positions, problems and perspectives], Solna: Liber AB.

Westlund, H. (2001), 'Social economy and development. The case of Sweden', paper presented at Uddevalla Symposium 2001 ('Regional Economies in Transition'), Vänersborg, Sweden, June 14–16.

Westlund, H. and R. Bolton (2003), 'Local social capital and entrepreneurship', *Small Business Economics*, **21**, 77–113.

Wiklund, J. (1998), 'Small firm growth and performance: entrepreneurship and beyond', doctoral thesis, Jönköping: Jönköping International Business School.

Winnicott, D.W. (1971), *Playing and Reality*, Harmondsworth: Penguin.

Wittgenstein, L. (1953), *Philosophical Investigations*, Oxford: Blackwell.

von Wright, G.H. (1971), *Explanation and Understanding*, London: Routledge & Kegan Paul.

Ylinenpää, H. (2002), 'Gränsöverskridande Triple-Helix-samverkan mellan Sverige och Finland' [Border-crossing Triple Helix co-operation between Sweden and Finland], paper presented at 12th Nordic Conference on Small Business Research, Kuopio, Finland, June 16–19.

Zafirovski, M. (1999), 'Probing into the social layers of entrepreneurship: outlines of the sociology of enterprise', *Entrepreneurship and Regional Development*, **11**, 351–71.

Ziff, P. (1960), *Semantic Analysis*, Ithaca, NY: Cornell University Press.

Zimmerer, T.W. and N.M. Scarborough (2002), *Essentials of Entrepreneurship and Small Business Management*, 3rd edition, Upper Saddle River, NJ: Prentice Hall.

Index